Lecture Notes in Economics and Mathematical Systems

For information about Vols. 1–183, please contact your bookseller or Springer-Verlag

Vol. 184: R. E. Burkard and U. Derigs, Assignment and Matching Problems: Solution Methods with FORTRAN-Programs. VIII, 148 pages. 1980.

Vol. 185: C. C. von Weizsäcker, Barriers to Entry. VI, 220 pages. 1980.

Vol. 186: Ch.-L. Hwang and K. Yoon, Multiple Attribute Decision Making – Methods and Applications. A State-of-the-Art-Survey. XI, 259 pages. 1981.

Vol. 187: W. Hock, K. Schittkowski, Test Examples for Nonlinear Programming Codes. V, 178 pages. 1981.

Vol. 188: D. Bös, Economic Theory of Public Enterprise. VII, 142 pages. 1981.

Vol. 189: A. P. Lüthi, Messung wirtschaftlicher Ungleichheit. IX, 287 pages. 1981.

Vol. 190: J. N. Morse, Organizations: Multiple Agents with Multiple Criteria. Proceedings, 1980. VI, 509 pages. 1981.

Vol. 191: H. R. Sneessens, Theory and Estimation of Macroeconomic Rationing Models. VII, 138 pages. 1981.

Vol. 192: H. J. Bierens: Robust Methods and Asymptotic Theory in Nonlinear Econometrics. IX, 198 pages. 1981.

Vol. 193: J. K. Sengupta, Optimal Decisions under Uncertainty. VII, 156 pages. 1981.

Vol. 194: R. W. Shephard, Cost and Production Functions. XI, 104 pages. 1981.

Vol. 195: H. W. Ursprung, Die elementare Katastrophentheorie. Eine Darstellung aus der Sicht der Ökonomie. VII, 332 pages. 1982.

Vol. 196: M. Nermuth, Information Structures in Economics. VIII, 236 pages. 1982.

Vol. 197: Integer Programming and Related Areas. A Classified Bibliography. 1978 – 1981. Edited by R. von Randow. XIV, 338 pages. 1982.

Vol. 198: P. Zweifel, Ein ökonomisches Modell des Arztverhaltens. XIX, 392 Seiten. 1982.

Vol. 199: Evaluating Mathematical Programming Techniques. Proceedings, 1981. Edited by J.M. Mulvey. XI, 379 pages. 1982.

Vol. 200: The Resource Sector in an Open Economy. Edited by H. Siebert. IX, 161 pages. 1984.

Vol. 201: P. M. C. de Boer, Price Effects in Input-Output-Relations: A Theoretical and Empirical Study for the Netherlands 1949–1967. X, 140 pages. 1982.

Vol. 202: U. Witt, J. Perske, SMS – A Program Package for Simulation and Gaming of Stochastic Market Processes and Learning Behavior. VII, 266 pages. 1982.

Vol. 203: Compilation of Input-Output Tables. Proceedings, 1981. Edited by J. V. Skolka. VII, 307 pages. 1982.

Vol. 204: K. C. Mosler, Entscheidungsregeln bei Risiko: Multivariate stochastische Dominanz. VII, 172 Seiten. 1982.

Vol. 205: R. Ramanathan, Introduction to the Theory of Economic Growth. IX, 347 pages. 1982.

Vol. 206: M. H. Karwan, V. Lotfi, J. Telgen, and S. Zionts, Redundancy in Mathematical Programming. VII, 286 pages. 1983.

Vol. 207: Y. Fujimori, Modern Analysis of Value Theory. X, 165 pages. 1982.

Vol. 208: Econometric Decision Models. Proceedings, 1981. Edited by J. Gruber. VI, 364 pages. 1983.

Vol. 209: Essays and Surveys on Multiple Criteria Decision Making. Proceedings, 1982. Edited by P. Hansen. VII, 441 pages. 1983.

Vol. 210: Technology, Organization and Economic Structure. Edited by R. Sato and M.J. Beckmann. VIII, 195 pages. 1983.

Vol. 211: P. van den Heuvel, The Stability of a Macroeconomic System with Quantity Constraints. VII, 169 pages. 1983.

Vol. 212: R. Sato and T. Nôno, Invariance Principles and the Structure of Technology. V, 94 pages. 1983.

Vol. 213: Aspiration Levels in Bargaining and Economic Decision Making. Proceedings, 1982. Edited by R. Tietz. VIII, 406 pages. 1983.

Vol. 214: M. Faber, H. Niemes und G. Stephan, Entropie, Umweltschutz und Rohstoffverbrauch. IX, 181 Seiten. 1983.

Vol. 215: Semi-Infinite Programming and Applications. Proceedings, 1981. Edited by A. V. Fiacco and K. O. Kortanek. XI, 322 pages. 1983.

Vol. 216: H. H. Müller, Fiscal Policies in a General Equilibrium Model with Persistent Unemployment. VI, 92 pages. 1983.

Vol. 217: Ch. Grootaert, The Relation Between Final Demand and Income Distribution. XIV, 105 pages. 1983.

Vol. 218: P. van Loon, A Dynamic Theory of the Firm: Production, Finance and Investment. VII, 191 pages. 1983.

Vol. 219: E. van Damme, Refinements of the Nash Equilibrium Concept. VI, 151 pages. 1983.

Vol. 220: M. Aoki, Notes on Economic Time Series Analysis: System Theoretic Perspectives. IX, 249 pages. 1983.

Vol. 221: S. Nakamura, An Inter-Industry Translog Model of Prices and Technical Change for the West German Economy. XIV, 290 pages. 1984.

Vol. 222: P. Meier, Energy Systems Analysis for Developing Countries. VI, 344 pages. 1984.

Vol. 223: W. Trockel, Market Demand. VIII, 205 pages. 1984.

Vol. 224: M. Kiy, Ein disaggregiertes Prognosesystem für die Bundesrepublik Deutschland. XVIII, 276 Seiten. 1984.

Vol. 225: T. R. von Ungern-Sternberg, Zur Analyse von Märkten mit unvollständiger Nachfragerinformation. IX, 125 Seiten. 1984

Vol. 226: Selected Topics in Operations Research and Mathematical Economics. Proceedings, 1983. Edited by G. Hammer and D. Pallaschke. IX, 478 pages. 1984.

Vol. 227: Risk and Capital. Proceedings, 1983. Edited by G. Bamberg and K. Spremann. VII, 306 pages. 1984.

Vol. 228: Nonlinear Models of Fluctuating Growth. Proceedings, 1983. Edited by R. M. Goodwin, M. Krüger and A. Vercelli. XVII, 277 pages. 1984.

Vol. 229: Interactive Decision Analysis. Proceedings, 1983. Edited by M. Grauer and A. P. Wierzbicki. VIII, 269 pages. 1984.

Vol. 230: Macro-Economic Planning with Conflicting Goals. Proceedings, 1982. Edited by M. Despontin, P. Nijkamp and J. Spronk. VI, 297 pages. 1984.

Vol. 231: G. F. Newell, The M/M/∞ Service System with Ranked Servers in Heavy Traffic. XI, 126 pages. 1984.

Vol. 232: L. Bauwens, Bayesian Full Information Analysis of Simultaneous Equation Models Using Integration by Monte Carlo. VI, 114 pages. 1984.

Vol. 233: G. Wagenhals, The World Copper Market. XI, 190 pages. 1984.

Vol. 234: B. C. Eaves, A Course in Triangulations for Solving Equations with Deformations. III, 302 pages. 1984.

Vol. 235: Stochastic Models in Reliability Theory. Proceedings, 1984. Edited by S. Osaki and Y. Hatoyama. VII, 212 pages. 1984.

continuation on page 203

Lecture Notes in Economics and Mathematical Systems

Managing Editors: M. Beckmann and W. Krelle

328

Werner Güth
Brigitte Kalkofen

Unique Solutions for Strategic Games

Equilibrium Selection Based on Resistance Avoidance

Springer-Verlag
Berlin Heidelberg New York London Paris Tokyo

Authors

Werner Güth
Brigitte Kalkofen
Professur für wirtschaftliche Staatswissenschaften I,
insbesondere Wirtschaftstheorie
Johann Wolfgang Goethe-Universität
Mertonstr. 17, D-6000 Frankfurt am Main 1, FRG

ISBN-13: 978-3-540-50974-5 e-ISBN-13: 978-3-642-48367-7
DOI: 10.1007/978-3-642-48367-7

Softcover reprint of the hardcover 1st edition 1989

2847/3140-543210

Acknowledgements

We are very indebted to John C. Harsanyi and Reinhard Selten who introduced Werner Güth to equilibrium selection theory and game theory in general. Cooperating with Reinhard Selten has, furthermore, improved our understanding of what equilibrium selection and game theory, in general, should be trying to accomplish. Thus, either directly or indirectly, both authors are strongly influenced by John C. Harsanyi and Reinhard Selten who, together with John F. Nash, are the true pioneers of equilibrium selection and who already explored the main conceptual ideas.

This study has been inspired and initiated by long and helpful discussions with Bezalel Peleg at the Hebrew University of Jerusalem in 1982. Later applications induced some improvements but did not change the basic idea.

Wilhelm Krelle inspired the nontechnical Introduction and asked us to discuss the differences between the refinement and the selection approach. We would also like to thank him and the Springer–Verlag for accepting our study for the 'Lecture Notes in Economics and Mathematical Systems'.

Last but not least, we thank Waltraud Kraft who has typed the manuscript with great care.

Contents

Introduction: On equilibrium selection

In this introductory chapter we first introduce the problem of equilibrium selection and outline the program of equilibrium selection theory (Section 1). Examples of strategic games with multiple equilibria are given in Section 2 which already indicate how to select between equilibria. In Section 3 we briefly review the most well–known refinements of the equilibrium concept and discuss the basic differences between the refinement and the equilibrium selection approach. The pioneering contributions to equilibrium selection theory by NASH (1950 and 1953) as well as HARSANYI and SELTEN (1988) are described in Section 4 where we try to avoid technical details as far as possible. In Section 5 we briefly review the remaining chapters of this study. By reading this Introduction the reader should already understand the program of equilibrium selection theory as well as the specific aspects of our approach.

1. The equilibrium concept

In the social sciences an equilibrium state is usually characterized by some kind of stability. At an equilibrium price on a competitive market, for instance, supply equals demand implying that there are no unsatisfied desires for trade which could destabilize the market price. In Figure 0.1.1 we have illustrated a simple exchange economy with two commodities 1 and 2 and two agents a and b. $e_a = (e_{a,1};e_{a,2})$ is the initial endowment vector of agent a, $e_b = (e_{b,1};e_{b,2})$ the one of agent b. The trade or offer curves T_a and T_b of agents a and b, respectively, have five points of intersection which all determine different price relations and trade vectors. Using the normalization rule $p_2 = 1$ we therefore face a multiplicity of equilibrium prices p_1 and, correspondingly, of trade amounts. If one wanted to know exactly the terms of trade, one would have to select one of the five equilibrium prices p_1 as the actual solution price. Multiplicity of equilibrium states and the problem of equilibrium selection is thus a familiar phenomenon on competitive markets.

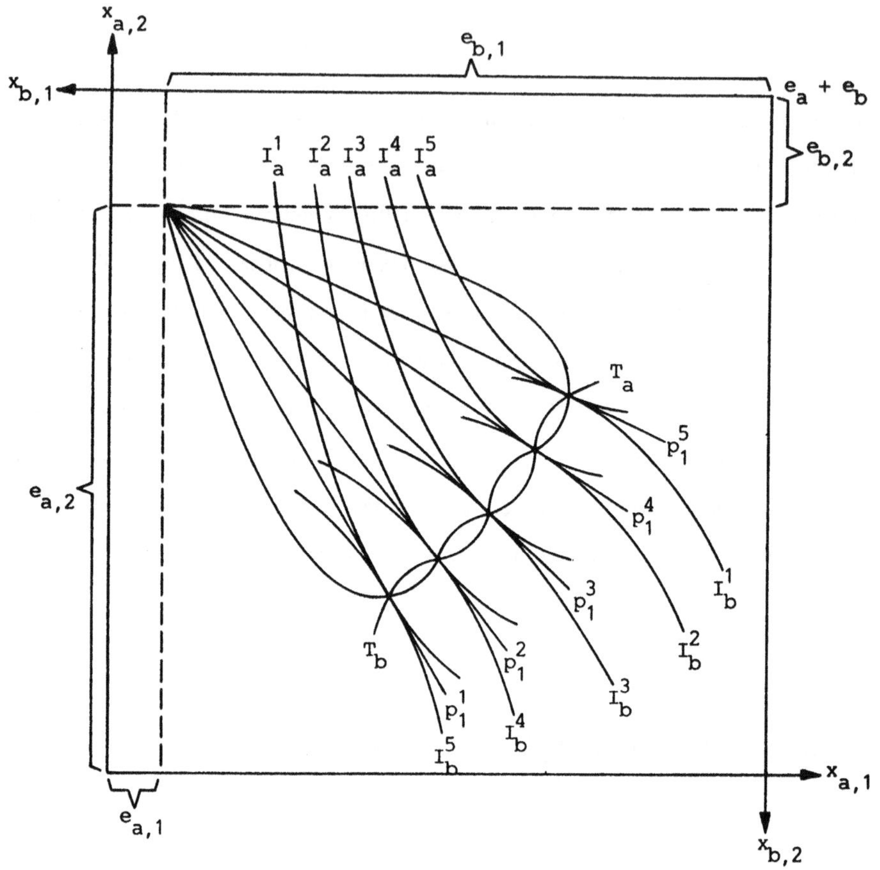

Figure 0.1.1: An exchange economy with two agents a and b and two commodities $l = 1, 2$ and five equilibrium prices p_1 given the normalization rule $p_2 = 1$ (I_i^m indicates an indifference curve of agent $i = a, b$ where a point on I_i^m is better than one on $I_i^{m'}$ if $m > m'$; T_i is the trade or offer curve of agent $i = a, b$).

Here we do not restrict ourselves to a specific class of decision problems, like competitive markets, but consider the whole variety of social decision problems. Instead of the specific equilibrium concept for competitive markets we therefore use a more general equilibrium notion. Now social decision problems, in general, are most adequately described as strategic games. For strategic models of markets or political conflicts see, for instance, FRIEDMAN (1977), KRELLE (1976),

SELTEN (1980a), SHUBIK (1982), and BRAMS (1985).

The equilibrium concept for strategic games is the equilibrium point as introduced by COURNOT (1838) and NASH (1951). If a strategy vector is an equilibrium point, no player can gain by unilaterally deviating from his equilibrium strategy. An equilibrium is therefore a self–stabilizing behavioral expectation. If all expect it to be the solution no player has a reason to destabilize this expectation. If however a nonequilibrium is expected, at least one player can gain by deviating from his expected behavior. Thus a nonequilibrium point is a self–destroying prophecy. When from now on we speak of an equilibrium without any further specification, we always mean an equilibrium point of a strategic game.

The main task of game theory, i.e. the theory of strategic games, is to determine for each player in a given strategic game the strategy which he should use. To resolve strategic uncertainty the solution has to give an unambiguous advice for every player. Therefore reducing strategic uncertainty means to increase predictive power. Now, unfortunately, the predictive power of the equilibrium concept is rather limited since many games have more than one equilibrium point. Although some market games (see, for instance, FRIEDMAN, 1977, SELTEN, 1980a, SHUBIK, 1985) have a unique equilibrium, the literature on markets with incomplete information (see, for instance, SPENCE, 1974, KREPS and WILSON, 1982, BANKS and SOBEL, 1987) indicates that this is due to special assumptions like complete information, single decision stages, continuous strategy spaces etc.

To resolve strategic uncertainty we must therefore try to develop solution requirements stronger than that of an equilibrium point. Although the solution of a game will have to be an equilibrium, not all equilibria are reasonable solution candidates. Equilibrium selection theory preassumes that the individually rational decision behavior can be uniquely defined for all social decision problems and thus for all strategic games. This is done by considering most carefully the various substructures and parameters of the given game situation. It seems justified to say that equilibrium selection theory is the most ambitious attempt to resolve strategic uncertainty.

Before proceeding we would like to comment on the usual, but unfortunate distinction between noncooperative and cooperative games. When speaking of a strategic game we always mean a noncooperative game. By this we do not exclude at all collusion among players. On the contrary, some of the most interesting strategic games with multiple equilibria deal with cooperative activities like coalition or cartel formation (see, for instance, NASH, 1953; SELTEN, 1973; HARSANYI and SELTEN, 1972; as well as Section 8 of Part II in this study).

A cooperative game assumes unrestricted self–commitment power for all players, i.e., every player can commit himself to any possible kind of behavior in the course of the game. Given a strategic game one derives its cooperative version by assigning to all possible sets/coalitions of players the sets of feasible payoff vectors which they can jointly assure themselves. All other strategic aspects, e.g. the individual choices implying such payoff results and the process of strategic interaction, are neglected. Correspondingly, the solution of a cooperative game is simply a payoff vector or a set of payoff vectors and not a strategy combination.

When selecting among equilibrium points nearly all strategic aspects will be relevant, especially those neglected by cooperative game theory. Furthermore, equilibrium selection theory is not restricted to games with unrestricted self–commitment power for all players, but wants to solve all strategic games with and without self–commitment power. It is therefore necessary to incorporate all aspects of a social decision problem as done in the theory of noncooperative games. Since this does not exclude collusion among players, we prefer to speak of the strategic approach instead of the noncooperative approach to model a social decision problem.

2. Examples of games with multiple equilibria

Consider a 2–person game where both players $i = 1, 2$ can choose between two strategies X_i and Y_i and where, furthermore, this has to be done simultaneously, i.e., no player knows the decision of the other when choosing his strategy. The payoff function of such a game can easily be illustrated in the form of a bimatrix whose components correspond to the strategy vectors $s = (s_1,s_2)$

with $s_i \in \{X_i, Y_i\}$ for $i = 1, 2$. In Table 0.2.1 the payoff of player 1 appears in the upper left corner and the payoff of player 2 in the lower right corner of the respective matrix component s. The games, illustrated in Table 0.2.1, are often named 'battle of sexes'–games; sometimes only the symmetric cases with $a = b$ are considered. Let, for instance, player 1 be a male–single and player 2 be a female–single living at distinct places x and y. Assume that both individuals prefer being together to being alone and being together at home to being together at the other's place. If in case of being alone they, furthermore, do not care where they are, the situation is the one described by the payoff function of Table 0.2.1 where we used the fact that cardinal utilities are only uniquely defined up to an arbitrary choice of the 0–point and the unit of the utility scales, i.e. up to positive linear transformations of the utilities.

	X_2	Y_2
X_1	1 / a	0 / 0
Y_1	0 / 0	b / 1

Table 0.2.1: The 'battle of sexes'–games: with $0 < a < 1$ and $0 < b < 1$ (player 1 (2) is the row (column) player whose payoff appears in the upper left (lower right) corner of each matrix component $s = (s_1,s_2)$ with $s_i \in \{X_i, Y_i\}$ for $i = 1, 2$).

The game of Table 0.2.1 has apparently two pure strategy equilibrium points, namely $X = (X_1,X_2)$ and $Y = (Y_1,Y_2)$. Furthermore, there is an equilibrium point $q = (q_1,q_2)$ in mixed strategies according to which player 1 uses his strategy X_1 with probability $q_1(X_1) = 1/(1+a)$ and player 2 his strategy X_2 with probability $q_2(X_2) = b/(1+b)$. Let $H(s) = (H_1(s),H_2(s))$ denote the payoff vector, i.e., the vector of the payoffs $H_1(s)$ of player 1 and $H_2(s)$ of player 2, implied by the strategy vector s. Whereas X and Y yield the payoff vector (1,a) and (b,1), respectively, the mixed strategy equilibrium point q implies the payoff vector $(b/(1+b),a/(1+a))$ which gives both players less than either X or Y.

Saying that the solution must be an equilibrium point would not resolve strategic uncertainty: Both players, $i = 1$ and $i = 2$, would not know whether to choose X or Y or to randomize between them. Any helpful strategic advice concerning the games of Table 0.2.1 has to distinguish between equilibria.

It is an obvious idea to exclude q as a solution candidate since it yields less for both players. An equilibrium point is said to payoff dominate another equilibrium point if it yields a higher payoff for all players. In the games of Table 0.2.1 both strict equilibrium points payoff dominate q, but none of them payoff dominates the other. Thus even the concept of payoff undominated equilibria does not resolve strategic uncertainty. Players $i = 1, 2$ will not know whether to use X_i or Y_i.

But again it is rather obvious that X and Y are not always equally reasonable candidates for the solution of the game. To illustrate this consider the cases where $a = 1 - \epsilon$ and $b = \epsilon$ and where ϵ is a small positive number. Here player 1 does not risk very much by sticking to his preferred solution candidate whereas maintaining on Y can be rather costly for player 2. One of the main tasks of equilibrium selection theory is to develop general solution requirements which would take into account these different incentives of players 1 and 2 for the two solution candidates X and Y.

Other special cases of Table 0.2.1 are the symmetric games with $a = b$. To select either X or Y as the solution of these games would then be completely arbitrary since these two equilibria differ only by an arbitrary choice of names for players and strategies. We call a game symmetric if there is a nontrivial way of renaming players and/or strategies without changing the game. An obvious solution requirement for the solution of such a game is that it should be symmetry invariant, i.e., a renaming of players and/or strategies, which does not change the game, should not change the solution of the game either. In the symmetric games of Table 0.2.1 with $a = b$ there is no payoff undominated and symmetry invariant equilibrium point. The three requirements (equilibrium property, payoff dominance, symmetry invariance) are therefore mutually inconsistent. This already indicates that equilibrium selection theory will have to establish hierarchies among solution requirements. To avoid an arbitrary selection of the solution it is natural to assume that symmetry invariance is more important than payoff dominance. Given this hierarchy of solution requirements the solution of the symmetric games will be the mixed strategy equilibrium point q.

Consider now a society with three individuals/players/voters 1, 2, and 3 who can realize any of the three social alternatives A, B, or C if a majority of them votes for this alternative (a closely related model has been analysed by GÜTH and SELTEN, 1988). Each player i = 1, 2, 3 must choose a strategy/vote $s_i \in \{A, B, C\}$. The payoff function $H(s) = (H_1(s),H_2(s),H_3(s))$ assigning a vector of individual payoffs $H_i(s)$ to all possible strategy vectors s is given by

$$H(s) = \begin{cases} (1, H_2^a, H_3^a) & \text{for } |\{i \in \{1,2,3\} \mid s_i = A\}| \geq 2 \;, \\ (H_1^b, H_2^b, 1) & \text{for } |\{i \in \{1,2,3\} \mid s_i = B\}| \geq 2 \;, \\ (H_1^c, 1, H_3^c) & \text{for } |\{i \in \{1,2,3\} \mid s_i = C\}| \geq 2 \;, \\ (0,0,0) & \text{otherwise} \end{cases}$$

where $1 > H_1^b > H_1^c > 0$, $1 > H_2^a > H_2^b > 0$, $1 > H_3^c > H_3^a > 0$ and where $|S|$ stands for the cardinality of the set S. Due to these conditions for the payoff parameters there is a majority cycle in the sense that two of three voters prefer A to B, B to C, and C to A. In case of no majority for any social alternative the status quo results which no voter prefers to any of the three social alternatives. Since cardinal utilities are only uniquely defined up to positive affine transformations it is no restriction that every player evaluates the status quo by '0' and his most preferred alternative by '1'.

In this game every strategy vector $s = (s_1,s_2,s_3)$ with two players agreeing on the worst alternative of the third player who can choose any strategy implying 0–probability for his second best alternative is an equilibrium point. Thus there are six pure strategy equilibrium points (three with tight 2 player–majorities, three with unanimous votes) and infinitely many mixed strategy equilibrium points. However, none of the equilibria described above implies a positive probability for the non–Pareto–efficient status quo.

Let ϵ be again a very small positive constant and assume that every player i = 1, 2, 3 must choose every strategy $s_i \in \{A, B, C\}$ at least with probability ϵ ($< 1/3$). A natural interpretation of this restriction for the sets of strategies is that due to his '<u>trembling hand</u>' a player cannot be sure to realize the strategy which he wants to use. Another obvious interpretation is that players are rational only with probability $1 - 3\epsilon$. A game with the restricted strategy sets is called an ϵ–uniformly perturbed game of the original strategic game (SELTEN, 1975; HARSANYI and

SELTEN, 1988). Instead of analysing the game directly we will often investigate it indirectly by solving its ϵ-uniformly perturbed games and investigating the limit solution for ϵ approaching 0.

In an ϵ-uniformly perturbed game every pure strategy vector is obviously realized with positive probability. Regardless how small one chooses the perturbance parameter ϵ (> 0) this can have drastic consequences for the equilibria of the game. Consider, for instance, the game, illustrated in Table 0.2.1, with a = b = 0. Clearly, in an ϵ-uniformly perturbed game player 1 will choose X_1 and player 2 will choose Y_2 with maximal probability since these strategies are always better than the other pure strategy. A pure strategy is called <u>weakly dominated</u> if there is another strategy which, for all pure strategy combinations of the other players, is never worse and better for at least one such strategy combination. A weakly dominated strategy is called <u>strictly dominated</u> if there is another strategy being a better reply to all pure strategy combinations of the other players. Although X and Y are still equilibria if a = b = 0, both require one player to choose a weakly dominated strategy. In every ϵ-uniformly perturbed game both players will choose their weakly dominated strategy only with the minimal probability ϵ. Consequently, only the equilibrium (X_1, Y_2) in the game of Table 0.2.1 with a = b = 0 can be approached by equilibria of its ϵ-uniformly perturbed games.

In the voting game the multiplicity of equilibria is even more reduced by perturbing the game. To see this consider the continuum of equilibria in the original game according to which $q_1(A) = q_2(A) = 1$ and $q_3(C) = 0$. It is the overwhelming multiplicity of mixed equilibrium strategies q_3 of player 3 which can dramatically collapse in an ϵ-uniformly perturbed game: If 1 and 2 vote for alternative A with maximal probability $1 - 2\epsilon$, player 3's only best reply is A if $H_3^a > .5(1-\epsilon)/(1-2\epsilon)$. Consequently, if $H_3^a > .5$ and if ϵ (> 0) is sufficiently small, player 3 will also vote for A with maximal probability $1 - 2\epsilon$. The continuum of equilibria in the original game, mentioned above, corresponds to a single equilibrium in the ϵ-uniformly perturbed game given that $H_3^a > .5$ and ϵ (> 0) is small.

The two examples illustrate that small perturbations can eliminate unreasonable equilibria. They avoid, for instance, the voluntary choice of weakly dominated strategies and arbitrary randomization based on the ultimate trust that the others will never err when picking their strategy. A mixed strategy equilibrium point q in the original game, which can be approximated by equilibrium points q^{ϵ} of its ϵ–uniformly perturbed games for a sequence of perturbance parameters ϵ tending to 0, is called a (uniformly) perfect equilibrium point (SELTEN, 1975). The main purpose of solving the game indirectly via the limit solution of its ϵ–uniformly perturbed games is to make sure that the solution of the game is a perfect equilibrium point. The two examples above illustrate why rational players should not want to follow the prescriptions of imperfect equilibrium points.

The substructures of a given game are another essential aspect which equilibrium selection theory has to take into account. For games in extensive form such strategically essential substructures are, for instance, the subgames. A subgame of an extensive game can loosely be described as the strategic situation resulting after a certain course of actions which is informationally closed, i.e. at any possible state of the play in the subgame every player knows that he is playing in this subgame. Since a strategy s_i of player i is a complete strategic plan in the sense that it prescribes a unique choice for all possible decision situations of player i, a strategy s_i induces a strategy s_i' of player i in the subgame G' of the original game G. Similarly, a strategy vector s of G induces a strategy vector s' of G' where, of course, some players might be strategically irrelevant. An equilibrium point s of G is called subgame perfect if it induces an equilibrium point s' for all subgames G' of G (SELTEN, 1965 and 1975). If one accepts that rational players will satisfy the equilibrium property, it is natural to assume that they will do so in all possible game situations. The concept of subgame perfect equilibria is therefore an intuitively convincing refinement of the equilibrium concept. Since perfect equilibria are always subgame perfect (SELTEN, 1975), our indirect approach of solving the game via the limit solution of its ϵ–uniformly perturbed games will guarantee subgame perfectness for the solution of the game and thereby take into account the subgames of a given game.

But even without proper subgames a game can have substructures which any reasonable concept of equilibrium selection should take into account. The following 3–person game in normal form describes, for instance, an extensive game where all three players i = 1, 2, 3 have to decide independently whether to use X_i or Y_i, i.e., no player i knows the decisions of the other players when determining his strategy $s_i \in \{X_i, Y_i\}$. Thus there exists no proper subgame. The payoff function is given by Table 0.2.2 where each box corresponds to a pure strategy vector $s = (s_1, s_2, s_3)$ and where player 1's (3's) payoff appears in the upper left (lower right) corner of each box and player 2's payoff in between. Investigating Table 0.2.2 more closely reveals that player 1's best reply to any possible behavior of his coplayers only depends on the strategy s_2 of player 2 and vice versa. Thus although there is no payoff dominance between the equilibria $X = (X_1, X_2, X_3)$ and $Y = (Y_1, Y_2, Y_3)$, players 1 and 2 will undoubtedly realize Y simply because it yields higher payoffs than X both for 1 and 2.

1 1 0	Y_3 / X_3	X_2	Y_2	0 0 0
	X_1	1 1 2	0 0 0	
	Y_1	0 0 0	2 2 0	
0 0 0				2 2 1

Table 0.2.2: A 3–person game with the primitive cell {1, 2} (player 1 is the row, player 2 the column player; player 3 chooses between 'in' (the inner matrix) and 'out' (the outer matrix); 1's (3's) payoff appears in the upper left (lower right) corner; player 2's payoff stands in between).

What the example demonstrates is that solution requirements as the equilibrium property or payoff dominance must not be restricted to the game itself. It can be even more important to apply them to those substructures representing game–like situations. The essential substructure of the game in Table 0.2.2 is apparently that strategic interaction is mainly restricted to players 1 and 2 only. Whether 1 and 2 should use X_1 and X_2 or Y_1 and Y_2, respectively, does not depend at all on the behavior of player 3. In close relation to the terminology of HARSANYI and SELTEN (1988) we call the subset {1, 2} of the player set a cell. A cell can be characterized as a substructure resulting from deleting players which is closed with respect to the best reply–correspondence, i.e. whether a given strategy of a cell player is a best reply does not depend on the behavior of the noncell players. A cell is called primitive if it contains no proper subcells. The cell structure of a game will be taken into account by first solving its primitive cell games and then determining the behavior of those players not contained in any primitive cell. Obviously this procedure closely resembles the recursive method of solving extensive games by first solving the last subgames and then proceeding to the earlier decision stages. As a matter of fact a subgame always generates a cell game but, as demonstrated by Table 0.2.2, not vice versa. Considering the cell structure can therefore be seen as an extension of the recursive solution method.

By our next example we want to illustrate that one might have to redefine a game before solving it. In the 2–person game, with the strategy sets $\{X_i, Y_i\}$ for both players i = 1, 2 whose payoff function is illustrated by Table 0.2.3 in the usual way, there are infinitely many equilibria since the payoff of a player does not depend at all on his own strategy. Although a player's payoff may depend on the strategy which the other player uses, one has to ask whether the two players encounter at all any strategic decision problem. Since their own strategy does not influence their own payoff, changing one's strategy appears like doing something which is completely inessential. In other words: A player will not loose anything if his vast multiplicity of mixed strategies in the game of Table 0.2.3 is substituted by just one mixed strategy. But if this is done the game of Table 0.2.3 becomes trivial since both players do not face a choice problem at all.

	X_2	Y_2
X_1	0 / 0	a / 0
Y_1	0 / b	a / b

Table 0.2.3: A 2–person game with a trivial irreducible form (player 1 (2)'s payoff appears in the upper left (lower right) corner; a, b $\in \mathbb{R}$).

As the example indicates the description of a game may include aspects which are strategically irrelevant. Usually an essential thing can be done in many ways differing in irrelevant details only. So why should the solution of a game depend on such inessential details? We will make the solution independent of strategically inessential aspects by reducing the game, e.g. by substituting the continuum of mixed strategies in the game of Table 0.2.3 by just one mixed strategy for both players. A game without proper cells from which all strategically inessential details are eliminated will be called an irreducible game or the irreducible form of the original game. By solving the irreducible game to determine the solution of the original game one clearly avoids that the solution depends on strategically inessential details by which the original game can differ from its irreducible form.

In the examples above our arguments how to select between equilibria are till now rather ad hoc in nature and incomplete. It is the main task of equilibrium selection theory to avoid ad hoc—principles and to consider, for every game, all relevant aspects when determining a unique solution. Here we only wanted to illustrate that there is a need to distinguish between equilibria and that there are natural convincing requirements which any reasonable concept of equilibrium selection will want to satisfy.

To define a general theory of equilibrium selection one has to impose more requirements than the ones discussed above, some of them are, unfortunately enough, also more debatable. But in our view such debates should not be avoided. If the main task of game theory is to resolve strategic uncertainty, such debates have to take place in order to clarify the impact of the possible solution requirements. It might well be that after such debates our present attempts to define a general concept of equilibrium selection will be considered as rather unacceptable or preliminary. The main purpose of our study is to induce such debates and to inspire new approaches how to select one of many equilibria as the solution of the game.

If one is able to select among equilibria one can often model a strategic conflict in the most obvious way whereas without this possibility one might be induced to look for game models with a unique equilibrium. Consider, for instance, RUBINSTEIN's (1982 and 1985) celebrated analysis of the bargaining model with alternating offers and no upper bound for the length of the play which has a unique equilibrium. Apart from the fact that infinite plays are impossible one has to ask why parties have to alternate in making offers. An alternative assumption would be that the size of previous concessions determines the one who is next to make a proposal. Even more important is that the unique equilibrium is based on very deliberate choices between two alternative moves yielding the same payoff (this can be avoided by studying a discrete version of the model but such a model would usually have a multiplicity of equilibria). One cannot imagine that anybody wants to rely on such fragile institutions. A more natural model might allow for simultaneous moves with the risk that no party makes a concession and that conflict can result after finitely many moves. Unfortunately, these models pathologically have multiple equilibria.

Of course, there are social decision problems where the most natural models have unique equilibria (see, for instance, FRIEDMAN, 1977, and BRAMS, 1985). But, if one is unable to distinguish among equilibria, one usually will be induced to neglect the most straightforward models with multiple equilibria in favor of more special models with unique equilibria. In this sense equilibrium selection as such seems to prepare the grounds for more unbiased modelling attempts.

3. Refinement concepts versus equilibrium selection theory

Contrary to BANKS and SOBEL (1987) we want to reserve the name 'equilibrium selection' exclusively for concepts defining a unique solution for every strategic game. Different from equilibrium selection theory the so-called 'refinement concepts' do not aim at unique solutions but restrict themselves to excluding only certain types of equilibria (for a survey see VAN DAMME, 1983 and 1987). A refinement concept defines a subclass of equilibria which all satisfy a stronger rationality requirement than just the equilibrium property. Thus both, equilibrium selection theories and refinement concepts, do not consider all equilibria as reasonable solution candidates. But whereas refinements confine themselves to rule out certain types of unreasonable equilibria, theories of equilibrium selection uniquely select a solution in order to resolve strategic uncertainty. In this sense equilibrium selection theory is clearly more ambitious and on the other hand, due to its early stage of development, far more speculative in nature.

If the rationality requirement underlying the refinement concept is an undebatable condition for individually rational decision making, any reasonable theory of equilibrium selection will try to guarantee it. In our view, an example for such a condition is the perfectness requirement defining the refinement concept of perfect equilibria (SELTEN, 1975). The situation is different if the requirement determining the refinement cannot always be satisfied (for examples see VAN DAMME, 1983, Sections 1.5 and 1.6). Equilibrium selection theory has to contradict any assumption endangering the existence of a solution in a well-defined game. Of course, even such over-restrictive conditions can serve as guidelines for selecting among equilibria in those games where these conditions are fulfilled. But only refinements without existence problems will provide general hints how to select a unique equilibrium solution.

Here we cannot describe and discuss all refinement concepts. Except for some recent proposals (e.g. KALAI and SAMET, 1984, KOHLBERG and MERTENS, 1986, BANKS and SOBEL, 1987) the monograph of VAN DAMME (1983) provides an excellent survey. We therefore confine ourselves to just mentioning some of the most essential concepts and to discussing their relevance for the theory of equilibrium selection.

The most basic and pathbreaking refinement concept is the perfect equilibrium point (SELTEN, 1975). It has already been mentioned that equilibrium selection theory satisfies perfectness by solving the game via the limit solution of its ϵ-uniformly perturbed games (HARSANYI and SELTEN, 1988). Since perfectness implies subgame perfectness, this also guarantees subgame perfectness of the solution. Similarly, all other refinements, based on weaker requirements than perfectness, e.g. sequentiality (KREPS and WILSON, 1982), are satisfied by the solution of the game.

Consider a strategic game in extensive form specifying unambiguously what a player knows when deciding in the course of the game. A behavioral strategy of a player in an extensive game assigns a unique probability distribution over the set of possible moves for each information set of this player. A behavioral strategy is completely mixed if in all information sets the probability for each move is strictly positive. Given a vector of completely mixed behavioral strategies a player can obviously deduce the probability for being in a certain decision node by applying Bayes' rule (BAYES, 1763). For a vector of noncompletely mixed behavioral strategies this is impossible since certain decision nodes may be reached with 0-probability. In such a case there is some freedom to formulate the posterior beliefs at such an information set specifying the probabilities of the different decision nodes. In other words: There is some arbitrariness in the beliefs about situations which occur with probability 0 although these beliefs may be strategically very important. A sequential equilibrium (KREPS and WILSON, 1982) is a strategy vector for which one can find consistent beliefs such that every local decision, i.e. move in an information set, is a best reply given the prescribed behavior and the beliefs. Consistency of beliefs is guaranteed if the vector of behavioral strategies can be approximated by vectors of completely mixed strategies such that the beliefs are the limiting conditional probabilities implied by these vectors according to Bayes' rule.

From the definition of sequentiality immediately follows that perfectness always guarantees sequentiality. In an ϵ-uniformly perturbed game all decision nodes in all information sets are reached with positive probability. Therefore any limit solution (for $\epsilon \to 0$) can be supported by consistent beliefs. On the other hand, not all sequential equilibria are perfect. Our procedure to solve the game indirectly via the limit of the solutions of its ϵ-uniformly perturbed games rules out equilibria which are sequential but not perfect.

But there are also refinements based on stronger requirements than perfectness of the equilibrium, e.g. the proper equilibrium proposed by MYERSON (1978). The well-known set inclusion diagram of VAN DAMME (1983) provides a list of some other refinements of this kind. Unfortunately, some of them cannot always be satisfied. But if existence is guaranteed, as for the proper equilibrium concept, one has to investigate whether such a refinement should guide how to select a solution from the set of perfect equilibria.

The basic idea of properness (MYERSON, 1978) is a rationality requirement for making mistakes in the sense that a more costly mistake has a much smaller probability than a less serious one. To explain this in more detail consider a vector $q^\epsilon = (q_1^\epsilon,...,q_n^\epsilon)$ of completely mixed strategies assigning strictly positive probabilities to all pure strategies in the game. Let ϵ be a small positive constant and s_i' be a worse reply of player i to q_{-i}^ϵ than s_i'' where q_{-i}^ϵ results from q^ϵ by eliminating its i-th component: The rationality of making mistakes requires that the probability $q_i^\epsilon(s_i')$ for the worse reply s_i' does not exceed $\epsilon q_i^\epsilon(s_i'')$. The vector q^ϵ is called an ϵ-proper equilibrium (KOHLBERG and MERTENS, 1986) if this condition is met by all n strategies q_i^ϵ. A strategy vector q is a proper equilibrium of the game if it can be approached by a sequence of ϵ-proper equilibria q^ϵ of the game in the sense of $q^\epsilon \to q$ for $\epsilon \to 0$. Thus in the limit all relative probabilities $q_i^\epsilon(s_i')/q_i^\epsilon(s_i'')$, with s_i' being a worse reply than s_i'', become 0.

It is rather questionable whether equilibrium selection should be based on the intuitively rather unacceptable idea that one tries to make mistakes in a rational way. Of course, if mistakes can only be avoided at high costs, it makes sense to speak of rationality in making mistakes. But VAN DAMME (1983) shows that only very special assumptions concerning the costs of controlling the probabilities of mistakes will yield perfect equilibria. Another aspect of properness is that the set of proper equilibria does not change when adding strictly dominated strategies to the game whereas the same is not true for the set of perfect equilibria (MYERSON, 1978). But this will be satisfied here by solving the irreducible form of a game.

In our view refinements of the perfect equilibrium point are also aiming at resolving strategic uncertainty but in a less systematic way than the equilibrium selection theory of HARSANYI and SELTEN (1988). Justifying such a refinement typically starts by demonstrating that a game may have a perfect equilibrium which is no reasonable solution of the game. But in our view the claim of the perfectness concept is to rule out imperfect equilibria as solution candidates and not that all perfect equilibria are reasonable. From the very beginning HARSANYI and SELTEN wanted to decide by an equilibrium selection approach whether a perfect equilibrium point should become the solution or not.

In this sense perfectness is, for them, a necessary but generally insufficient condition for the solution of the game. Therefore refining the refinement concept 'perfect equilibria' means to tackle problems HARSANYI and SELTEN want to treat more systematically by their theory of equilibrium selection. As shown for the properness concept the basic ideas underlying these refinements are often quite debatable and speculative in nature and therefore provide no clear guideline for designing a theory of equilibrium selection. It will be shown below that many aspects of present equilibrium selection theories are also quite debatable and speculative in nature. But we claim that here the debates and speculative arguments are more systematic and provide a sound basis for considering, in a consistent way, all the aspects deciding whether a given perfect equilibrium is a reasonable solution or not.

KOHLBERG and MERTENS (1986) propose a set valued equilibrium concept for normal form games for which they prove existence. Let $\delta = (\delta_1,...,\delta_n)$ with $0 < \delta_i < \delta_0$ be a vector of positive constants smaller than δ_0 and $q = (q_1,...,q_n)$ a vector of completely mixed strategies in the normal form game G. The δ,q–perturbed game $G^{\delta,q}$ of G is the game where every player i is restricted to completely mixed strategies of the form $(1 - \delta_i)s_i + \delta_i q_i$ where s_i is any possible strategy of player i in game G. For any $\delta_0 > 0$ the set of all such δ,q–perturbed games $G^{\delta,q}$, i.e. the set of games $G^{\delta,q}$ with $0 < \delta_i < \delta_0$ for $i = 1,...,n$ and q being any vector of completely mixed strategies in G, is called the δ_0–perturbed neighborhood G^{δ_0} of G. For any $\epsilon > 0$ we say that $G^{\delta,q}$ has an equilibrium ϵ–close to an equilibrium s of G if there is an equilibrium q* of $G^{\delta,q}$ such that the (Eucledian) distance of s and q* in the space of mixed strategy vectors in G is smaller than ϵ. KOHLBERG and MERTENS (1986) consider a closed set S of equilibria in G as stable if for every $\epsilon > 0$ there exists $\delta_0 > 0$ such that all δ,q–perturbed games $G^{\delta,q}$ in G^{δ_0} have an equilibrium ϵ–close to one of the equilibria in S and if the set S is minimal with respect to this requirement.

For any vector $\hat{q}$ of completely mixed strategies in G the set of $\delta,\hat{q}$–perturbed games $G^{\delta,\hat{q}}$ can be loosely described as the $\hat{q}$–tremble class of perturbed games. Whereas perfectness of an equilibrium s requires stability in the sense that only the games of one $\hat{q}$–tremble class have equilibria ϵ–close to s, KOHLBERG and MERTENS demand a more global type of stability by demanding ϵ–close equilibria in the games of all q–tremble classes. Thus the essence of perfectness is that one can perturb the game without a drastic change in the solution. Stability in the sense of KOHLBERG and MERTENS rules out such a drastic change (in the set valued–sense) for all possible perturbances.

It should be noted that, when developing our approach, the stability concept of KOHLBERG and MERTENS was not yet available since it came out later than the first version of this study which was already circulated in 1982. But even now one would face two major difficulties when trying to develop a theory of equilibrium selection satisfying stability. First of all one would have to translate set valued stability to single valued stability. Although KOHLBERG and MERTENS show that stable sets reduce to single points in all generic games, equilibrium selection wants to solve all well–defined games, i.e. also degenerate ones.

The other difficulty results from representing a strategic game by its normal form which implies that two strategic games are considered as strategically equivalent if their normal forms coincide. The main argument of KOHLBERG and MERTENS (1986) for this point of view is that one can find refinements, e.g. properness, for normal form games which guarantee the fulfilment of certain refinements for extensive form games, like sequentiality or perfectness. Since one cannot be sure about all strategically relevant aspects before having completely resolved strategic uncertainty, this argument seems rather premature. According to our approach the complete agent normal form which will be defined later on includes all strategically relevant aspects, i.e. two strategic games with the same complete agent normal form are considered as strategically equivalent. But we can well imagine that further applications may reveal weaknesses of our present concept which can only be cured by more complex theories treating different games with the same complete agent normal form differently.

Only an approach which completely resolves strategic uncertainty can make a valid claim concerning which aspects of a strategic game are relevant or not. For less ambitious concepts it is no surprise that they will find fewer aspects to be relevant. To check, for instance, the equilibrium property, one only needs the normal form. KOHLBERG and MERTENS (1986) themselves present a one parameter–family of strategic games with the same normal form whose only sequential equilibrium depends on the game parameter neglected by the normal form.

There are many ways to select a unique equilibrium point as the solution of a strategic game and even some of the most fundamental requirements are far from being generally accepted. Often these different approaches will rely on different forms of presenting the strategic decision problem. Thus the problem of how to present a game is closely related to that of solving it. Before having resolved strategic uncertainty it therefore appears premature to argue that the normal form is a sufficient representation of a strategic decision problem.

4. The state of the art in equilibrium selection

In spite of the impressive multiplicity of game theoretic studies there are only very few contributions to the theory of equilibrium selection. There are mainly two conceptional milestones in the development of equilibrium selection, namely the solution of NASH (1950, 1953) for unanimity bargaining games and the Harsanyi–Selten theory of equilibrium selection (HARSANYI and SELTEN, 1988, for a brief description of this theory see also HARSANYI, 1976). Concerning applications of equilibrium selection theory it seems useless to mention all applications of NASH's bargaining solution (an influential early application was certainly MAYBERRY, NASH, and SHUBIK, 1953). But also the Harsanyi–Selten theory has been applied to various problems (e.g., HARSANYI, 1976, 1980, and 1982, SELTEN and GÜTH, 1978, 1982a and c, and 1988, SELTEN and LEOPOLD, 1982, GÜTH, 1978, LEOPOLD–WILDBURGER, 1982 and 1985, GÜTH and SEIFERT, 1984, GÜTH and STEPHAN, 1984).

In the following we will first describe the ad hoc–concept NASH (1950, 1953) offers for unanimity bargaining games and how, with a few introductory remarks, he outlined the program of equilibrium selection. Afterwards the Harsanyi–Selten theory of equilibrium selection will be introduced which is the first general approach to equilibrium selection and which will certainly have a major impact on all later studies in the field of equilibrium selection.

4.1 NASH's selection approach for unanimity bargaining games

With the following remark NASH (1953, pp. 131 and 132) outlined the program of equilibrium selection theory:

> "Thus the equilibrium points do not lead us immediately to a solution of the game. But if we discriminate between them by studying their relative stabilities we can escape from this troublesome nonuniqueness."

Let n (≥ 2) denote the number of players i engaged in the game and let B ($\subseteq \mathbb{R}^n_+$) be a compact and convex set of utility vectors $H = (H_1,...,H_n)$ with nonnegative components which has a nonempty interior and which, furthermore, satisfies the assumption that $u \in B$ implies $u' \in B$ for all $0 \leq u' \leq u$. In Figure 0.4.1 we have graphically illustrated for n = 2 some standard cases of the set B which is often called the feasible set. Case a) with a smooth upper–right boundary/efficiency frontier could, for instance, result from seller cooperation on a duopoly market where side payments are prohibited (see MAYBERRY, NASH, and SHUBIK, 1953).

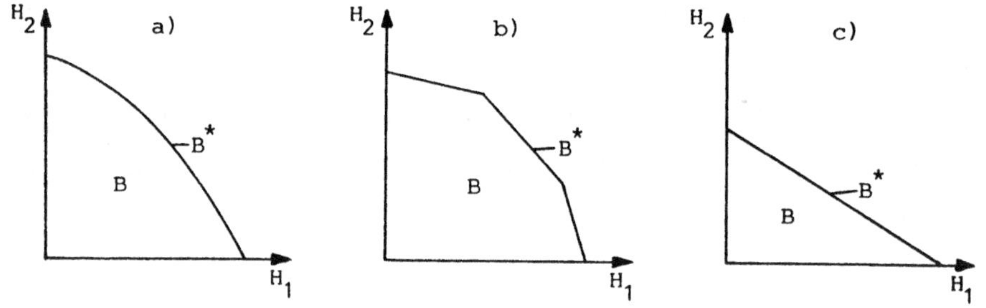

Figure 0.4.1: Some standard cases of the feasible set B in unanimity bargaining games.

Case b) typically represents the set of feasible payoff vectors in normal form games where all linear combinations of possible payoff vectors can be reached since players can jointly randomize their decision behavior. Case c) would result in any of the situations underlying a) and b) if side payments are possible.

In an n–person unanimity bargaining game the n players i determine their demands s_i (≥ 0) independently. If the demand vector $s = (s_1,...,s_n)$ is feasible, i.e. if $s \in B$, then each player i's payoff is s_i. Otherwise conflict results with 0–payoffs for all players i = 1,...,n. Let $\delta : \mathbb{R}^n_+ \to \{0, 1\}$ be the function such that $\delta(s) = 1$ for $s \in B$ and $\delta(s) = 0$ otherwise. With the help of this notation player i's payoff function $H_i(s)$ in the n–person unanimity game can be written as $H_i(s) = s_i\delta(s)$ for i = 1,...,n.

Denote by B^* the subset of B such that for all $s \in B^*$ there exists no $s' \in B$ with $s' \geq s$ and $s' \neq s$.

B^* is often called efficiency frontier or Pareto–frontier of B. Given a demand vector $s \in B^*$ no player i can gain by increasing his individual demand. As a matter of fact he will even loose if $s_i > 0$ since a higher demand of player i will result in an infeasible demand vector and therefore imply 0–payoffs for all n players. Thus all demand vectors s in B^* are equilibrium points (if $s_i > 0$ for i = 1,...,n they are also perfect equilibrium points) which shows the vast multiplicity of (perfect) equilibrium points in unanimity bargaining games. Here a strategy vector in a continuous game is called a perfect equilibrium point if it is a perfect equilibrium point for every finite discrete approximation of the continuous games not excluding the strategy vector under consideration.

To select a unique solution s^* in B^* NASH (1953) "smoothes the game" by approximating the discontinuous function $\delta(.)$ by continuous functions $d : \mathbb{R}^n_+ \to (0,1]$ with $d(s) = 1$ if $s \in B$, and which quickly converge to zero for growing $s \notin B$. In the "smoothed game" with d(.) for $\delta(.)$ an equilibrium point $s = (s_1,...,s_n)$ requires that for all $i = 1,...,n$ the strategy s_i maximizes the payoff $s_i d(s)$ at least locally.

Due to our assumptions concerning B there is a unique point s^* in B which maximizes the product of dividends, i.e. $\prod_{i=1}^n s_i^* > \prod_{i=1}^n s_i$ for all $s \in B$ (see Figure 0.4.2 where the situation is graphically illustrated for n = 2). The name 'dividend' is justified since, due to the normalization of payoffs, s_i is player i's difference between his agreement and his conflict payoff. Consider now the sequence of those equilibrium points s^d in the smoothed games with d(.) approaching $\delta(.)$ for which $d(s)\prod_{i=1}^n s_i$ is maximal (if $d(s)\prod_{i=1}^n s_i$ is maximal, obviously no player can gain by changing his demand). Clearly, no such equilibrium point s^d can lie below the hyperbola $\prod_{i=1}^n H_i = \prod_{i=1}^n s_i^*$, (for n = 2 the situation is again graphically illustrated in Figure 0.4.2). Furthermore, with d(.) approaching $\delta(.)$ the sequence $\{s^d\}$ has to converge to its unique limit point s^*.

Assume that all functions d(.) of the sequence $\{d(.)\}$ approaching $\delta(.)$ are continuously differentiable. Let, furthermore, $d(s)\prod_{i=1}^n s_i$ have a unique local maximum in $\mathbb{R}^n_+$ and let $d(s)\prod_{i=1}^n s_i \to 0$ for $\sum_{i=1}^n s_i^2 \to \infty$: Under these assumptions any equilibrium point s in the smoothed game must maximize $d(s)\prod_{i=1}^{n} s_i$. Thus s^* is the only necessary limit of equilibrium points in the smoothed games with d(.) approaching δ(.).

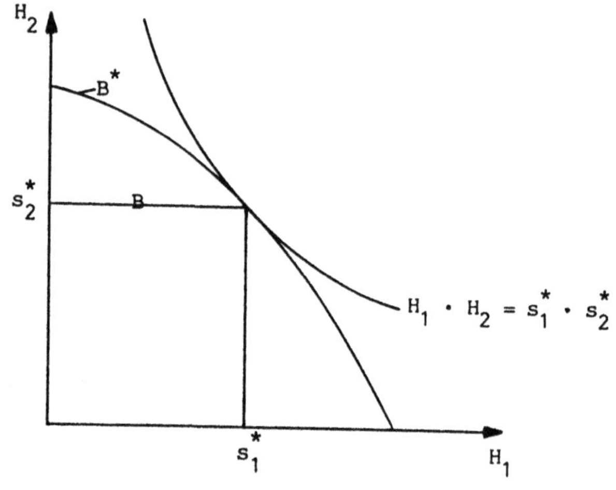

Figure 0.4.2: The solution point s^* of 2–person unanimity bargaining games which maximizes the product s_1s_2 of dividends over the feasible set B.

According to NASH (1953, p. 133) the equilibrium point s^* should therefore be selected as the solution of the n–person unanimity bargaining game since it is the only necessary limit of equilibrium points in smoothed games. An obvious interpretation of the functions d(.) is that they represent some slight uncertainties concerning the feasible set B, i.e. d(s) should be understood as the probability that the demand vector s is feasible (see NASH, 1953, p. 132). Thus the solution point s^* can be viewed as the (perfect) equilibrium point which is most immune against such slight uncertainties about the feasible set B.

In addition to his selection approach NASH provides an axiomatic characterization of the solution s^* which also became very influential (see, for instance, ROTH, 1985, PETERS, 1986, AUMANN, 1985). By now there are also other possible characterizations of NASH's solution point s^* (e.g. LENSBERG, 1987 and 1988, LENSBERG and THOMSOM, 1988) indicating that the philosophical justification of the various axioms can only be decided by looking at broader classes of bargaining games. The main axioms of NASH (1950) are efficiency, independence of positive affine transformations of the utility scales, symmetry, and independence of irrelevant alternatives (for the variable threat–problem NASH (1953) had to impose two more requirements).

NASH's ingenious contribution and his admirable conceptual long–sightedness became very influential in several respects: It was the first concept for bargaining games without side payments (see AUMANN, 1985, and ROTH, 1979, for a recent discussion of games without transferable utilities). It outlined the program for the so–called noncooperative approach to bargaining theory: "... one makes the players' steps of negotiation in the cooperative game become moves in the non–cooperative model" (NASH, 1953, p. 129). More recent milestones in this field are certainly RUBINSTEIN (1982 and 1985), for a survey see SUTTON (1985). And most importantly for us NASH influenced decisively the method of equilibrium selection theory: As NASH equilibrium selection theory looks at noncooperative games, studies their equilibria and selects a unique solution by discriminating between them according to their "relative stabilities". We will refer to this as the procedural approach of equilibrium selection. On the other hand, equilibrium selection theory also tries to find axiomatic characterizations of selection procedures (see HARSANYI and SELTEN, 1988, Chapter 5). Unfortunately, the axiomatic approach of equilibrium selection theory is till now less successful than NASH's approach for unanimity bargaining games. Up to now one can give axiomatic characterizations only for very limited classes of games. The generally known properties of selection theories do not suffice to eliminate all other selection procedures.

As NASH (1953, p. 129) equilibrium selection theory considers both, the procedural and the axiomatic approach, as complementary ways to illuminate a given selection concept:

> "The two approaches to the problem via the negotiation model or via the axioms, are complementary; each helps to justify and clarify the other."

Although in different ways, both, the Harsanyi–Selten theory and our concept, use NASH's solution for unanimity bargaining games as one of the most crucial guidelines by requiring that in n–person unanimity bargaining games s^* is selected as the solution. Thus NASH did not only outline the program of equilibrium selection theory. With his ingenious solution for unanimity bargaining games he also provided a benchmark for more general selection concepts. Thus it seems justified to say that NASH is the founder and the first contributor to the field of equilibrium selection theory.

4.2 The Harsanyi–Selten theory of equilibrium selection

The first general attempt to accomplish the program outlined by NASH is the theory of equilibrium selection developed by JOHN C. HARSANYI and REINHARD SELTEN. Already in 1973 when one of the authors of this study attended the seminars of HARSANYI and SELTEN at the University of Bielefeld their concept seemed to be nearly fully developed. But although it has already been applied to various games with multiple equilibria (see the references mentioned in the introduction of Section 4), "their book", by which they always wanted to describe and discuss their theory, came out only recently. On the one hand, the delay is certainly due to the many conceptual and mathematical difficulties which one faces when trying to define a nontrivial selection concept. So the Harsanyi–Selten theory for the first time investigates important substructures of games which were unknown before and which every reasonable theory of equilibrium selection will carefully consider. On the other hand, HARSANYI and SELTEN apparently wanted to come out with the concept of equilibrium selection. This induced them to revise their concept several times after considering more and more examples (see, for instance, GÜTH, 1978, who describes one of the earlier versions of the Harsanyi–Selten theory). Another reason for the delay is, of course, that it is difficult to design a concept and to write one of the most ambitious books satisfying the aspirations of two of the most distinguished game theorists.

In our view, there are also considerable costs caused by the delay in publishing their concept. Until now the group of scholars who are familiar with their concept or at least with its main aspects is very small. Thus over the years HARSANYI and SELTEN had to live with rather few reactions by other game theorists who could have provided other ideas, new examples etc.

Although many aspects of the Harsanyi–Selten theory have already been described in previous publications (HARSANYI, 1975 and 1976, SELTEN, 1975) or applications (e.g. SELTEN and GÜTH, 1978, 1982a and c, HARSANYI, 1976, LEOPOLD–WILDBURGER, 1982) the most recent and impressing account of their pioneering approach is certainly their book (HARSANYI and SELTEN, 1988) which, in our view, will become one of the major milestones in the development of game theory:

In Chapter 1 HARSANYI and SELTEN justify the need for a general theory of equilibrium selection. Since finally all cooperative activities have to be modelled by noncooperative bargaining models such a general theory must define a solution concept for all noncooperative games. The equilibrium concept for such games is most thoroughly discussed by surveying some of its most important interpretations and critical discussions. The main shortcoming is, of course, the nonuniqueness of the equilibrium point solution which causes the need to select among equilibria.

The formal representation of strategic conflicts is developed in Chapter 2 where HARSANYI and SELTEN introduce the standard form as well as important substructures of such games. Chapter 3 contains a very deep philosophical and mathematical discussion of desirable properties for a general solution theory which, in our view, will be influential beyond the scope of equilibrium selection theory. The general theory of HARSANYI and SELTEN, here called the Harsanyi –Selten theory, is fully defined and described in Chapters 4 and 5. Applications, mostly already published before, can be found in Chapters 6 and 7 (games with complete information) as well as in Chapters 8 and 9 (two person bargaining games with incomplete information). In the final Chapter 10 the philosophical aspects of the Harsanyi–Selten theory are once again discussed by reconsidering some of its most crucial conceptual decisions.

Chapters 1, 3, and 10 together provide a very thorough and probably pathbreaking discussion for any general theory resolving strategic uncertainty. It is especially this profound philosophical analysis for which we have been waiting so long. Compared to this the remaining chapters naturally are not as 'new' since many aspects of the Harsanyi–Selten theory have been sketched before (HARSANYI, 1975 and 1976, SELTEN, 1975) and since several applications contained in the book are already published elsewhere.

In the following we give a brief and mostly verbal description of the Harsanyi–Selten theory. On the one hand, this will demonstrate that our approach often follows ideas originally introduced by HARSANYI and SELTEN. On the other hand, it will allow us to discuss the main differences between the Harsanyi–Selten theory and our approach.

4.2.1 Uniformly perturbed games in standard form

The most detailed description of a game is certainly the extensive form consisting of the game tree, the player partition, the information partition, the move partition, the probability assignment for chance moves, and the payoff function (see SELTEN, 1975, for details). The extensive form can even be overspecified since it requires, for instance, to specify the time order for simultaneous moves. The main advantage of the extensive form is obviously its adequate representation of the decision process in case of sequential decisions which is neglected by the normal form. According to the normal form all dynamic aspects are captured by strategies which players are assumed to choose independently and simultaneously at the beginning of the game. An important formal game representation between those two extremes is the agent normal form which considers the same person in different decision situations as different players or agents. Although, as for the normal form, all players are assumed to choose their strategies independently and simultaneously at the beginning of the game, an agent who chooses a move later than another agent of the same player will base his decision purely on local considerations, i.e. on whether his decision is good or bad given that his information set has been reached.

Formally, the normal form has to specify the strategy sets of all players and the payoff function which assigns a vector of cardinal utilities to all strategy vectors expressing how the different players evaluate such a result of the game. In the agent normal form the strategy set of an agent is the set of possible choices in his information set. Furthermore, all agents of the same player evaluate the results of the game as the player himself. Although both, the Harsanyi–Selten theory and our concept of equilibrium selection, do not consider the agent normal form as a sufficient description of a strategic game, the agent normal form is their main starting point of presenting a game.

Unlike an earlier version of the Harsanyi–Selten theory (see GÜTH, 1978), HARSANYI and SELTEN (1988, Chapter 2) now model strategic conflicts as games in standard form. Loosely speaking the standard form differs from the agent normal form by an additional component which preserves the identity of players, i.e. in the standard form an agent is assumed to know the coagents of "his player". In other words: The decision behavior of a player is not simply composed by the locally optimal decisions of his agents but, at least sometimes, also by global considerations. Technically, the reason for preserving the identity of players is that different agents of the same player should share the same views concerning their opponents.

In our view, it is at least debatable whether different agents of the same player must view their opponents' decision behavior in the same way. At later stages a player knows more and may therefore have different expectations about his opponents. Even more important might be that in games with incomplete information the notion of a player is quite meaningless since it only reflects the possible expectations of others. Here only the (true) agents/types are real. The player is just a result of closing the game informationally (HARSANYI, 1967/68), i.e. a purely theoretical construct of presenting the game.

When solving the game according to the Harsanyi–Selten theory one actually analyses sequences of games converging to the game in question. Let ϵ be a positive small number. The ϵ–uniformly perturbed game G^ϵ in standard form of the game G in standard form results from G by narrowing down the set of mixed strategies in G to completely mixed strategies in the sense that in G^ϵ every move of every (personal) player will be realized at least with probability ϵ. Instead of applying their selection procedure directly to G HARSANYI and SELTEN determine the solution of G via the limit of the solutions s^ϵ of the games G^ϵ approximating G. The main purpose of solving G via the limit solution of games G^ϵ is to guarantee the perfectness of the solution for G. Since all solutions s^ϵ are equilibria of their respective games G^ϵ, an equilibrium point s of G satisfying $s = \lim_{\epsilon \to 0} s^\epsilon$ is a perfect equilibrium point of G. On the other hand, the indirect way of solving G implies various mathematical difficulties related to the existence of a limit solution for a given solution concept. HARSANYI and SELTEN think that the existence of the limit solution can be proved with the help of algebraic geometry though they did not show this explicitly. They only state (HARSANYI and SELTEN, 1988, Section 2.9):

> "In an unpublished paper the authors have achieved a result on iterated limits of piecewise algebraic functions, which suggest that no difficulties should arise with respect to the existence of the limit solution. [HARSANYI and SELTEN, 1977]".

Since, in this respect, our concept closely follows the ideas of HARSANYI and SELTEN, we think that a similar argument can be provided to justify our hope that the limit solution exists.

4.2.2 The tracing procedure

A major tool of the Harsanyi–Selten theory is the tracing procedure (HARSANYI, 1975, and HARSANYI and SELTEN, 1988). The tracing procedure is an equilibrating process in the sense that, for a given game, the procedure will end with an equilibrium state regardless whether its starting point is an equilibrium point or not. Intuitively it can be seen as a combination of decision theory and game theory since its starting point results from the 'naive' decision theoretic approach whereas its end point satisfies the game theoretic equilibrium property.

Here we restrict ourselves to the description of the tracing procedure for those games having an equal number of agents and players. In spite of this simplification the main ideas will become clear and we avoid an even more technical presentation (see HARSANYI and SELTEN, 1988, Section 4.15).

Formally, the starting point is determined by a vector $p = (p_1,\dots,p_n)$ of prior beliefs, i.e. the mixed strategy p_i of player i is assumed to reflect all other players' beliefs about i's decision behavior. The 'naive' decision theoretic approach implies that every player $j = 1,\dots,n$ chooses the strategy which is a best reply to his <u>prior beliefs</u> $p_{-j} = (p_1,\dots,p_{j-1},p_{j+1},\dots,p_n)$ concerning the other players' behavior. For the game theoretic approach the prior beliefs are meaningless since all players analyse the game according to the equilibrium concept, i.e. by searching for behavioral constellations which are self-enforcing.

Let $G = (S_1,...,S_n;H)$ be a game in (agent) normal form and $p = (p_1,...,p_n)$ the vector of prior beliefs.The games $G^t = (S_1,...,S_n;H^t)$ in the one-parameter family $\{G^t\}_{t\in[0,1]}$ differ from G only with respect to their payoff functions $H^t = (H_1^t,...,H_n^t)$ which are defined by

$$H_i^t(q_i,q_{-i}) = t\, H_i(q_i,q_{-i}) + (1-t)\, H_i(q_i,p_{-i}) + (1-t)\, \delta \sum_{s_i\in S_i} \log(q_i(s_i))$$

where δ is positive. Thus, only for $t = 1$ player 1's payoff $H_i^t(q_i,q_{-i})$ is the same as in G for any mixed strategy vector (q_i,q_{-i}) consisting of player i's strategy mixture q_i as well as the mixed strategy constellation $q_{-i} = (q_1,...,q_{i-1},q_{i+1},...,q_n)$ of his opponents. For $t = 0$ the game G^t is obviously an adequate representation of the 'naive' decision theoretic apporach since i's payoff does not depend at all on the other players' strategies q_{-i} but only on his prior beliefs p_{-i} concerning his opponents' behavior. The last term of the payoff function H_i^t is a penalty guaranteeing a unique equilibrium point as the solution of the tracing procedure. With t increasing from $t = 0$ to $t = 1$ the degree of strategic interaction increases till it reaches the analysis of the game G itself with $t = 1$.

For sufficiently small $\delta > 0$ it is due to the logarithmic penalty term that one can always find a unique algebraic curve of equilibria $s^t = s^t(\delta)$ in the games G^t ($t \in [0,1]$) connecting the vector $s^0 = s^0(\delta)$ of best replies to p to an equilibrium point $s^1 = s^1(\delta)$ of G. Then the limit $\delta \to 0$ yields a piecewise algebraic curve whose endpoint $T(G,p) = \lim_{\delta\to 0} s^1(\delta)$ is always well-defined and an equilibrium point of G. It is called the tracing result for G with respect to the prior beliefs p.

4.2.3 The method of how to solve a game

Consider a small perturbance parameter $\epsilon > 0$. From what has been said above one has to determine the solution s^ϵ for any game G^ϵ which results from perturbing a given game G uniformly according to ϵ. The first step in solving G^ϵ is to decompose G^ϵ if possible. A subset C of the player set is said to yield a cell (game) if the best reply of all players in C does not depend at all on the strategies chosen by players outside C, i.e. the subset C is closed with respect to the best reply correspondence. A game G^ϵ is called decomposable if a proper and nonempty subset C of the player set satisfies the requirement for a cell. If the game G^ϵ is decomposable, one first solves the primitive cell games, i.e. the cell games which are not further decomposable. Given the solutions for these cell games one then solves the residual game which results from G^ϵ by fixing the cell players to their cell solution strategies. We call this procedure of decomposing G^ϵ in primitive cells, which are solved first in order to determine and to solve the residual game, the <u>decomposition subroutine</u>. The decomposition procedure of HARSANYI and SELTEN, which is used by our approach without change, will be described in more detail in Section 4 of Part II.

For the decomposition subroutine to be well–defined one has to specify how to solve a decomposable game. Now the formal representation of a decomposable game may still contain superfluous aspects. If, for instance, the strategy set of player i contains an inferior strategy s_i for which another strategy s_i' exists which is a best reply whenever s_i is one and which is a best reply to some behavior of the others when this is not true for s_i, the inferior strategy appears to be superfluous. Similarly, the strategy set may contain strategies which are strategically equivalent since they always yield the same payoffs for all players (duplicate strategies) or only for the player himself (semi–duplicate strategies) regardless what the others decide to do. The <u>reduction subroutine</u>, which has to be applied to the indecomposable substructures of G^ϵ and simultaneously for all players, starts with an iterated elimination of inferior strategies followed by a decomposition of the game if necessary. If there are no more inferior strategies, this is followed by substituting sets of duplicate strategies by their centroids, i.e. the mixed strategy which asssigns the same positive probability to all strategies in this set and only to them. Having done so one has to eliminate inferior strategies as before and possibly to repeat the substitution of duplicate sets till the game contains neither duplicate sets nor inferior strategies. Then the sets of semi–duplicate strategies are substituted by their centroids in the same way. Since all strategy sets are finite, the reduction procedure has to stop after finitely many steps with an irreducible game structure which is indecomposable and contains neither inferior nor duplicate or semi–duplicate strategies for any of its players.

The reduction subroutine of HARSANYI and SELTEN is also used by our approach except that we do not distinguish between duplicate and semi–duplicate strategies. The reason for this is that we do not see any justification for giving lexicographically more weight to the substitution of duplicate strategies as compared to the substitution of semi–duplicate strategies. All what a rational player cares for is expressed by his own payoff function. So whether a strategy should be eliminated or substituted should only be based on his own payoff function. Already the decomposition procedure, which has to be applied before, is based purely on how the choice of a strategy affects the own payoff. Taking this seriously we do not see any need to distinguish between duplicate and semi–duplicate strategies.

Given an irreducible game one can now apply the essential <u>solution subroutine</u> of the Harsanyi—Selten theory. The solution subroutine first investigates the formation structure of such a game. A formation F is a subset of the set of all possible strategy vectors of the game which results from eliminating individual strategies and which is closed with respect to the best reply—correspondence, i.e. if all players are assumed to choose among strategies permissible in F all best replies are included in F. A formation F is called primitive if it contains no proper subformation. Now, the games determined by primitive formations F may not be irreducible whereas the original game is. Thus one first has to apply the decomposition and reduction subroutine before solving the irreducible games without proper subformations. According to the Harsanyi–Selten theory the most primitive form of strategic interaction is a game which cannot be decomposed nor reduced and which does not fall apart into a formation substructure. For these most primitive games F they determine the solution in the most primitive way, namely by tracing the centroid c(F), i.e. the mixed strategy in F whose components give equal weights to all possible strategies of the respective player. The tracing results T(F,c(F)) for the games F resulting from applying the decomposition and reduction subroutine to the primitive formations of the game are the first solution candidates. If there is only one first candidate, this is the solution of the game. Otherwise HARSANYI and SELTEN first investigate whether candidates are payoff dominated. The restricted game F(X,Y) for the comparison of X and Y is the smallest formation game of the original irreducible game containing X as well as Y. An element X of the candidate set is said to be payoff dominated if another candidate Y yields a higher payoff for every active player in F(X,Y).

In case of a unique payoff undominated candidate, this is the solution. Otherwise HARSANYI and SELTEN investigate what they call the risk dominance relation between the payoff undominated solution candidates. Let X and Y be two different such solution candidates. The dominance relation between X and Y is determined by tracing the so-called bicentric prior beliefs p(X,Y). The definition of p(X,Y) is based on the assumption that every player i thinks that all other players know whether X or Y is the solution and that he himself expects the solution to be X with probability z and Y with probability 1–z where z is a uniformly distributed random variable on the interval [0,1]. Obviously this implies that player i expects the jointly randomizing behavior $zX_{-i} + (1-z)Y_{-i}$ on behalf of his opponents although the rules of the game do not permit such a coordinated decision behavior (the critical discussion of the Harsanyi–Selten theory in GÜTH (1985) exactly exploits this fact). The component $p_i(X,Y)$ of the bicentric prior beliefs p(X,Y) is then simply the mixed strategy $p_i(X,Y)$ of player i in F(X,Y) according to which every strategy s_i is chosen with the probability of being a (central) best reply to $zX_{-i} + (1-z)Y_{-i}$.

If the tracing result T(F(X,Y),p(X,Y)) is the equilibrium point X, HARSANYI and SELTEN say that X risk dominates Y. If neither X risk dominates Y nor vice versa one cannot discriminate between X and Y by risk dominance. Risk dominance is an intransitive partial order on the set of solution candidates. According to HARSANYI and SELTEN payoff and risk dominance relations should be weighted by what they call the strategic distance e(X,Y) between solution candidates X and Y. Let $e_i(X,Y)$ be the number of critical values $z \in [0,1]$ where player i's best reply in F(X,Y) to $z X_{-i} + (1-z)Y_{-i}$ changes. The strategic distance e(X,Y) is determined by the sum of all $e_i(X,Y)$ over the set of active players i in F(X,Y) who have more than just one strategy in F(X,Y). A solution candidate X is called maximally stable if i) or ii) are true:

i) X is undominated, i.e. neither payoff nor risk dominated in the set of solution candidates Ω.

ii) There is no undominated solution candidate in Ω and the minimal net strategic distance of X to another solution candidate Y in Ω, which dominates X, is maximal.

Here the net strategic distance of X and Y in Ω is closely related to the strategic distance e(X,Y) and the dominance relationship is a combination of payoff and risk dominance giving precedence to payoff dominance [if X is a next neighbor of Y the converse must not be true!]. More precisely, X dominates Y if i) or ii) are true:

i) $H_i(X) > H_i(Y)$ for all active players $i \in N$ with $X_i \neq Y_i$.

ii) X risk dominates Y and there is an active player i for whom $H_i(X) \geq H_i(Y)$.

First all candidates which are not maximally stable, are eliminated. If there exists only one such maximally stable element, this is the solution. Otherwise HARSANYI and SELTEN distinguish whether all or not all previous solution candidates are maximally stable. In the first case one substitutes the set of maximally stable candidates by the tracing result of their centroid in the original game, i.e. the new candidate set only consists of candidates, which were eliminated (and not substituted) before, and the tracing result of the centroid of those strategies which have not been excluded before. If not all previous candidates are maximally stable the set of maximally stable elements is the new candidate set to which one again applies the concepts of payoff and risk dominance till after finitely many steps one finally obtains a unique candidate which is the Harsanyi–Selten solution of the game.

So far we have described how HARSANYI and SELTEN solve a game which cannot be decomposed or reduced. Given the solutions of these substructures which are determined by first solving the primitive cell games and then the residual game, the solution of the game itself is simply the composition of the solutions of these substructures. In this way one can solve all uniformly perturbed games G^ϵ of the original game G for all sequences of perturbance parameters ϵ converging to 0. The limit of these solutions is the Harsanyi–Selten solution of the original game G.

Our description shows that the Harsanyi–Selten theory is extremely complex and based on many very different ideas, e.g. those underlying the definition of bicentric prior beliefs, the tracing procedure, and the strategic distance. Some other fundamental philosophical decisions are, furthermore, revealed by the list and time order of principles according to which one discriminates among solution candidates. So it is, for instance, assumed that payoff dominance is lexicographically more important than risk dominance.

Till now we have tried to describe the Harsanyi–Selten theory by avoiding technicalities as far as possible. Knowing the various subroutines on which the solution is based the complete procedure of how to compute the Harsanyi–Selten solution for a given game G in standard form is most conveniently described with the help of flow chart diagrams. This will be done in Section 4.2.5 below.

4.2.4 Properties of the Harsanyi–Selten theory

In our view, the major difficulty of the Harsanyi–Selten theory is that it uses so many different tools like the tracing procedure, bicentric or centroid prior beliefs, strategic distance and a complicated process of candidate elimination and substitution (see the terrifying example of LEOPOLD–WILDBURGER, 1982 and 1985) which is mainly due to the intransitivity of risk dominance. Of course, most of these tools are based on their two essential philosophical ideas, namely Bayesianism and the equilibrium concept, which serve as the main guidelines for nearly all game theoretic studies of HARSANYI and SELTEN. But nevertheless one can hardly judge whether the various "stories" underlying the different tools mentioned above are methodologically consistent or not. Especially therefore it is extremely important to justify the selection procedure also axiomatically, i.e. to develop an axiomatic approach complementing the procedural approach as NASH has done it. Fortunately, HARSANYI and SELTEN were ingenious enough to derive some very encouraging results (HARSANYI and SELTEN, 1988, Chapter 3) although a full axiomatic characterization of the Harsanyi–Selten theory is still out of sight.

Properties of the Harsanyi–Selten solution following directly from the solution procedure are, for instance, <u>invariance with respect to inferior, duplicate, and semi–duplicate strategies</u>, where the hierarchy of these properties is given by the time order of the reduction subroutine. By this we mean that adding or eliminating such strategies for one or more players will not change the Harsanyi–Selten solution in an essential way (if a duplicate or semi–duplicate strategy is used according to the Harsanyi–Selten solution the solution changes, of course, since now the centroid is chosen). Similarly, the decomposition subroutine implies decomposition consistency meaning that the solutions which the Harsanyi–Selten solution implies for the cell games as well as for the residual game coincide with the Harsanyi–Selten solutions of these games. Decomposition consistency is closely related to the more familiar axiom of subgame consistency (see SELTEN and GÜTH, 1982b, and GÜTH, LEININGER, and STEPHAN, 1988).

Another property satisfied by the Harsanyi–Selten solution is invariance with respect to isomorphisms implying invariance with respect to positive linear payoff transformations and symmetry invariance. The property is satisfied since all steps which have to be performed according to the solution procedure are not influenced if the game is transformed isomorphically. Payoff dominance, which is used to discriminate between solution candidates as risk dominance, is thus considered as less important than symmetry invariance, i.e. the Harsanyi–Selten solution satisfies payoff dominance only within the set of symmetry invariant solution candidates. For the 'battle of sexes' with $a = b$ in Table 0.2.1 this implies that the Harsanyi–Selten solution is the mixed strategy equilibrium point which is payoff dominated by both pure strategy equilibria. Since any solution which is not symmetry invariant would imply an arbitrary selection, the absolute priority of symmetry invariance is, in our view, undebatable. More difficult to justify is the priority of payoff dominance over risk dominance meaning that even the slightest payoff advantages will offset all risk considerations. We have tried to illustrate this by the 2–person game in Table 0.4.1 where e is assumed to be a very small and E a very large positive number. Clearly, players 1 and 2 can be sure to loose nothing as long as they use s_1^1 and s_2^1, respectively, whereas choosing the strategies s_1^2 and s_2^2 of the Harsanyi–Selten solution means to risk a fortune. HARSANYI and SELTEN (1988, Sections 10.11 and 10.12) are aware that this is one of their more critical decisions. As a matter of fact an earlier version of their theory did not impose payoff dominance (see GÜTH, 1978).

	s_2^1		s_2^2	
s_1^1	e	e	0	−E
s_1^2	−E	0	2e	2e

Table 0.4.1: A 2–person normal form game with E > e > 0 and two strict equilibria, namely $s^1 = (s_1^1, s_2^1)$ and $s^2 = (s_1^2, s_2^2)$, of which s^2 is the Harsanyi–Selten solution.

As already mentioned before a major guideline for designing the Harsanyi–Selten theory is to generalize NASH's selection procedure (see Section 4.1 above), i.e. the Harsanyi–Selten solution for unanimity bargaining games introduced in Section 4.1 should be the equilibrium point s^* which maximizes the dividend product over the feasible set B. As shown by HARSANYI (1975) the Harsanyi–Selten solution satisfies this requirement which from now on will be called the Nash–property. An immediate consequence of the Nash–property is that at least for the class of unanimity bargaining games the axiomatic approach can use all respective results of NASH's ingenious and influential axiomatic approach. In other words: The Nash–property guarantees a convincing axiomatic characterization of the Harsanyi–Selten theory for unanimity bargaining games.

In addition to the Nash–property focussing on unanimity bargaining games HARSANYI and SELTEN provide an axiomatic characterization of risk dominance for 2×2–bimatrix games (2–person normal form games with 2 pure strategies for each player) with two strict equilibria, i.e. both players loose by unilaterally deviating from a pure strategy equilibrium. There is only one (risk dominance) relationship which satisfies invariance with respect to isomorphisms, best reply invariance, and payoff monotonicity. The two latter properties are not generally satisfied by the Harsanyi–Selten solution. Best reply invariance means that the solution should not change with transformations preserving the best reply structure. Payoff monotonicity is guaranteed if higher payoffs for the solution do not endanger the prospects of becoming the solution.

In their brilliant discussion of possible selection properties HARSANYI and SELTEN (1988, Chapter 3) also consider other reasonable properties, e.g. best reply invariance and payoff monotonicity, which are not satisfied by the Harsanyi–Selten solution in general. Here we will not enter the discussion of those requirements not satisfied by the Harsanyi–Selten theory. For the time being any such discussion will have to restrict itself to the most basic properties as those discussed by HARSANYI and SELTEN. New solution theories and further examples will certainly yield new insights according to which any such discussion at this early stage will be viewed as incomplete and premature.

4.2.5 The solution procedure

In the preceding sections we have concentrated on the description of the main ideas and the most important properties of the Harsanyi–Selten theory without going into technical details. In what follows, we will explain the solution procedure of the Harsanyi–Selten theory by means of the flow chart diagrams in Figure 0.4.3 because this is the easiest and the most comprehensive description. Furthermore, it will be much easier to compare the Harsanyi–Selten solution procedure with the one of the ESBORA–concept given later on in Figure II.6.1.

The subroutine TRACE describes only one of several operations by which one determines the set $\mathcal{M}(\Omega)$ of maximally stable elements in Ω as required by ELIMSUB. If dominance within Ω is decided by payoff dominance alone, one does not use TRACE at all in order to compute $\mathcal{M}(\Omega)$. Here we avoided to design a special subroutine for determining $\mathcal{M}(\Omega)$. This rather complex subroutine would have to define how one determines for every solution candidate q in Ω its stability radius in Ω. It therefore would have to rely on the following operations for any pair of two different candidates in Ω: determination of their strategic distance, check for payoff dominance, determination of bicentric priors to which TRACE can be applied, comparing the stability radii of all solution candidates.

Similarly, one might face great difficulties when trying to determine an algebraic curve consisting of indexed combinations (t,q^t) with q^t being an equilibrium point of the auxiliary game G^t (see

TRACE). Thus the complete algorithm to compute the Harsanyi–Selten solution of a numerically specified game would require much more detailed subroutines than those presented above and will encounter new conceptual difficulties as, for instance, the ones involved in the numerical computation of an algebraic curve.

a) Main program

Input: $G = (S_1,\dots,S_n;H)$ game in standard form

Output: q, solution of G

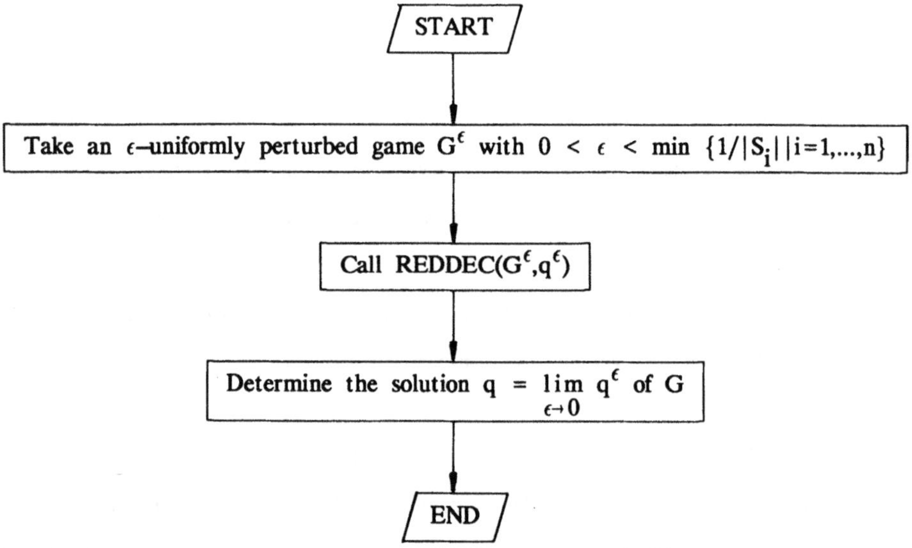

b) Subroutine REDDEC(G^ϵ,q^ϵ)

Input: G^ϵ, ϵ–uniformly perturbed game in standard form

Output: q^ϵ, solution of G^ϵ

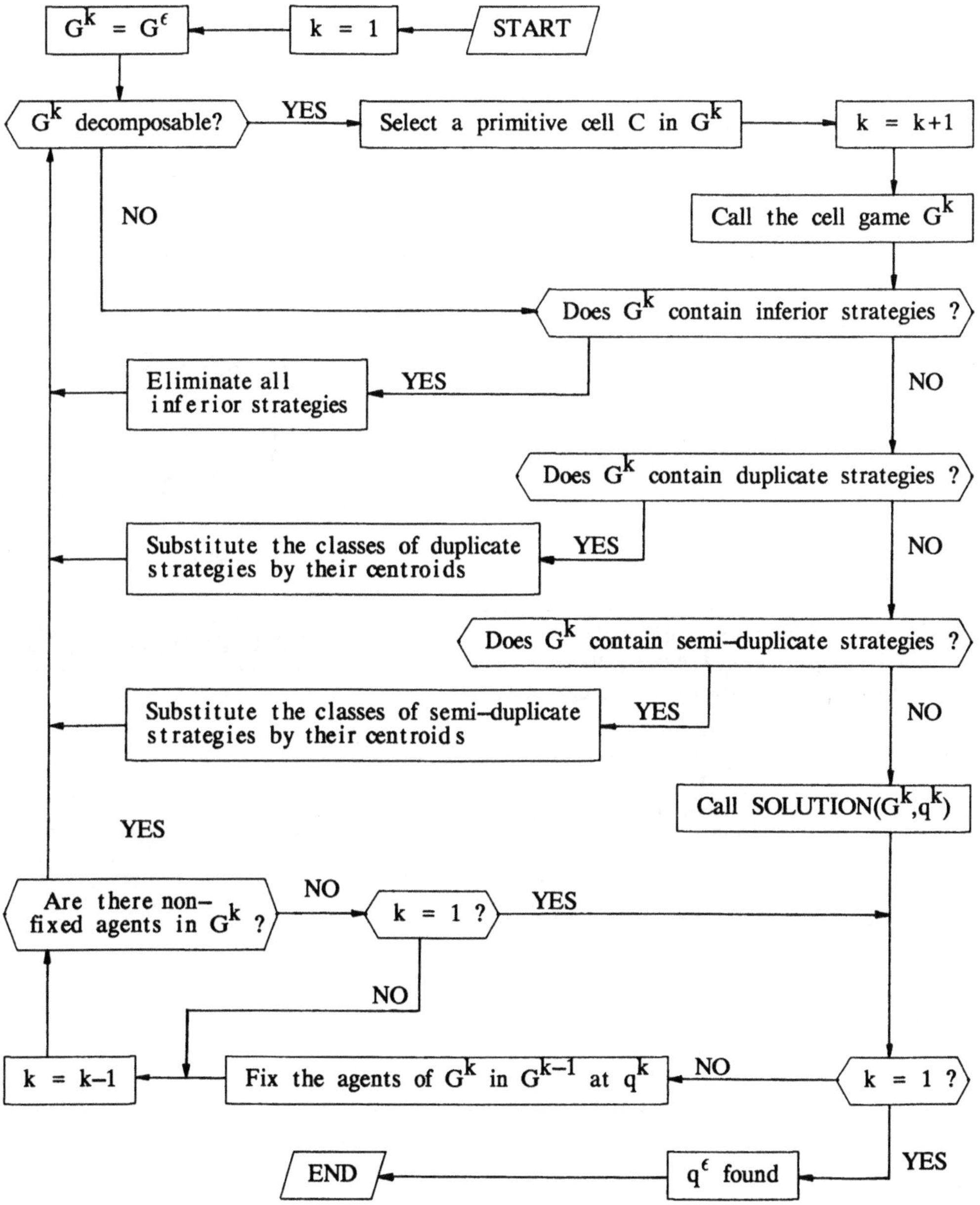

c) Subroutine SOLUTION(G,q)

Input: G, irreducible uniformly perturbed game

Output: q, solution of G

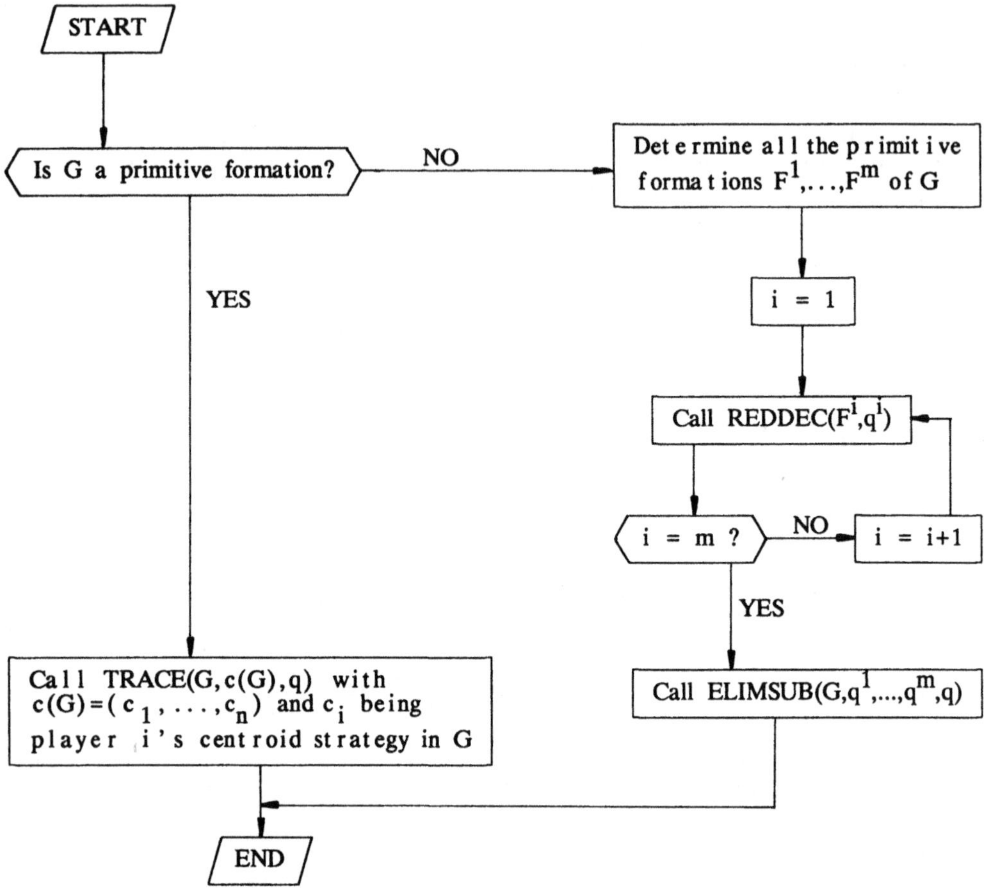

d) Subroutine TRACE(G,c,q)

Input: $G = (S_1^\epsilon,\ldots,S_n^\epsilon;H)$, irreducible uniformly perturbed primitive formation

c, prior probability distribution

Output: q, solution of G

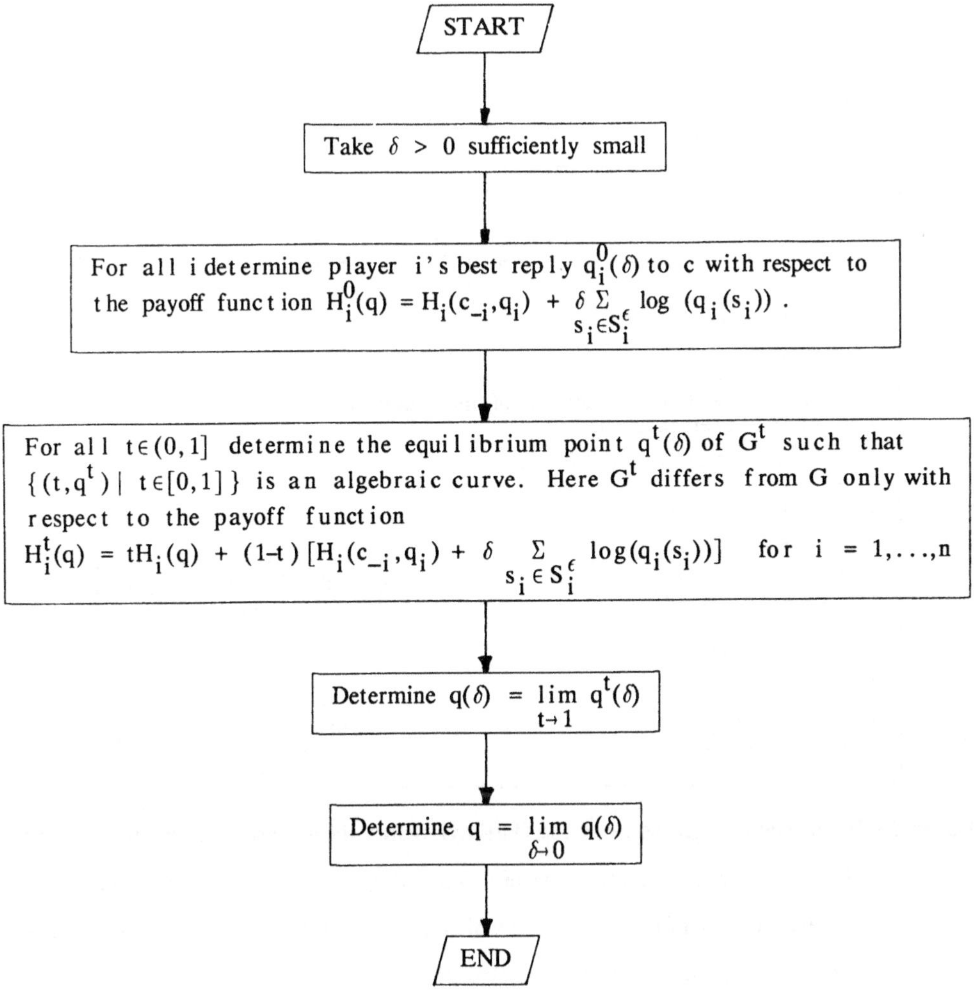

e) Subroutine ELIMSUB(G,q^1,...,q^m,q)

Input: G, irreducible uniformly perturbed game

$q^1,\dots,q^m$, solution candidates

Output: q, solution of G

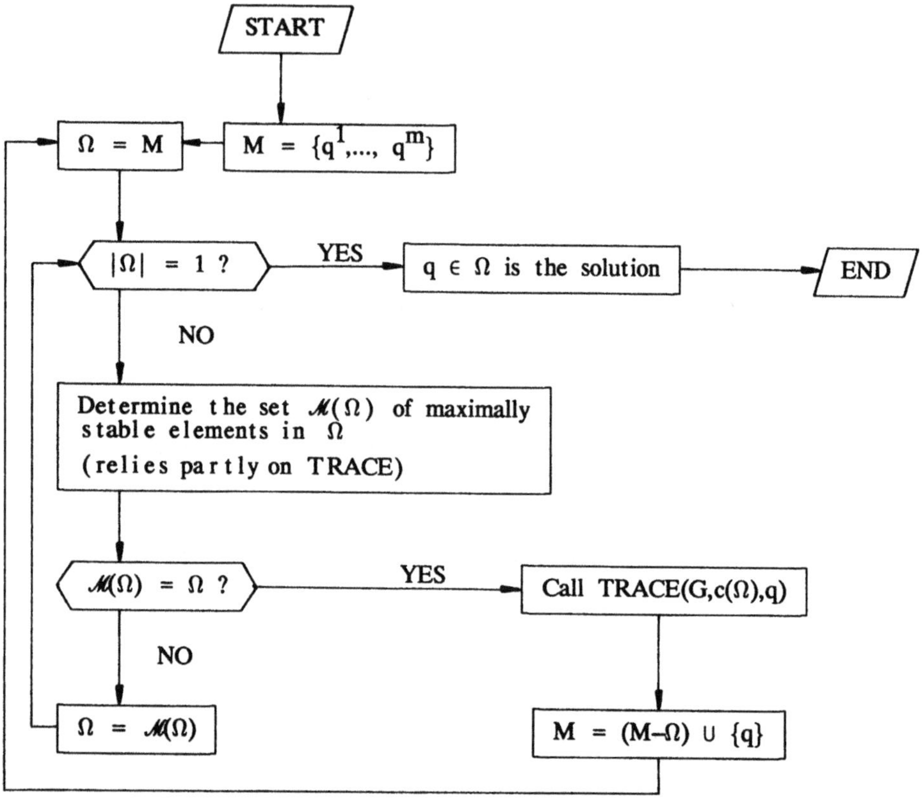

Figure 0.4.3: The solution procedure of the Harsanyi–Selten theory, given in algorithmic form by flow chart diagrams, consisting of a Main Program, where the algorithm starts and finally ends, and four subroutines which are called up in the course of the procedure and which are thereby part of the algorithm:

a) Main Program

b) Subroutine REDDEC (the reduction and decomposition program),

c) Subroutine SOLUTION (the "proper" solution procedure),

d) Subroutine TRACE (a simplified version of the tracing procedure),

e) Subroutine ELIMSUB (the elimination and substitution program).

5. Equilibrium selection based on resistance avoidance (ESBORA)

Before describing how we will introduce and apply our theory of equilibrium selection it should be stated clearly that this approach is mainly based on methods which were already considered by HARSANYI and SELTEN themselves. But by combining these tools in a different way we often derive results which differ considerably from those implied by the Harsanyi–Selten theory.

5.1 The general motivation

One of the reasons for developing our own concept was certainly that one got tired to learn new versions of the Harsanyi–Selten theory without being able to influence the way of changing their concept. Another reason is that, in our view, the Harsanyi–Selten theory is based on too many procedural ideas whose philosophical consistency is difficult to see: The two initial ideas of the Harsanyi–Selten theory, namely the definiton of the so–called 'prior strategy combinations' and the tracing procedure, are, for instance, now completed by a distance measure, a most complicated procedure of eliminating and substituting solution candidates (see LEOPOLD–WILDBURGER, 1982 and 1985). Furthermore, we never liked the idea that in a strictly noncooperative game best replies to jointly randomizing decisions of other players should be of any importance (see the more detailed discussion in GÜTH, 1985).

Our approach does not offer a single concept since its basic ideas can be complemented in different ways. Even when discussing our basic ideas we will mention alternative conceptual ideas. Thus we do not claim that we have developed the concept of equilibrium selection. For such a justified claim we would have had to explore the alternative concepts more thoroughly by applying them to some of the most crucial examples of games with multiple equilibria (reading this study should indicate how much work would be involved in doing so). But we claim that our approach, together with the Harsanyi–Selten theory of equilibrium selection, will help to span the space of possible selection concepts. It therefore should be more easy for new scholars to enter the field and to see the various conceptual possibilities so that they can understand the advantages and disadvantages of competing ideas and maybe improve previous concepts or even develop new concepts based on superior conceptual ideas. We would consider it a great success if our study helps to lower the barriers of entry into the field of equilibrium selection theory.

Whereas the main idea of the Harsanyi–Selten theory is the risk dominance relationship between solution candidates, our approach can be described as

Equilibrium Selection Based On Resistance Avoidance, or, in abbreviated form: ESBORA

which explains why we use the name "ESBORA–concept" for our theory of equilibrium selection. Work on the ESBORA–concept started in spring 1982 when one of the authors was visiting Jerusalem where he had many long discussions with BEZALEL PELEG who strongly encouraged this work (also GÜTH (1985) was a result of these discussions with BEZALEL PELEG).

In this introductory chapter we will describe the ESBORA–concept in a nontechnical way by surveying the remaining parts of this study which contain many examples of games with multiple equilibria. For these examples we compare the results of the Harsanyi–Selten theory with those implied by the ESBORA–concept. Before starting to do so we would like to mention already here that not all mathematical details, necessary to show that the ESBORA–solution is always uniquely defined, are fully elaborated. Partly the uniqueness of the ESBORA–solution is based rather on conjectures than on theorems.

Equilibrium selection theory as such is based on the a priori–assumption that the individually rational decision behavior can always be uniquely defined. Therefore one has to discriminate between equilibria, which are the possible solution candidates, according to their relative "stabilities". One can also imagine that every player when analysing the game puts himself into the position of an arbitrator who has to give a unique strategic recommendation for every player. Sometimes we will interpret our definitions and concepts by imagining an arbitrator who is asked to recommend a unique solution. In view of equilibrium selection theory his considerations should be viewed as intellectual considerations of every individual player who tries to resolve his strategic uncertainty by analysing the game in an impartial way. There is no assumption that players try to solve the game by asking an arbitrator for his advice (according to our apporach such a possibility would have to be modelled explicitly as a possible move in the course of the game).

Till now the ESBORA-concept is only a constructive procedure to solve finite games which satisfies certain desirable properties, i.e. we have mainly worked out the procedural approach to equilibrium selection. For the axiomatic approach our results are very limited. The main difference to the Harsanyi-Selten theory is that their intransitive relationship of risk dominance is substituted by the transitive relation of resistance dominance among solution candidates. To see why resistance avoidance is important imagine a player considering a certain solution candidate. Except for special games he will have to fear that some players will oppose to the solution whatever solution candidate he considers. Assume now that he proposes the solution candidate for which the "opposition by all players" is minimal. Any other proposal can apparently be turned down by the argument that it would have to face an even greater resistance.

By an axiomatic approach, similarly to NASH (1953), we could justify our way of measuring "resistance" by general philosophical requirements for individually rational decision behavior. Since we can give only few results in this respect, we consider many different games to illustrate and test the selection behavior of the ESBORA-concept. Many of these examples have already been analysed with the help of the Harsanyi-Selten theory, some of them are new. They mostly describe social decision problems with their own scientific interest and demonstrate thereby the need to follow and to accomplish the program as outlined by NASH. Equilibrium selection theory provides new interesting paradigms of social decision problems which could hardly be analysed without equilibrium selection therory. We hope that this book helps to demonstrate the richer possibilities in analysing social conflict situations.

5.2 The idea of resistance avoidance

After describing finite strategic games formally and analysing the possible substructures of such games in Section 1 of Part I the relation of resistance dominance is introduced in Section 2. We consider strategic games in complete (agent) normal form. Given an extensive game its agent normal form is the normal form game where each information set of a personal player is represented by one agent, i.e. a player whose strategies are the possible moves at this information set and whose payoff coincides with the evaluation of the play by the respective player. The complete agent normal form contains, in addition to the agent normal form, a probability assignment which assigns to every strategy vector the vector probabilities measuring how likely it is for a given agent/player that he actually will have to move, i.e. how likely it is that a given information set will be reached. When comparing two solution candidates a given player's preference for one of the two candidates might weigh less if according to both candidates his decision is very unlikely to change the course of the play. This explains why we use the complete agent normal form to represent a strategic game.

For the purpose of these introductory remarks a solution candidate can be understood as a strict equilibrium point, i.e. an equilibrium point where any player will loose by deviating unilaterally. One basic idea of the ESBORA–concept is to determine for every candidate s a resistance vector R(s) whose components r(s',s) measure the resistance against s resulting from any other competing solution candidate s'. To define r(s',s) we consider the restricted game for the comparison of s' and s whose only active players are the ones who use different strategies in s and s'. For each active player i we measure how much weight can be put on s without endangering that s'_i is a best reply to that strategy combination. Let $r_i(s',s)$ denote the maximum of such weights, i.e. if all other active players j ($\neq$ i) use their strategy s_j with probability $r_i(s',s)$, and their strategy s'_j with probability $1 - r_i(s',s)$, then player i is just indifferent between using s'_i and his best alternative strategy. Thus $r_i(s',s)$ measures how stable the choice of s'_i is in the restricted game.

It should be noted that the (Lebesgue–)measure of the stability set for the strategy s'_i would be another and, probably, an even more convincing concept to measure player i's stickiness to s'_i. The stability set of s_i' is the set of all strategy combinations for the other players to which s_i' is a best reply. As a matter of fact we first have used this measure for $r_i(s',s)$. But unfortunately it was mathematically very difficult to compute the (Lebesgue–)measure of stability sets when there are more than two players engaged in the game, e.g. in an n–person unanimity bargaining games with $n > 2$. One way to avoid these difficulties would have been to use a definition of the restricted game with only two players j and i and to aggregate the individual resistance $r_i^{(j)}(s',s)$ over all such games with players j and i such that $j \neq i$ and over all players i instead of aggregating the individual resistance $r_i(s',s)$ only over all players i. We still think that this is an alternative to our approach which one should explore more deeply, especially since it could try to generalize the axiomatic approach of HARSANYI and SELTEN (1988) for 2×2–bimatrix games with two strict equilibria. But here we refrained from allowing only 2–person restricted games. Instead of the (Lebesgue–)measure we have therefore used the "diagonal length" $r_i(s',s)$ of the stability set, defined above, to quantify player i's individual resistance against s in view of s'.

Call $r_i(s',s)/r_i(s,s')$ the <u>normalized individual resistance</u> of player i against s in view of s'. The normalized individual resistances are weighted by the mean $P_i(s',s)$ of the probabilities $P_i(s')$ and $P_i(s)$ of s' and s that player i will actually have to move in the course of the game, i.e. a player i's individual resistance will be neglected if player/agent i's information set will not be reached regardless whether s or s' is chosen.

In this study we use exponential weights $P_i(s',s)$ and aggregate the individual resistance by multiplying the weighted normalized individual resistances $(r_i(s',s)/r_i(s,s'))^{P_i(s',s)}$ over all active players in the restricted game. The result is denoted by $r(s',s)$ and called the <u>resistance against s in view of s'</u>.

An interesting alternative to aggregate individual resistances would be to weigh the normalized individual resistances by multiplying them with $P_i(s',s)$ and to add the terms $P_i(s',s)\cdot r_i(s',s)/r_i(s,s')$ instead of multiplying them. Our reason for not choosing this aggregation procedure was that from the very beginning we wanted our concept to satisfy a "<u>generalized Nash–property</u>". By this we mean that in a certain class of unanimity bargaining games with incomplete information (see HARSANYI and SELTEN, 1972, SELTEN, 1975b, and Section 4.1

below) our concept should select the generalized Nash–solution (HARSANYI and SELTEN, 1972). Since HARSANYI and SELTEN provide an axiomatic characterization of the generalized Nash–solution this seems to be a very promising guideline in view of the axiomatic approach. But as MYERSON (1984) has pointed out the Harsanyi–Selten axioms contradict one of the most fundamental axioms of decision theory. Thus our aggregation procedure might not be the best one. Certainly we would have considered other methods more carefully if, when developing our concept, we would have been aware of the study by MYERSON (1984).

Now for any solution candidate s one may have (finitely) many resistance values r(s',s) resulting from competing solution candidates s'. We therefore define for every solution candidate s a resistance vector R(s) by arranging the resistance levels r(s',s) with s' $\neq$ s in a nonincreasing order, i.e. the highest level first, then the second highest level etc. Thus the first component of R(s) expresses the strongest opposition against the solution s in view of all competing solution candidates s' $\neq$ s. It seems natural to select the candidate s as the solution for which this strongest resistance is minimal. Formally this is done by selecting the candidate s as the solution of the game whose resistance vector R(s) is lexicographically minimal, i.e. for the solution the loudest resistance (the first component of R(s)) is minimal, in case of more candidates with minimal loudest resistance the second loudest resistance (the second component of R(s)) is minimal over the set of these candidates etc. The idea to compare solution candidates by means of lexicographical minimization has already been exploited in cooperative game theory (SCHMEIDLER, 1969). Generically there will always be a unique solution candidate s whose vector R(s) is lexicographically minimal. Typical exceptions are symmetric games with several solution candidates which can only be distinguished by the names of players and/or strategies.

Consider a game with the solution s^*, i.e. $R(s^*)$ is lexicographically minimal. If we change the game only by increasing an individual player i's payoff $H_i(s^*)$ for s^*, the solution of the new game will be s^*, too. This will be described by saying that the selection behavior of resistance avoidance is monotonic. Another obvious property of resistance avoidance is invariance with respect to positive affine utility transformations and symmetry invariance (the resistance vectors of "symmetric candidates" are equal). One can further show that our way of aggregating individually weighted resistances can be characterized axiomatically. Another important property is the generalized Nash–property mentioned above.

In Section 4 of Part I the idea of resistance avoidance is applied to several games with complete and incomplete information. The first example is a 2–person game with three pure strategy equilibria X, Y, and Z where X payoff dominates Y and Y payoff dominates Z. Since Y is the only resistance undominated solution candidate, the example shows that resistance dominance and payoff dominance are mutually inconsistent. The next example is the one which has been more thoroughly discussed in GÜTH (1985) where it was argued that the definition of the bicentric prior–strategies (HARSANYI and SELTEN, 1988) could be improved if one avoids the expectation of correlated decision behavior. Interestingly enough our concept determines the same solution for these games as the Harsanyi–Selten theory if one uses the bicentric prior–strategies proposed in GÜTH (1985). The next example is a 3–person bargaining game which is a unanimity bargaining game except that a deviation of player 3 does not imply the conflict payoff for 1 and 2 but only a utility loss c (≥ 0) not depending on the solution candidate from which 3 is defecting (GÜTH and SEIFERT, 1984). Whereas for an interesting subclass the ESBORA–solution does not depend on the parameter c, the same is not true for the Harsanyi–Selten theory. The last example with complete information is a game in extensive form which illustrates the influence of the weights $P_i(s',s)$ on the ESBORA–solution as the probabilities by which the different information sets are reached are different for different solution candidates.

In a game with <u>incomplete information</u> not all players are sure about what their opponents can do (incomplete information about strategy sets), what they know when deciding (incomplete information about information standards), and how they evaluate the possible results of the game (incomplete information about payoffs). HARSANYI (1967/68) has shown that all these information deficits can be remodelled as incomplete information about payoff functions. Clearly, the definition of strategy sets has to rely on a specific information structure, i.e. information deficits about information standards are reflected by information deficits about strategy sets. Imagine, furthermore, that player 2 does not know whether player 1 can choose a certain move X_1 or not where he expects the possibility to use X_1 with probability p. This can be remodelled by assuming that 1 can always use X_1. But whereas the use of X_1 yields the normal payoff, in case 1 can do so, it implies a terrifying loss in case of the (1–p)–probability event that 1 cannot use X_1. Thus the payoff functions of player 1 will prevent the choice of X_1 whenever it is not available. This illustrates that all information deficits about strategy sets, information standards, and payoff functions can be remodelled as incomplete information about payoff functions.

Usually the possible payoff functions of a player i, i.e. the payoff functions expected by any other player, are called the different types of player i. The game with incomplete information is transformed into one with complete information by adding a fictitious initial chance move determining the vector of types of all players i whose result is only partially revealed to the different players as to capture their information deficits concerning the types of other players (HARSANYI, 1967/68). Instead of determining the decision behavior of the true type vector only, one thus solves the game for all possible type vectors. As a matter of fact the individual decision behavior can only be reasonably defined in such an expectationally closed system where every player considers any possible type constellation.

Nearly all social decision problems are characterized by incomplete information since usually a player will have some private information. It is therefore important to demonstrate how equilibrium selection theory can remove strategic uncertainty also in games with incomplete information or in their analogues with complete but imperfect information described above. As a matter of fact many refinement concepts were induced by attempts to derive more specific results in games with incomplete information, e.g. the sequential equilibrium concept (KREPS and WILSON, 1982). It is probably a weakness of many refinement concepts that they restrict themselves to games with incomplete information.

The first example of games with incomplete information, considered in Part I, is an n–person unanimity bargaining game with incomplete information in order to prove a generalized Nash–property. The next game is the wage bargaining situation with incomplete information analysed by SELTEN and LEOPOLD (1982a) with the help of the Harsanyi–Selten theory. Here the Harsanyi–Selten solution and the ESBORA–solution coincide whereas the same is not true for the art forgery situation SELTEN and GÜTH (1982c) have analysed. The examples demonstrate that there can be subclasses of games where the two selection theories coincide although their selection behavior is generically different.

5.3 The selection procedure

Part II mainly serves to determine for every strategic game the set of solution candidates to which one can then apply the relationship of resistance dominance. Especially here we rely on procedures of the Harsanyi–Selten theory as, for instance, the cell composition and the generation of irreducible games mentioned above. To ensure the perfectness of the solution and the strictness of solution candidates (a player has to loose from any deviation) a game is not solved directly but solved by determining the limit $s^* = \lim_{\epsilon \to 0} s^\epsilon$ of the solutions s^ϵ of its ϵ–uniformly perturbed games. In an ϵ–uniformly perturbed game every strategy has to be used with at least ϵ–probability, i.e. there are no unreached information sets, which, by definition, ensures the perfectness of the limit solution s^* and that all weights $P_i(s',s)$ are positive. Furthermore, the payoff function is modified by including a small fine for using extreme (pure) strategies where we are interested only in the limit result for the fine approaching 0. This ensures that for any strategy constellation of the other players a player's best reply is always unique, i.e. all equilibria in ϵ–uniformly perturbed games including such a fine are strict.

Given the (strict) equilibria of such an ϵ–uniformly perturbed game the candidate set is the set of all equilibria which are not payoff dominated by other equilibria. Application of resistance avoidance then yields the set of resistance undominated candidates which generically contains only one element. If this set contains more than just one element, e.g. in case of a symmetric game, all resistance undominated candidates are eliminated as solution candidates since any selection among them would be completely arbitrary. The new candidate set is therefore the set of all not previously excluded equilibria which are not payoff dominated by a not previously excluded other equilibrium and so forth. Thus the generation of candidate sets considers symmetry invariance (no arbitrary selection of the solution in symmetric games) as more important than payoff dominance among equilibria and payoff dominance as more important than resistance dominance. If symmetry invariance were not satisfied, the solution would obviously be disqualified as completely arbitrary, it would distinguish "indistinguishables". Payoff dominance is relevant since the expectations of players will naturally focus on such equilibria and not on payoff dominated equilibria which yield for all players less than another equilibrium. Why should a player resist to a proposed solution if it gives him and all the others more? We therefore think that considerations of resistance avoidance should be restricted to equilibria among which one cannot distinguish by payoff dominance.

One of the main conjectures, i.e. not yet completely asserted theorems, is that the limit $s^* = \lim_{\epsilon \to 0} s^\epsilon$ of the solutions s^ϵ of the ϵ–uniformly perturbed games always exists, i.e. is the same for all sequences $\{\epsilon_k\}$ with ϵ_k approaching 0. Another important but still unproved conjecture is related to the following problem: In which cases can the rather complicated way of solving the ϵ–uniformly perturbed games and the way of determining the limit solution be avoided by applying the considerations of payoff dominance and resistance avoidance directly to the unperturbed game? Observe that most applications (e.g. HARSANYI, 1982, SELTEN and GÜTH, 1978, 1982a and c, SELTEN and LEOPOLD, 1982a) of the Harsanyi–Selten theory are based on similar conjectures. An early example where the Harsanyi–Selten solution is determined via solving the perturbed games is LEOPOLD–WILDBURGER (1982 and 1985). Our first conjecture supposes that one can solve the game directly by applying first payoff dominance and then resistance dominance if all payoff undominated equilibria are strict and if the payoff undominated equilibrium with minimal loudest resistance is unique. Our next conjecture is concerned with those games which must be solved via perturbed games but where one does not need a penalty term to ensure strictness of equilibria.

At the end of Part II we consider again all previously analysed examples and discuss their solutions. By symmetric 'battle of sexes'–games it is, furthermore, demonstrated how symmetry invariance can imply a solution which is payoff dominated by other strict equilibria. Another example, a strategic game in extensive form, is used to illustrate the whole solution procedure (deriving the complete agent normal form, reducing the game, decomposing it if possible etc.). The so–called Condorcet paradox (CONDORCET, 1785), a game model related to the one analysed by GÜTH and SELTEN (1988) with the help of the Harsanyi–Selten theory, finally serves to demonstrate how helpful it is if certain games can be solved via solving perturbed games without penalties for using extreme strategies. In the voting game, which has already been mentioned in Section 2 above, the three voters/players have cardinal preferences over the social alternatives A, B, and C implying a majority cycle, i.e. always two voters prefer A to B, B to C, and C to A. It is assumed that any of the three social alternatives payoff dominates the prevailing status quo. The game is pathological in the sense that it has infinitely many equilibria but that only few equilibria exist if one perturbs the game slightly by requiring that every pure strategy must be used with at least ϵ–probability. Interestingly enough the set of equilibria in these perturbed games depends crucially on the cardinal utilities by which the players evaluate the social alternatives.

5.4 Possible modifications of the ESBORA–concept

In Part III it is first shown that the weights $P_i(s',s)$ used to aggregate the individual normalized resistances $r_i(s',s)/r_i(s,s')$ can yield counterintuitive results. This is demonstrated by the 'one seller and n–1 buyers'–problem (HARSANYI, 1982, and GÜTH and STEPHAN, 1984), an n–person game in which the seller wants to sell an indivisible commodity to one of the n–1 potential buyers. The rules of the game require that the seller as well as all potential buyers independently propose a price and that the object is sold if the seller and at least one of the n–1 symmetric potential buyers have named the same price. In case that more potential buyers have proposed the same price as the seller each of them has an equal chance to make the deal. The counterintuitive result is that the ESBORA–solution price decreases when the number n–1 of potential buyers increases. This is true since the relative weight of the demand side of the market increases with the number of potential buyers although a monopolistic seller does not loose market power when facing more potential buyers.

This counterintuitive result is no real surprise since the weights $P_i(s',s)$ are not sophisticated enough to capture all relevant strategic aspects. That is why we call them preliminary weights. But since there are many possibilities to improve the weighting concept starting from the preliminary weights $P_i(s',s)$, it is important to explore the preliminary weights in more detail. By the so–called generalized weights, introduced in Section 2 of Part III, one can easily avoid the counterintuitive result for the 'one seller and n–1 buyers'–game without endangering the most important properties of our theory as, for instance, the generalized Nash–property. According to the generalized weights a player i's objection against a solution candidate s can be neglected if player i's deviation to the competing solution candidate s' does not hurt any other active player in the restricted game for the comparison of s and s'. More specifically, the generalized weight $P_i(s',s)$ is the product of players i's preliminary weight and the sum of preliminary weights of all other players who suffer when i deviates from s_i to s_i', i.e. $P_i(s',s)$ is the product of i's preliminary weight and the total preliminary weight of those players $j \neq i$ who have reasons to listen to player i's objection.

By some examples it is demonstrated that due to 0–generalized weights it might happen that the considerations of resistance avoidance are completely neglected, e.g. in a game where all other players gain if a player defects from any equilibrium. To avoid this the generalized weights $P_i(s',s)$ are assumed to have at least a small value $\tilde{\epsilon}$ (> 0) in all ϵ,δ–perturbed games where one is, of course, again interested in the limit results for $\tilde{\epsilon} \to 0$. An ϵ,δ–perturbed game is an ϵ–uniformly perturbed game where the payoff function includes a fine that is weighted by a small positive number δ. In Section 5 of Part II we will give a more detailed description of these double–perturbed games. Thus when solving the game via determining the limit s^ϵ of solutions $s^{\epsilon,\delta}$ of its ϵ,δ–perturbed games considerations of resistance avoidance will never be completely neglected when comparing two solution candidate. Of course, the lower bound $\tilde{\epsilon}$ for $P_i(s',s)$ is irrelevant when all generalized weights are strictly positive even without this bound.

Again several examples are used to illustrate how the ESBORA–concept is changed by substituting preliminary weights by generalized weights. In the 'one seller and n–1 buyers'–game the generalized weights of all potential buyers are zero whenever there are at least two potential buyers whereas the generalized weight of the monopolistic seller is given by the number n–1 of potential buyers. Thus the solution price is the 'equal split of surplus'–price in case of n = 2 and the 'give all the surplus to the seller'–price if $n \geq 3$. Since for $n \geq 3$ the competitive price is the highest price a buyer can accept this clearly confirms our intuitive expectations about the result in the 'one seller and many buyers'–game. Interestingly enough, the sharp increase in the competitiveness of the market when changing from n = 2 to n > 2 is not so clearly reflected by the Harsanyi–Selten theory (GÜTH and STEPHAN, 1984). Only for $n = \infty$ the Harsanyi–Selten solution price equals the (constant) competitive price in the whole range $n > 2$.

By a rather simple 3–person game with three solution candidates it is then demonstrated that the generalized weights can make the solution far more reactive to payoff parameters which are neglected if one uses preliminary weights. Of course, this also increases the difficulties of solving the game.

Another example is a situation by which SELTEN and GÜTH (1978) have tried to investigate the problem whether in a bargaining situation it pays more to bargain with the other side in a decentralized way or in a centralized way. In the decentralized case we have a 3–player game where 1 and 2 as well as 1 and 3 can share an amount of 100. In case of no bilateral agreement conflict results with 0–payments to 1 and 2 whereas player 3's conflict payoff is $b \geq 0$. Thus for $b > 0$ the isolated bargaining agreements of 1 and 2 as well as 1 and 3 would differ since player 3 will be more tough than player 2. But since player 1 is restricted to offer the same terms to both his opponents, players 2 and 3 find themselves involved in the same game although they interact strategically only via player 1.

The ESBORA–solution agreement always assigns a higher amount to players 2 and 3 if one uses preliminary weights instead of generalized weights. Furthermore, for $b > 0$ and for both weighting concepts players 2 and 3 together get more than they would receive if they merged and 'bargained centrally' with player 1 about how to share the total amount of 200. Thus it never pays to bargain centrally in case of asymmetric conflict payoffs.

The final examples analysed in Part III are the market entry games as introduced by SELTEN and GÜTH (1977 and 1982a). In a market entry game the n players must independently decide whether to enter a market or not. If player i enters the market his entry cost will be C_i which is opposed to his entry incentive A_m depending only on the number m of sellers who have already entered the market. Assuming that A_m does not increase with m one can show that there is a unique equilibrium number m of market entrants although there may be many different pure strategy equilibria. If entry costs differ for different players, obviously the m players with lowest entry costs should enter the market. This shows that market entry games can serve as a crucial test for equilibrium selection concepts. If the solution does not prescribe entry for the m players with lowest entry costs, the concept certainly has to be modified accordingly as to avoid such a counterintuitive result. The ESBORA–concept passes the test of selecting the right solution candidate in market entry games regardless whether one uses preliminary or generalized weights. Of course, the same is true also for the Harsanyi–Selten solution (SELTEN and GÜTH, 1977 and 1982a).

In Part IV we discuss further possibilities to modify the ESBORA–concept of equilibrium selection. But whereas it is quite apparent that substituting preliminary weights by generalized weights is an improvement, it is less obvious whether the modifications discussed in Part IV are equally desirable. The changes would make it far more difficult to compute the ESBORA–solution even for rather simple games. One might argue, of course, that a theory of individually rational decision behavior should not depend on computational difficulties since the computational abilities of rational decision makers are by definition unlimited. However, if one is not only interested in the philosophical aspects of individual rationality but also in analysing the rational decisions in various social decision situations, one has to give up this ideal position and look for a compromise. As a matter of fact, some aspects of the Harsanyi–Selten theory are clearly attempts to limit the computational difficulties of applying it, e.g. the use of jointly randomized strategies, the distance measure etc.

Often the solution will not change if one uses a more sophisticated concept. But in complex games a more sophisticated concept will certainly be more reactive to the various strategically relevant aspects. Here we do not want to decide once and for ever how the concept of resistance avoidance should be defined since a final decision would obviously be premature. Thus Part IV should be considered as an offer: If you consider the ESBORA–concept, described above, as too simple and not reactive enough to capture all strategic aspects, here are some perspectives how to improve the concept!

According to the generalized weights one considers whether or not another player j suffers from a deviation by player i. It is however completely neglected how serious player j's loss is. The continuous weighting approach tries to capture both aspects: It does not only take into account who suffers from a deviation by player i but also how much he suffers. We distinguish two variants of the continuous approach. The new weights differ from the generalized weights by multiplying the preliminary weights of players j suffering from i's deviation by their relative losses.

The alternative weights differ from the new weights since they do not only account for players j who suffer from player i's deviation but also for those players j who gain from it. More specifically, the alternative weight $P_i(s',s)$ is defined as the product of player i's preliminary weight and the sum of the preliminary weights of all other active players j times the relative payoff effects for these players j caused by i's deviation. Both, the new and the alternative weights, will make it rather difficult to solve games which are not numerically specified as most of the examples considered before. Except for rather special classes of games like, for instance, n–person unanimity bargaining games, it will be quite complicated to derive the solution based on new or alternative weights.

By a simple 3–person game with two solution candidates it is demonstrated that the selection behavior can differ drastically for the different weighting approaches corresponding to the preliminary, generalized, new, and the alternative weights. In the 'one seller and n–1 buyers'—game with $n \geq 3$ the solution price for all weighting concepts is the competitive price. Also in the 3–person game with an unbiased threat, introduced in Part I, the solution does not change if one weighting concept is substituted by another. Of course, the continuous weighting approaches also satisfy our generalized Nash–property.

Another possible improvement, discussed in Part IV, is to rely on a more sophisticated definition of the restricted game for the resistance comparison of two solution candidates s' and s. Instead of assuming that all active players i can only use their strategies s_i' and s_i or any mixture of the two HARSANYI and SELTEN (1988) define the restricted game as the smallest formation containing s_i' and s_i for every active player i. Let us repeat that a formation is a substructure of a game resulting from elimination of strategies which is closed with respect to the best reply correspondence of the original game, i.e., no player will want to use a strategy not available in the formation if all other players use strategies admissible in the formation.

To illustrate the difference of the two definitions of restricted games we apply them to a class of 2–person bargaining games with an outside option for both players. LEOPOLD–WILDBURGER (1982 and 1985) has analysed these games very thoroughly with the help of the Harsanyi–Selten theory. In these games both players can decide not to bargain at all and thereby achieve a higher payoff than in case of conflict in bargaining. The example demonstrates that our simpler definition of the restricted game might neglect essential threat possibilities although the more sophisticated notion of restricted games will not yield different solutions in many of the previously discussed examples.

In the last section of Part IV we consider 3–person games having a strict equilibrium point which payoff or resistance dominates all other strict equilibria but where the ESBORA–solution is nevertheless a mixed strategy equilibrium. This shows that mixed strategy equilibria are qualified as initial candidates even if they are not solutions of primitive formations. As a matter of fact the Harsanyi–Selten theory will not select the mixed strategy equilibrium point as the solution in these games although it payoff dominates all other equilibria, i.e. "formation stability" (a candidate has to be the solution of a primitive formation) is more important than payoff dominance. Therefore it seems justified to say that the Harsanyi–Selten theory discriminates mixed strategy equilibria whereas for the ESBORA–concept this is not true.

The Final Remarks summarize the essential differences of the Harsanyi–Selten theory and the ESBORA–concept and list the main properties of the ESBORA–approach. It is stressed again that the new concept owes most of its tools and ideas to the previous pioneering work of HARSANYI and SELTEN. But by combining these aspects in a different way we have derived a concept which determines the solution in a more direct way by the parameters of the game.

Part I: The concept of resistance avoidance

First it will be shown how to represent a finite (noncooperative) game. With the help of this basic terminology it is then easy to describe how equilibrium selection can be based on resistance avoidance. The relation of resistance dominance between solution candidates is the central idea of the ESBORA–concept. We will show some general properties of resistance dominance and apply it to several examples. By these examples we illustrate the computational aspects of resistance avoidance as well as its important selection properties.

1. Modelling finite noncooperative games

The most general form to represent a finite noncooperative game is the extensive form. An extensive game $\Gamma = (B,P,U,Z,p,h)$ consists of the following elements: B is the game tree, i.e. a connected graph (consisting of nodes and branches) without loops and with a special node o which is the origin of the tree. P is the player partition, i.e. a partition of the set X of decision nodes x into subsets $P_0, P_1, \ldots, P_{\bar{n}}$ where $1,\ldots,\bar{n}$ are personal players and '0' stands for chance moves. U is the information partition being a refinement of P, i.e. for every player i the set P_i is divided into subsets u, the so–called information sets, which are characterized by the following two facts:

i) Every play intersects u at most once.

ii) The alternatives at x are the same for all $x \in u$.

We denote by U_i the set of all information sets u ($\subseteq P_i$) of player i. Z is the choice partition (of the branches of B) which assigns the set Z(u) of possible choices at u to every information set $u \in U_i$ of a personal player $i = 1,\ldots,\bar{n}$. The probability assignment p determines a probability distribution p(x), governing the decision at x, for all $x \in P_0$. By the payoff function h an $\bar{n}$–vector $h(y) = (h_1(y),\ldots,h_{\bar{n}}(y))$ of von Neumann–Morgenstern utilities is attached to each end point y in the set Y of all end points (for more details see KUHN, 1953, and SELTEN, 1975).

Given a finite game Γ in extensive form its agent normal form is the normal form game $\tilde{G}(\Gamma) = (S_1,\ldots,S_n;H)$ where

$$n = \sum_{i=1}^{\bar{n}} |U_i| \qquad (I.1.1)$$

is the number of information sets of personal players in Γ. Given the 1–1–mapping

$$\pi : \begin{cases} \bigcup_{i=1}^{\bar{n}} U_i & \longrightarrow \{1,\ldots,n\} \\ u & \longmapsto \pi(u) \quad , \end{cases} \qquad (I.1.2)$$

which attaches a player index $\pi(u)$ to every information set u of a personal player, the (pure) strategy sets $S_{\pi(u)}$ in $\tilde{G}(\Gamma)$ are simply the choice sets Z(u). Let $q = (q_1,\ldots,q_n)$ be a mixed strategy vector in $\tilde{G}(\Gamma)$. For any node x of B the probability $P(x|q)$ that x is reached if all players behave according to q is simply the product of the probabilities of all the moves which are necessary to come from o to x. With the help of this notation we can define the expected payoff function

$$H : \begin{cases} S = \times_{i=1}^{n} S_i & \longrightarrow \mathbb{R}^n \\ s = (s_1,\ldots,s_n) & \longmapsto H(s) = (H_1(s),\ldots,H_n(s)) \end{cases} \qquad (I.1.3)$$

of $\tilde{G}(\Gamma)$ by

$$H_{\pi(u)}(s) = \sum_{y \in Y} P(y|s) h_i(y) \qquad (I.1.4)$$

for all $u \in U_i$ and $i = 1,\ldots,\bar{n}$. According to (I.1.4) all agents of player i in Γ, i.e. all players $\pi(u)$ with $u \in U_i$ in $\tilde{G}(\Gamma)$, receive the same payoff in $\tilde{G}(\Gamma)$ as player i in Γ.

In comparison to $\tilde{G}(\Gamma)$ the complete agent normal form $G(\Gamma) = (S_1,\ldots,S_n;P;H)$ of Γ has an additional component

$$P : \begin{cases} S \longrightarrow [0,1]^n \\ s \longmapsto P(s) = (P_1(s),...,P_n(s)) \end{cases} \tag{I.1.5}$$

which is the probability assignment P of G(Γ) attaching to each vector s of pure strategies the probability vector P(s). Here $P_{\pi(u)}$ is defined according to

$$P_{\pi(u)}(s) = \sum_{x \in u} P(x|s), \tag{I.1.6}$$

for $s \in S$, i.e. $P_{\pi(u)}(s)$ is the probability that a decision node in u is reached if all players behave according to s. When dealing with complete agent normal form games P will always denote the probability assignment whereas for extensive form games it is an abbreviation for the player partition.

It is easy to see that two different extensive games might have the same complete agent normal form. Especially in case of simultaneous decisions the time order of these moves (which can be arranged in several ways to generate an extensive game) in the extensive game will not be reflected by the complete agent normal form. Our theory will treat finite extensive games Γ as strategically equivalent if they yield the same finite game G(Γ) in complete agent normal form.

The only novelty of our approach in modelling noncooperative games is that we complete the agent normal form by including the probability assignment P. Since it is inessential whether the complete normal form has been originally given or derived as a complete agent normal form from an extensive game we will, in the following, speak of (finite) games in complete (agent) normal form $G = (S_1,...,S_n;P;H)$ without referring to an underlying extensive form game Γ. Except for an example used to illustrate the whole solution procedure starting from an extensive game we will not come back to games in extensive form.

We will rely on the following notation which partly has already been introduced when defining G(Γ). A probability distribution q_i on S_i, where $q_i(s_i)$ is the probability that the (pure) strategy s_i is chosen, is called the <u>mixed strategy</u> q_i of player i. Q_i denotes the set of all mixed strategies q_i of player i and $Q = Q_1 \times ... \times Q_n$ the set of all mixed strategy vectors $q = (q_1,...,q_n)$. The set of all (n–1)–vectors $s_{-i} = (s_1,...,s_{i-1},s_{i+1},...,s_n)$ and $q_{-i} = (q_1,...,q_{i-1},q_{i+1},...,q_n)$ will be denoted by S_{-i} and Q_{-i}, respectively. S_i, S_{-i}, and S are embedded into Q_i, Q_{-i}, and Q, respectively, in the natural way. It is convenient to write the n–vector, which results from q_{-i} by adding q_i as the i–th component, simply in the form (q_i,q_{-i}). Let C be a proper subset of $N = \{1,...,n\}$. $Q_C = \mathop{X}_{i \in C} Q_i$ and $Q_{N-C} = \mathop{X}_{i \notin C} Q_i$ are the sets of mixed strategy vectors q_C and q_{N-C} of the players in C and N–C, respectively. $Q_{C-i} = \mathop{X}_{j \in C-\{i\}} Q_j$ is the set of mixed strategy vectors q_{C-i} for all players in C but player $i \in C$. By (q_i,q_{C-i},q_{N-C}) we denote the mixed strategy vector in Q according to which player i chooses q_i, the other players $j \in C-\{i\}$ play q_{C-i} and the players outside C use their mixed strategies defined by q_{N-C}.

When solving (finite) games in complete (agent) normal form it is essential to notice that two different games may be strategically equivalent. This indicates that it might be necessary to disregard certain aspects of such game situations. Let $G = (S_1,...,S_n;P;H)$ be a (finite) game in complete (agent) normal form. For $s_i \in S_i$ the set

$$R_i(s_i) = \{q_{-i} \in Q_{-i} |\ H_i(s_i,q_{-i}) \geq H_i(\bar{s}_i,q_{-i}) \text{ for all } \bar{s}_i \in S_i\} \tag{I.1.7}$$

is called s_i's <u>stability set</u>. A strategy $s_i \in S_i$ is said to be <u>inferior</u> if there exists another strategy $\bar{s}_i \in S_i$ with $R_i(\bar{s}_i) \supset R_i(s_i)$. A <u>rational</u> player i will obviously never consider to use an inferior strategy s_i since $\bar{s}_i$ is always best whenever s_i is best and sometimes best when s_i is not.

Observe that this definition of inferior strategies preassumes that a player will always choose a best reply. For other concepts like maximin–strategies, which do not require best replies, this definition would not be useful. The unique maximin–strategy of a player can, for instance, be an inferior strategy.

On the other hand, a player i might have different strategies which are essentially equivalent. If for s_i, $\bar{s}_i \in S_i$ it is true that

$$H_i(\bar{s}_i,q_{-i}) = H_i(s_i,q_{-i}) \qquad \text{for all } q_{-i} \in Q_{-i} \tag{I.1.8}$$

we say that s_i and $\bar{s}_i$ are <u>duplicate</u> strategies.

In case of duplicate strategies any decision for using either one of them would be arbitrary. Like HARSANYI and SELTEN (1988) we therefore substitute a class $D_i \subsetneq S_i$ of duplicate strategies with $|D_i| \geq 2$, by their centroid (mixed strategy) c_i given by

$$c_i(s_i) = \begin{cases} 1/|D_i| & \text{for all } s_i \in D_i , \\ 0 & \text{otherwise} , \end{cases} \tag{I.1.9}$$

i.e. all strategies in D_i will be chosen with the same probability.

A (finite) game $G = (S_1,...,S_n;P;H)$ in complete (agent) normal form might have game–like substructures which are closed with respect to the best reply correspondence of game G. HARSANYI and SELTEN (1988) distinguish between cells and formations. Whereas cells result from excluding players, formations result from excluding strategies.

Let C be a nonempty subset of the player set $N = \{1,...,n\}$ in G. C is a <u>cell</u> of G if for all $i \in C$ and for all $q_{C-i} \in Q_{C-i}$ the following is true: If s_i is a best reply against (q_{C-i},q_{N-C}), i.e.

$$H_i(s_i,q_{C-i},q_{N-C}) \geq H_i(\bar{s}_i,q_{C-i},q_{N-C}) \qquad \text{for all } \bar{s}_i \in S_i , \tag{I.1.10}$$

s_i is a best reply against $(q_{C-i},\bar{q}_{N-C})$ for all $\bar{q}_{N-C} \in Q_{N-C}$. This shows that strategic interaction is restricted to players within the same cell. Whatever the players outside the cell choose does not affect the best replies of the cell players. If a cell C contains no proper subcell, it is called <u>primitive</u>. Since an intersection of two cells is again a cell, it is easy to see that a (finite) game G in complete (agent) normal form has a unique cell decomposition into primitive cells $C_1,...,C_k$, $k \geq 1$. Observe that subgames in extensive form games correspond to cell games in agent normal form games. But an agent normal form might have proper cells C, i.e. $\emptyset \neq C \neq N$, although its extensive form has no proper subgames.

The set $F = \overset{n}{\underset{i=1}{X}} F_i$ of strategy vectors $s = (s_1,\ldots,s_n)$ in G satisfying $\emptyset \neq F_i \subseteq S_i$ $(i = 1,\ldots,n)$ is called a <u>formation</u> of G if for all players $i = 1,\ldots,n$ and for all mixed strategy vectors q_{-i} with carrier in $F_{-i} = \overset{n}{\underset{\substack{j=1\\j\neq i}}{X}} F_j$, i.e. with $q_{-i}(s_{-i}) = (0,\ldots,0)$ for all $s_{-i} \notin F_{-i}$, it is true that

$$\{s_i \in S_i \mid H_i(s_i,q_{-i}) \geq H_i(\bar{s}_i,q_{-i}) \text{ for all } \bar{s}_i \in S_i\} \subseteq F_i \ . \qquad \text{(I.1.11)}$$

This shows that every player i will restrict himself to strategies in F_i if he expects that all other players restrict themselves to a behavior within the formation F. A formation F is called <u>primitive</u> if it contains no proper subformation. Let $(s_1^+,\ldots,s_n^+)$ be a <u>strict equilibrium point</u> in the following sense:

$$H_i(s^+) > H_i(s_i,s_{-i}^+) \qquad \text{for all } s_i \in S_i - \{s_i^+\} \text{ and } i = 1,\ldots,n. \qquad \text{(I.1.12)}$$

It is easy to see that $F^+ = F_1^+ \times \ldots \times F_n^+$, with $F_i^+ = \{s_i^+\}$ for $i = 1,\ldots,n$, is a primitive formation. To avoid unnecessary notation we will identify a strict equilibrium point s^+ and the formation F^+ generated by s^+. A (finite) game G must have at least one primitive formation, since S is a formation, and it can obviously have only finitely many primitive formations. From a well–known existence theorem (NASH, 1951) follows that every primitive formation contains at least one equilibrium point.

1, –1	–1, 1	0, 0	0, 0
–1, 1	1, –1	0, 0	0, 0
0, 0	0, 0	2, –2	–2, 2
0, 0	0, 0	–2, 2	2, –2

Table I.1.1: A 2–person game G in (agent) normal form (player 1 (2) is the row (column) player; player 1's (2's) payoff is given in the upper left (lower right) corner).

In degenerate cases a primitive formation might contain infinitely many equilibrium points as it is shown by the 2–person game with no proper subformation in Table I.1.1. If player 1 chooses the first and second row with probability .5, all four pure strategies of player 2 yield the maximal payoff expectation. Since a similar statement is true for player 1, this proves that game G of Table I.1.1 has no proper subformation. Define the mixed strategy

$$q_i^{\lambda_i} = (\lambda_i/2, \lambda_i/2, (1-\lambda_i)/2, (1-\lambda_i)/2) \tag{I.1.13}$$

of player i by the constant λ_i with $0 \leq \lambda_i \leq 1$. It is easy to see that for all pairs (λ_1,λ_2) the mixed strategy vector $(q_1^{\lambda_1},q_2^{\lambda_2})$ is an equilibrium point of game G in Table I.1.1.

2. The definition of resistance dominance

Let $G = (S_1,\dots,S_n;P;H)$ be a finite game in complete (agent) normal form. S_i is player i's set of (pure) strategies, P the probability assignment

$$P : \begin{cases} S = S_1\times\dots\times S_n \rightarrow [0,1]^n \\ s = (s_1,\dots,s_n) \mapsto P(s) = (P_1(s),\dots,P_n(s)) \end{cases} \tag{I.2.1}$$

and H the (expected) payoff function

$$H : \begin{cases} S = S_1\times\dots\times S_n \rightarrow \mathbb{R}^n \\ s = (s_1,\dots,s_n) \mapsto H(s) = (H_1(s),\dots,H_n(s)) \end{cases} \tag{I.2.2}$$

of G.

In the following it will be described how one can possibly select one out of many solution candidates to be the solution of the game G. For the time being it will simply be assumed that the set of solution candidates is given. In Part II it will be shown how to generate the set of solution candidates. Let C be a nonempty set of strict equilibrium points $s^j = (s_1^j,...,s_n^j)$ in G, i.e.

$$C = \{s^1,...,s^m\} \qquad \text{with } m \in \mathbb{N} \text{ .} \tag{I.2.3}$$

In Part I the (strict) equilibrium points in C will be called solution candidates.

In general, the concept of resistance avoidance does not require that all candidates are strict equilibrium points. The relation of resistance dominance is well–defined for all nonempty sets of equilibrium points which all lie in different primitive formations.

The basic idea of our concept is to define for every solution candidate $s^k \in C$ a resistance vector $R(s^k) \in \mathbb{R}^{m-1}$. The components of $R(s^k)$ are (nonnegative) resistance values $r(s^{k'},s^k)$ which are derived by measuring the resistance of every other solution candidate $s^{k'}$ in C against s^k and which are arranged in a nonincreasing order. If $R(s^k)$ is lexicographically smaller than $R(s^{k'})$, we will say that s^k resistance dominates $s^{k'}$ which will be written as

$$s^k \mathcal{R} s^{k'}. \tag{I.2.4}$$

Since $\mathcal{R}$ is a complete and transitive preordering on C, the nonempty set C^+ of resistance undominated solution candidates can be defined for every nonempty set C of solution candidates. For $|C^+| = 1$ the only element in C^+ will be called the resistance dominating solution candidate which will be selected as the solution of the game if certain other conditions are satisfied.

Consider a given pair of two different solution candidates s^k and $s^{k'}$ in C. Define

$$S_i' = \{s_i^k, s_i^{k'}\} \qquad (i \in N = \{1,...,n\}) \tag{I.2.5}$$

and

$$H_i' = H_i \Big|_{\substack{n \\ X \\ i=1} S_i'} \qquad \text{for all } i = 1,\dots,n \ . \tag{I.2.6}$$

If f is a function with domain D and if $A \subseteq D$, the notation $f_{|A}$ stands for the restriction of f to the smaller domain A. The normal form game $G' = (S_1',\dots,S_n';H')$ with $H' = (H_1',\dots,H_n')$ is called the <u>restricted game</u> for the resistance comparison of s^k and $s^{k'}$. In G' only the players i in

$$M = \{i \in N |\ s_i^k \neq s_i^{k'}\} \tag{I.2.7}$$

who use different strategies in s^k and $s^{k'}$ are active players. The payoff function H' of G' is simply the restriction of H to the possible strategy vectors s in G'. The definition of the restricted game differs from the one of HARSANYI and SELTEN (1988). In Part IV it will be investigated in more detail how our concept would change if our definition of the restricted game were substituted by the one of HARSANYI and SELTEN.

The resistance value $r(s^{k'},s^k)$ is defined by considering how every player $i \in M$ is opposed against s^k to become the solution of G' instead of $s^{k'}$. Let us consider a given player $i \in M$. Define

$$\begin{aligned} &r_i(s^{k'},s^k) \\ &= \max \{z \in [0,1] \mid H_i'(s_i^{k'},(zs_j^k+(1-z)s_j^{k'})_{j\neq i}) \geq H_i'(s_i^k,(zs_j^k+(1-z)s_j^{k'})_{j\neq i})\} \ . \end{aligned} \tag{I.2.8}$$

Here $(s_i^k,(zs_j^k+(1-z)s_j^{k'})_{j\neq i})$ is the strategy vector according to which player i chooses his (pure) strategy s_i^k whereas all other players $j \in M$ use their (pure) strategy s_j^k with probability z and their (pure) strategy $s_j^{k'}$ with probability 1–z. Then $r_i(s^{k'},s^k)$ is measuring how much bias z toward s^k player i can stand in the sense that $s_i^{k'}$ is still a best reply if he expects all other players $j \in M-\{i\}$ to use their strategy s_j^k with probability z.

HARSANYI and SELTEN call the set of all mixed strategy vectors $q_{-i} = (zs_j^k+(1-z)s_j^{k'})_{j\neq i}$ the diagonal line in the restricted game. But according to their concept they do not measure the incentives to deviate on the diagonal line but in the set of expectations $zs_{-i}^k+(1-z)s_{-i}^{k'}$ with $0 \leq z \leq 1$ about the behavior of player i's opponents (see GÜTH, 1985, for a more detailed discussion about this aspect of the Harsanyi–Selten theory).

Since all solution candidates are strict equilibrium points, it is immediate that the following lemma holds.

Lemma 1:

For all possible pairs of different solution candidates s^k and $s^{k'}$ in C and all players $i \in M$ the values $r_i(s^{k'},s^k)$ are greater than 0 and smaller than 1.

For a given pair s^k and $s^{k'}$ of two different solution candidates in C we define

$$P_i = (P_i(s^k) + P_i(s^{k'})) / 2 \quad (i \in M) . \tag{I.2.9}$$

P_i can be described as the average probability in G' that player i's information set is reached. The <u>resistance value</u> $r(s^{k'},s^k)$ is defined by

$$r(s^{k'},s^k) = \prod_{i \in M} (r_i(s^{k'},s^k)/r_i(s^k,s^{k'}))^{P_i} \tag{I.2.10}$$

which is well–defined because of Lemma 1. We will refer to $r(s^{k'},s^k)$ as the resistance of $s^{k'}$ against s^k. Again because of Lemma 1 one has

Lemma 2:

For all possible pairs of different solution candidates s^k and $s^{k'}$ in C the resistance values $r(s^{k'},s^k)$ are positive.

Before proceeding let us shortly discuss some other ways to measure player i's resistance $r_i(s^{k'},s^k)$ of $s^{k'}$ against s^k. Instead of determining $r_i(s^{k'},s^k)$ by the maximal z on the diagonal line one could have defined it by the maximal z for which $s_i^{k'}$ is still a best reply in S_i' against $zs_{-i}^k+(1-z)s_{-i}^{k'}$. This would greatly simplify to compute $r_i(s^{k'},s^k)$ and the <u>normalized individual resistance</u> $r_i(s^{k'},s^k)/r_i(s^k,s^{k'})$ of player i. But it has been shown elsewhere (GÜTH, 1985) that this approach would also neglect strategically important parameters of the game.

Another possibility to determine $r_i(s^{k'},s^k)$ is given by the Lebesgue–measure of the stability set $R'_i(s_i^{k'})$ in the set Q'_{-i} of admissible mixed strategy vectors q_{-i} in G'. The set $R'_i(s_i^{k'})$ is the set of admissible vectors q_{-i} in G' to which $s_i^{k'}$ is a best reply in S'_i. Since $s^{k'}$ is a strict equilibrium point, $R'_i(s_i^{k'})$ has full dimensionality in Q'_{-i} and therefore positive Lebesgue–measure. We believe that this is the most natural approach to measure individual resistance. Unfortunately, it is often very difficult to calculate the so defined resistance values if M contains more than 2 players. Of course, one might consider restricted games G'_{ij} with only two active players and aggregate the normalized individual resistances of the active players i and j in G'_{ij} first and then aggregate these "aggregates" for all games G'_{ij} with i, j $\in$ M and i $\neq$ j. But this would not reflect the risk of deviations by more than one player.

Considering all possible pairs s^k and $s^{k'}$ of two different solution candidates in C and arranging them in a nonincreasing order yields a unique (m–1)–vector $R(s^k)$ whose components are all positive:

$$R(s^k) = (r(s^{k_1},s^k),\dots,r(s^{k_{m-1}},s^k)) \in \mathbb{R}^{m-1}_{>0} \tag{I.2.11}$$

where the indices $k_1,\dots,k_{m-1}$ have been chosen so that for i = 2,...,m–1

$$r(s^{k_{i-1}},s^k) \geq r(s^{k_i},s^k) \ . \tag{I.2.12}$$

We call $R(s^k)$ the <u>resistance vector</u> against s^k. For u, v $\in \mathbb{R}^{m-1}$ the lexicographic order $u \leq_L v$ is defined by: There is $i_0 \in \{1,\dots,m\}$ such that for all $i \in \{1,\dots,i_0-1\}$ we have $u_i = v_i$ and $u_{i_0} < v_{i_0}$. We define the resistance dominance relation $\mathcal{R}$ on C by

$$s^k \,\mathcal{R}\, s^{k'} \quad \Leftrightarrow \quad [\, R(s^k) \leq_L R(s^{k'}) \text{ and } R(s^{k'}) \neq R(s^k)\,] \tag{I.2.13}$$

and the set C^+ of <u>resistance undominated solution candidates</u> in C according to

$$C^+ = \{s^k \in C | \text{ There is no } s^{k'} \in C \text{ so that } s^{k'} \mathcal{R} s^k\} \quad . \tag{I.2.14}$$

If C^+ contains a single element the latter will be called the resistance dominating solution in C and will be selected as the solution of G with respect to the candidate set C. An obvious property of C^+ is described by Lemma 3.

Lemma 3:

For all nonempty sets C of solution candidates, which are all strict equilibrium points in G, the set C^+ of resistance undominated solution candidates is nonempty.

Since $\leq_L$ is transitive the preordering $\mathcal{R}$ on C is transitive. Rewriting $r_i(s^k,s^{k'})$ according to

$$\begin{aligned} & r_i(s^k,s^{k'}) \\ & = \max\{z \in [0,1] \mid H_i'(s_i^k,(zs_j^{k'} + (1-z)s_j^k)_{j \neq i}) \geq H_i'(s_i^{k'},(zs_j^{k'} + (1-z)s_j^k)_{j\neq i})\} \\ & = 1 - \max\{z \in [0,1] \mid H_i'(s_i^{k'},((1-z)s_j^{k'} + zs_j^k)_{j\neq i}) \geq H_i'(s_i^k,((1-z)s_j^{k'} + zs_j^k)_{j\neq i})\} \end{aligned} \tag{I.2.15}$$

and comparing this to the definition of $r_i(s^{k'},s^k)$ given in (I.2.8) shows that

$$r_i(s^{k'},s^k)/r_i(s^k,s^{k'}) = z^+/(1-z^+) \tag{I.2.16}$$

where z^+ is the greatest value in $[0,1]$ solving

$$H_i'(s_i^{k'},(z^+s_j^k + (1-z^+)s_j^{k'})_{j\neq i}) = H_i'(s_i^k,(z^+s_j^k + (1-z^+)s_j^{k'})_{j\neq i}) \quad . \tag{I.2.17}$$

For many examples it is easier to compute the relative resistance values $r_i(s^{k'},s^k)/r_i(s^k,s^{k'})$ directly by solving for $z^+/(1-z^+)$ than to determine the resistance values $r_i(s^{k'},s^k)$ and $r_i(s^k,s^{k'})$ themselves. Equation (I.2.16) is therefore a helpful result when analysing specific game situations to illustrate the concept of resistance dominance.

Let us look at the class of all 2–person games in (agent) normal form with $u > 0$ which are illustrated in Table I.2.1 in the usual way and completed by $P_1(s) = P_2(s) = 1$ for all strategy vectors $s = (s_1,s_2)$. All these games have two strict equilibrium points only, namely $X = (X_1,X_2)$ and $Y = (Y_1,Y_2)$. Therefore consider

$$C = \{X, Y\} \tag{I.2.18}$$

as the set of solution candidates.

	X_2	Y_2
X_1	1 / u	0 / 0
Y_1	0 / 0	u / 1

Table I.2.1: 2–person games in (agent) normal form with u > 0 (player 1 (2) is the row (column) player, player 1's (2's) payoff is given in upper left (lower right) corner).

Because of the symmetry of G follows that

$$C^+ = \{X, Y\}\,, \tag{I.2.19}$$

i.e. there is no unique resistance undominated solution candidate in C. In Part II it will be shown how by determining C^+ for a finite sequence of candidate sets C one can define a unique solution also for situations as illustrated by Table I.2.1. We will, furthermore, prove that the result of a nonunique resistance undominated candidate is very exceptional.

To have a more intuitive description of our concept, one might refer to $r_i(s^{k'},s^k)$ as the "noise of resistance" on behalf of player i which has to be encountered if s^k instead of $s^{k'}$ is selected as the solution. Since not all players are equally important, every relation $r_i(s^{k'},s^k)/r_i(s^k,s^{k'})$ of normalized noise levels is weighted by P_i, the average probability that player i will actually show up in the play. $r(s^{k'},s^k)$ aggregates the normalized individual resistances of all players whose decisions are different in $s^{k'}$ and s^k and can, accordingly, be interpreted as the noise of resistance of $s^{k'}$ against selecting s^k as the solution.

Arranging all $r(s^{k'},s^k)$–values in a nonincreasing order to define $R(s^k)$ and minimizing lexicographically the vector $R(s^k)$ on C amounts to minimize the loudest noise of resistance by any other possible solution candidate when selecting a solution of game G in complete (agent) normal form with the candidate set C.

Imagine that an unbiased arbitrator has to decide which solution candidate in C should be selected as the solution of the game. An obvious motivation of the arbitrator is to make a proposal which meets the least resistance if compared to any other possible decision. This shows that the concept of resistance dominance can be understood as a choice theory for a fictitious unbiased arbitrator who wants to keep the loudest resistance against his proposal as low as possible. Accordingly, players will derive the solution of the game by imagining which candidate such an arbitrator would propose.

3. General properties of resistance dominance

Let $G = (S_1,...,S_n;P;H)$ be a game in complete (agent) normal form and C be a set of solution candidates of game G, i.e. C is nonempty and all elements in C are strict equilibrium points of G. We refer to the mapping

$$\varphi : (G,C) \longmapsto \varphi(G,C) \subseteq C \ , \tag{I.3.1}$$

which assigns to any such pair (G,C) a nonempty subset of C, as a selection φ.

Consider two games $G = (S_1,...,S_n;P;H)$ and $G' = (S_1,...,S_n;P;H')$ which only differ because of

$$H_{i_0}(\bar{s}) = H'_{i_0}(\bar{s}) + \delta \text{ with } \delta > 0 \tag{I.3.2}$$

for some specific player i_0 and strategy vector $\bar{s} \in S_1 \times ... \times S_n$. Let, furthermore, C and C' be candidate sets of G and G', respectively, satisfying $C = C'$. A selection φ is said to be monotonic if

$$\bar{s} \in \varphi(G',C') \quad \Rightarrow \quad \bar{s} \in \varphi(G,C) \ . \tag{I.3.3}$$

Increasing the payoff of a player for a given solution candidate $\bar{s}$ will never exclude $\bar{s}$ from the selection if the selection is monotonic.

Let us assume that $\bar{s}$ is a solution candidate in both games. For all $s' \in C = C'$, $s' \neq \bar{s}$, the noise of resistance $r_i(\bar{s},s')$ of $\bar{s}$ against s' by player i is greater in G than in G'. $r(\bar{s},s')$ is therefore in G at least not smaller than in G'. From this one can conclude:

Lemma 4:

The selection $\varphi(G,C) = C^+$ implied by the concept of resistance dominance is monotonic.

Lemma 4 is of limited importance since the candidate sets in the games G and G' may, of course, be different. Only for those values of δ (> 0) for which the candidate set is the same in both games, the lemma implies that $\bar{s}$ is selected in G if this is true in G'.

Let $\mathcal{G}$ denote the class of all games $G = (S_1,...,S_n;P;H)$ which only differ in the component H. A specific game $G \in \mathcal{G}$ can be described by the vector

$$H = (H_1(s)_{s \in S},...,H_n(s)_{s \in S}) \in \mathbb{R}^{n|S|} \tag{I.3.4}$$

where $S = S_1 \times ... \times S_n$ is the (finite) set of (pure) strategy vectors $s = (s_1,...,s_n)$. Assume that G(H) $= (S_1,...,S_n;P;H) \in \mathcal{G}$ is determined by choosing a point $H \in \mathbb{R}^{n|S|}$. For any such game G(H) a nonempty set $\tilde{C}$ of equilibrium points is called a possible candidate set if all points in $\tilde{C}$ lie in different primitive formations of G(H). The following theorem says that generically there is always a unique resistance undominated candidate in $\tilde{C}$.

Theorem 1:

The subset $\mathcal{G}^0$ of $\mathcal{G}$ defined by

$\mathcal{G}^0 = \{G(H) \in \mathcal{G} \mid G(H)$ has a possible candidate set $\tilde{C}$ with $|\tilde{C}^+| > 1\}$

is of Lebesgue–measure 0 in $\mathcal{G}$.

To prove Theorem 1 one first of all has to observe that for almost all $H \in \mathbb{R}^{n|S|}$ the game G(H) has only finitely many possible candidate sets $\tilde{C}$. We can therefore restrict our attention to those games G(H) with finitely many possible candidate sets. For any such game G(H) and possible candidate set $\tilde{C}$ of G(H) to satisfy $|\tilde{C}^+| > 1$ it is necessary that there are at least two candidates s' and s" in $\tilde{C}$ such that $R(s') = R(s")$. For this to be true the components of H have to satisfy $|\tilde{C}|-1 = m-1 \geq 1$ equalities. This shows that $\mathcal{G}^0$ is of lower dimensionality than $\mathcal{G}$ which is isomorphic to $\mathbb{R}^{n|S|}$ and that Theorem 1 holds.

It should be mentioned that the definition of a possible candidate set $\tilde{C}$ does not require that the elements $s \in \tilde{C}$ are strict equilibrium points. But since all elements of $\tilde{C}$ lie in different primitive formations, all $r_i(s^{k'},s^k)$–values are positive and smaller than 1. This shows that the relation of resistance dominance is well–defined also for possible candidate sets.

Cardinal utility functions are uniquely determined up to positive linear transformations. A minimal requirement of any game theoretic solution concept is therefore that positive linear transformations of the players' payoff functions do not change the result of the game. From the definition given in (I.2.8) it is easy to see that $r_i(s^{k'},s^k)$ is independent of positive linear transformations of player i's payoff H_i and therefore of H_i'. This implies that all resistance vectors $R(s^k)$ are invariant under positive linear transformations of every player's payoff function. It is therefore an obvious property of resistance dominance that it is not influenced by positive linear transformations of the players' payoff functions.

As mentioned in our Introduction it would be desirable to rely on axioms supporting the constructive procedure of selecting the solution. Although we do not envisage a complete characterization of our solution concept, an axiomatic characterization of resistance dominance alone seems to be a much simpler task. Let

$$r = (r_1,...,r_n) \in \mathbb{R}^n_{>0} \tag{I.3.5}$$

be a vector of positive numbers and

$$P = (P_1,...,P_n) \in \mathbb{R}^n . \tag{I.3.6}$$

We do not require $P_i \geq 0$ for $i = 1,...,n$ since later on we will also consider negative weights (see Section 1.2 of Part IV on alternative weights). We want to characterize axiomatically our way of aggregating the normalized individual resistances r_i of players $i = 1,...,n$ with weights P_i in the form of

$$R(r,P) = \prod_{i=1}^{n} r_i^{P_i} . \tag{I.3.7}$$

For that we introduce the following requirements:

Axiom 1: ("Independence of positive transformations")

If $f: \mathbb{R} \rightarrow \mathbb{R}$ is a strictly increasing function, $f(R(r,P))$ is also a total resistance measure.

Since all what matters comparing two solution candidates is whether the aggregate resistance level against one candidate is greater, equal, or smaller than the aggregate resistance level against the other; independence of positive transformations is clearly an innocent requirement. Due to Axiom 1 we can restrict ourselves to the axiomatic characterization of the function

$$\tilde{R}(\tilde{r},P) = \beta \sum_{i=1}^{n} P_i\tilde{r}_i \quad \text{with } \beta > 0 , \tag{I.3.8}$$

where $\tilde{r}_i = \log(r_i)$ $(i = 1,...,n)$, instead of the original function R in (I.3.7). The following requirements for a function $F : \mathbb{R}^n \times \mathbb{R}^n \rightarrow \mathbb{R}^n$ imply that it must be exactly of the form (I.3.8).

Axiom 2: ("Anonymity")

For every permutation π of $N = \{1,...,n\}$:

$$F(\pi(\tilde{r}), \pi(P)) = F(\tilde{r},P) \ . \tag{I.3.9}$$

Here $\pi(\tilde{r})$ and $\pi(P)$ are the vectors resulting from $\tilde{r}$ and P, respectively, by exchanging the components according to the permutation π. Axiom 2 says that the name of a player should not matter.

Axiom 3: ("Bilinearity")

F is a linear function with respect to the first and to the second variable,

i.e. for all $\tilde{r}$, $\tilde{s}$, P, $\bar{P} \in \mathbb{R}^n$, λ, $\mu \in \mathbb{R}$:

$$F(\lambda\tilde{r} + \mu\tilde{s},P) = \lambda F(\tilde{r},P) + \mu F(\tilde{s},P)$$

$$F(\tilde{r}, \lambda P + \mu\bar{P}) = \lambda F(\tilde{r},P) + \mu F(\tilde{r},\bar{P}) \ . \tag{I.3.10}$$

The axiom essentially requires that F is bilinear and can thus be written in the form

$$F(\tilde{r},P) = \tilde{r}^t Q P \tag{I.3.11}$$

where $Q = (q_{ij})$ is an n×n–matrix. Let $e^i = (0,...,0,1,0,...,0)$ denote the i–th unit vector in $\mathbb{R}^n$, i.e. $e^i_i = 1$ and $e^i_j = 0$ for $j \neq i$. Axioms 2 and 3 imply that $q_{ii} = q_{jj} = \beta$ since $F(e^i,e^i) = F(e^j,e^j)$ for all $i,j = 1,...,n$. Similarly, because of $F(e^i,e^j) = F(e^k,e^j)$ for all $j = 1,...,n$, and $i, k \in \{1,...,n\}-\{j\}$, it follows that there is $\alpha \in \mathbb{R}$ such that $q_{ij} = \alpha$ $(i,j = 1,...,n,\ i \neq j)$. Now the matrix

$$Q = \begin{bmatrix} \beta & \alpha & \cdots & \alpha \\ \alpha & \beta & \cdots & \alpha \\ \vdots & & \ddots & \vdots \\ \alpha & \alpha & \cdots & \beta \end{bmatrix} \tag{I.3.12}$$

can obviously be decomposed into a matrix with equal elements and a diagonal matrix:

$$Q = \begin{bmatrix} \alpha & \alpha & \cdots & \alpha \\ \alpha & \alpha & \cdots & \alpha \\ \vdots & & \ddots & \vdots \\ \alpha & \alpha & \cdots & \alpha \end{bmatrix} + \begin{bmatrix} \beta-\alpha & 0 & \cdots & 0 \\ 0 & \beta-\alpha & \cdots & 0 \\ \vdots & & \ddots & \vdots \\ 0 & 0 & \cdots & \beta-\alpha \end{bmatrix} . \tag{I.3.13}$$

This shows that Axioms 2 and 3 together imply

$$F(\tilde{r},P) = \alpha \, (\sum_{i=1}^{n} \tilde{r}_i) \, (\sum_{i=1}^{n} P_j) + (\beta-\alpha) \sum_{i=1}^{n} \tilde{r}_i P_i \; . \tag{I.3.14}$$

Axiom 4: ("Proportionality with respect to the number of players")

If $\tilde{r}$ and P are uniform, i.e. $\tilde{r}_i = c$, $P_i = d$ for $i = 1,\dots,n$, then

$$F(\tilde{r},P) = n \, F(c,d) \tag{I.3.15}$$

where on the right-hand side of (I.3.15) F is a function $\mathbb{R}\times\mathbb{R} \longrightarrow \mathbb{R}$.

For the uniform vectors $\tilde{r}$ and P defined in Axiom 4 equation (I.3.14) becomes

$$F(\tilde{r},P) = \alpha \, n^2 \, c \, d + (\beta-\alpha) \, n \, c \, d \tag{I.3.16}$$

which shows that, due to Axiom 4, the parameter α must be zero. Thus any function F satisfying Axioms 2, 3, and 4 can be written as

$$F(\tilde{r},P) = \beta \sum_{i=1}^{n} \tilde{r}_i P_i \; . \tag{I.3.17}$$

Axiom 5: ("Monotonicity")

If $\tilde{r} \in \mathbb{R}^n$, $\epsilon > 0$, and $P \in \mathbb{R}^n$ with $P_{i_0} > 0$ for some $i_0 \in \{1,\dots,n\}$, then

$$F(\tilde{r} + \epsilon e^{i_0},P) > F(\tilde{r},P) \; . \tag{I.3.18}$$

Monotonicity requires that if, due to $P_i > 0$, player i is not negligible, an increase of his individual resistance should increase total resistance. Axiom 5 implies that the parameter β in function (I.3.17) must be positive. Thus we have shown

Lemma 5:

Only functions given by (I.3.8) satisfy Axioms 2–5. Since the aggregate resistance measure R in (I.3.7) is a positive monotone transformation of $\tilde{R}$, it is uniquely determined up to such a transformation.

The axiomatic characterization of risk dominance by HARSANYI and SELTEN (1988, Section 3.9) for 2×2–bimatrix games with two strict equilibria also applies to resistance dominance. Here a 2–person game $G = (S_1,S_2;P;H)$ in complete (agent) normal form will be called a 2×2–bimatrix game if $|S_1| = |S_2| = 2$ and $P(s) = 1$ for all $s \in S_1 \times S_2 = S$. Let G be the restricted game for the resistance comparison of two equilibria s and s' which lie in different primitive formations and assume that game G has only two active players i and j. Obviously, G is a 2×2–bimatrix game with two strict equilibria. From the argument above neither s resistance dominates s' nor vice versa if G is symmetric, i.e. resistance dominance in G is symmetry invariant. Furthermore, the proof of Lemma 4 shows that resistance dominance is monotonic in the sense of HARSANYI and SELTEN (1988, Section 3.8).

To prove the equivalence of risk and resistance dominance between two strict equilibria s, s' in 2×2–bimatrix games G and to provide thereby an axiomatic characterization of resistance dominance for this special class of games, it remains to show that resistance dominance between s and s' in G only depends on the best reply structure of the game. HARSANYI and SELTEN (1988, Section 3.5) call this property best reply invariance. Obviously, we do not change a player's pure best reply if we add a constant to his payoff for those pure strategy vectors which rely on the same behavior on behalf of his opponent. The change from game G to game $\hat{G}$ in Table I.3.1 can obviously be justified as such a payoff transformation preserving the best reply correspondence of the game (see HARSANYI and SELTEN, 1988, Section 3.4). Comparing $r_1(s',s)$ and $r_2(s',s)$ for G and $\hat{G}$ according to our basic formula (I.2.8) shows that resistances are not changed by this payoff transformation. The change from G to $\hat{G}$ results from applying the principle of best reply invariance, the change from $\hat{G}$ to $\breve{G}$ in Table I.3.1 is simply a result of positive linear transformations of 1's and 2's payoff function.

G	s_2	s'_2
s_1	$H_1(s)$ / $H_2(s)$	$H_1(s_1, s'_2)$ / $H_2(s_1, s'_2)$
s'_1	$H_1(s'_1, s_2)$ / $H_2(s'_1, s_2)$	$H_1(s')$ / $H_2(s')$

$\hat{G}$	s_2	s'_2
s_1	u_1 / u_2	0 / 0
s'_1	0 / 0	v_1 / v_2

$\breve{G}$	s_2	s'_2
s_1	u / 1	0 / 0
s'_1	0 / 0	1 / v

Table I.3.1: Applying best reply invariance to change G into $\hat{G}$ and a positive linear payoff transformation to change $\hat{G}$ into $\breve{G}$ ($u_i = H_i(s) - H_i(s'_i, s_j)$, $v_i = H_i(s') - H_i(s_i, s'_j)$ for i, j $\in$ {1, 2}, j $\neq$ i and $u = u_1/v_1$, $v = v_2/u_2$).

Now consider game $\breve{G}$. If u = v, i.e. both sides in (I.3.19) are equal, neither s resistance dominates s' nor vice versa since resistance dominance is symmetry invariant. If u > v resistance dominance of s over s' follows from the monotonicity of resistance dominance. Thus s resistance dominates s' in G whenever

$$\frac{H_1(s) - H_1(s'_1, s_2)}{H_1(s') - H_1(s_1, s'_2)} > \frac{H_2(s') - H_2(s'_1, s_2)}{H_2(s) - H_2(s_1, s'_2)} \tag{I.3.19}$$

and vice versa if the reverse inequality is true. This proves the following theorem on the resistance comparison of two strict equilibria in a 2×2–bimatrix game.

Theorem 2:

i) In any restricted game G' with only two active players, a strict equilibrium point resistance dominates the other strict equilibrium point if and only if it risk dominates the other equilibrium point.

ii) Resistance dominance in restricted games with only two active players is uniquely characterized by the principles of symmetry invariance, best reply invariance and payoff monotonicity.

That risk and resistance dominance coincide for strict equilibria in 2×2–bimatrix games partly results from the fact that we have used ideas closely related to the Harsanyi–Selten theory.

Another reason is that the class of 2×2–bimatrix games with two strict equilibria is very limited. It does not matter, for instance, whether risk dominance is transitive or not or whether opponents jointly randomize or not. The following examples will demonstrate that the selection behavior of resistance dominance greatly differs from the one of risk dominance although both concepts coincide for the class of 2×2–bimatrix games with two strict equilibria.

4. Applying the principle of resistance avoidance

Before describing how the concept of resistance avoidance will be used in selecting a unique solution of a game G in complete (agent) normal form we want to illustrate the concept and its underlying definitions by applying it to specific examples. In this section only strict equilibria are considered as solution candidates. Although in general mixed strategy equilibria may become solution candidates as well, this cannot happen in the examples analysed below since all mixed strategy equilibria are payoff dominated by pure strategy equilibria.

4.1 Games with complete information

To get an impression of how the principle of resistance avoidance selects one equilibrium point out of a given set of solution candidates, we first look at some simple classes of 2–person and 3–person games. As such games are quite easy to deal with and do not require complex computations they best reveal how resistances depend on the game parameters.

4.1.1 A simple 2–person game with three strict equilibrium points

Let us consider the game illustrated in Table I.4.1 with the parameter restrictions

$$3 > a, \quad 3 > d, \quad 1 > c, \quad 1 > b, \quad \frac{(1-b)(1-c)}{(3-a)(3-d)} > 9/4, \tag{I.4.1}$$

which are obviously not exclusive, and with the probability assignment P given by

$$P_i(s) = 1 \qquad \text{for all } s \in S \text{ and } i = 1, 2 . \tag{I.4.2}$$

	X_2		Y_2		Z_2	
X_1	3	3	0	0	c	d
Y_1	0	0	2	2	0	0
Z_1	a	b	0	0	1	1

Table I.4.1: A 2–person game in (agent) normal form with parameter restrictions given by (I.4.1) (player 1's (2's) payoff is in the upper left (lower right) corner; 1 (2) is the row (column) player).

Game G in complete (agent) normal form has three strict equilibrium points, namely

$$X = (X_1,X_2), \quad Y = (Y_1,Y_2), \quad Z = (Z_1,Z_2). \tag{I.4.3}$$

Therefore one has to consider

$$C = \{X, Y, Z\} \tag{I.4.4}$$

as the set of solution candidates for the game G. One derives

$$r_1(Z,X) = \max\{z \in [0,1] \mid az+1-z \geq 3z+(1-z)c\} = (1-c)/(4-c-a) \tag{I.4.5}$$

$$r_2(Z,X) = \max\{z \in [0,1] \mid dz+1-z \geq 3z+(1-z)b\} = (1-b)/(4-d-b) \tag{I.4.6}$$

and, analogously,

$$r_1(X,Z) = (3-a)/(4-c-a) \tag{I.4.7}$$

$$r_2(X,Z) = (3-d)/(4-d-b)\ . \tag{I.4.8}$$

From these equations follows that

$$r(Z,X) = r(X,Z)^{-1} = \frac{(1-c)(1-b)}{(3-a)(3-d)}\ . \tag{I.4.9}$$

In the same way one computes

$$r(X,Y) = r(Y,X)^{-1} = 9/4 \tag{I.4.10}$$

and

$$r(Y,Z) = r(Z,Y)^{-1} = 4\ . \tag{I.4.11}$$

The example shows that the relation $\frac{r(s^{k'},s^k)}{r(s^k,s^{k'})}$ of the relative "noise of resistance" is neither transitive nor consistent with Pareto–optimality since

$$\frac{r(X,Y)}{r(Y,X)} > 1\,,\quad \frac{r(Y,Z)}{r(Z,Y)} > 1\,,\quad \text{but}\quad \frac{r(X,Z)}{r(Z,X)} < 1\,. \tag{I.4.12}$$

Although the resistance of X against Y is louder than vice versa and the resistance of Y against Z is louder than vice versa, this does not imply that also the resistance of X against Z is louder than vice versa. To derive the set C^+ of resistance undominated solution candidates one has to compare

$$R(X) = (r(Z,X),r(Y,X)) \quad , \tag{I.4.13}$$

$$R(Y) = (r(X,Y),r(Z,Y)) \quad , \tag{I.4.14}$$

$$R(Z) = (r(Y,Z),r(X,Z)) \quad . \tag{I.4.15}$$

In all three vectors the first component is greater and the second component is smaller than 1 which shows that the "noise levels" are arranged in a nonincreasing order. Since

$$r(X,Y) < \min \{r(Z,X), r(Y,Z)\} \tag{I.4.16}$$

it follows that

$$C^+ = \{Y\} \quad , \tag{I.4.17}$$

i.e. Y is the only resistance undominated candidate in C.

This shows that the relation $\mathcal{R}$ of resistance dominance is not consistent with payoff dominance on C. Y resistance dominates X although X payoff dominates Y in the sense that every player receives more in X than in Y.

4.1.2 A 3–person game with two solution candidates

Consider the family of 3–person games with $x > 1.25$ illustrated in Table I.4.2 and completed by the probability assignment

$$P_i(s) = 1 \qquad \text{for all } s \in S \text{ and } i = 1, 2, 3 \ . \tag{I.4.18}$$

0, 0, 0	Y_3 / X_3	X_2	Y_2	0, 2, 0
	X_1	1, 1, 1+x	2, 0, 0	
	Y_1	0, 2, 0	2, 2, 0	
2, 0, 0				2, 2, 1

Table I.4.2: A 3–person game in (agent) normal form (player 1 chooses between above (X_1) and below (Y_1), player 2 between left (X_2) and right (Y_2), player 3 between inside (X_3) and outside (Y_3); payoffs are given for player 1 (3) in the upper left (lower right) corner and for player 2 in between; $x > 1.25$).

There are only two strict equilibrium points $X = (X_1,X_2,X_3)$ and $Y = (Y_1,Y_2,Y_3)$. Thus

$$C = \{X, Y\} \tag{I.4.19}$$

has to be considered as the set of solution candidates. From

$$\begin{aligned} & r_1(Y,X) = r_2(Y,X) \\ & = \max \{z \in [0,1] \mid 4z(1-z) + 2(1-z)^2 \geq z^2 + 2z(1-z)\} \end{aligned} \tag{I.4.20}$$

and

$$r_3(Y,X) = \max \{z \in [0,1] \mid (1-z)^2 \geq (1+x)z^2\} \tag{I.4.21}$$

follows that

$$\frac{r_1(Y,X)}{r_1(X,Y)} = \frac{r_2(Y,X)}{r_2(X,Y)} = 1+\sqrt{3} \ , \tag{I.4.22}$$

$$\frac{r_3(Y,X)}{r_3(X,Y)} = 1/\sqrt{1+x} \quad . \tag{I.4.23}$$

The condition

$$r(Y,X) = r(X,Y)^{-1} > 1 \tag{I.4.24}$$

is therefore equivalent to

$$(1+\sqrt{3})^2 > \sqrt{1+x} \tag{I.4.25}$$

or

$$x < 27+16\sqrt{3} \, . \tag{I.4.26}$$

This implies that $C^+ = \{Y\}$ for $1.25 < x < 27+16\sqrt{3}$ and $C^+ = \{X\}$ for $x > 27+16\sqrt{3}$.

The above calculations are also valid for $x > -1$ so that we could have substituted 1.25 by –1. But to assure that the mixed strategy equilibrium is payoff dominated we need the above assumption on x. Already for $x > 5$ the Harsanyi–Selten theory selects X as the solution of the game, due to the fact that X risk dominates Y (GÜTH, 1985).

It is interesting to observe that for $x > 5$ the very same result is also implied by the Harsanyi-Selten theory if their definition of bicentric prior–strategies is replaced by one which avoids the expectation of correlated decision behavior (GÜTH, 1985). The new bicentric prior–strategies can be described as mixed strategies in the restricted game G' according to which $s_i^{k'}$ and s_i^k are used with probabilities $r_i(s^{k'},s^k)$ and $r_i(s^k,s^{k'})$, respectively.

4.1.3 A 3–person game with an unbiased threat

For a 3–person bargaining game with two strict equilibrium points the rules of unanimity bargaining are assumed except for player 3. If player 3 deviates, this does not necessarily imply that his opponents receive their conflict payoffs. Instead it is assumed that player 1's and 2's payoffs are decreased by a given amount c regardless from which of the two unanimous agreements player 3 deviates. Since the payoff effects of 3's deviation are the same for both solution candidates, we say that player 3 has an unbiased threat. A more thorough discussion of bargaining games with unbiased threats can be found in GÜTH and SEIFERT (1984) and GALAHN (1984).

Consider the class of games $G = (S_1,S_2,S_3;P;H)$ in complete (agent) normal form with

$$S_i = \{X_i, Y_i\} \qquad \text{for } i = 1, 2, 3\,, \tag{I.4.27}$$

$$P_i(s) = 1 \qquad \text{for all } s \in S \text{ and } i = 1, 2, 3\,, \tag{I.4.28}$$

and

$$H_1(s) = H_2(s) = \begin{cases} u & \text{for } s = X = (X_1,X_2,X_3) \\ 1 & \text{for } s = Y = (Y_1,Y_2,Y_3) \\ u-c & \text{for } s = (X_{-3},Y_3) \\ 1-c & \text{for } s = (Y_{-3},X_3) \\ 0 & \text{otherwise} \end{cases} \tag{I.4.29}$$

and

$$H_3(s) = \begin{cases} 1 & \text{for } s = X \\ v & \text{for } s = Y \\ 0 & \text{otherwise} \end{cases} \tag{I.4.30}$$

where $v > 0$, $u > 1$ and $c \geq 0$. It is easy to see that X and Y are the only strict equilibrium points of any such game.

Considering

$$C = \{X, Y\} \tag{I.4.31}$$

as the candidate set one easily derives that

$$C^{+} = \{X\} \qquad \text{if } u^{2}/\sqrt{v} > 1 \tag{I.4.32}$$

and that $C^{+} = \{Y\}$ if the reverse inequality of (I.4.32) is true.

It is an interesting result that it does not depend at all on the parameter c whether X resistance dominates Y or vice versa. If $v \leq 1$, then only X is resistance undominated. In case of $v > 1$ the solution candidate X will resistance dominate Y only if $u^{4} > v$. Usually the parameter v has to be much higher than u to yield Y as the solution of the game.

When comparing the ESBORA–solution, which will be introduced later on, with the result determined by the Harsanyi–Selten theory, we restrict our attention to those games with $u = v$ where the ESBORA–solution is always X. Although the prior–probabilities do not depend on the parameter c, the same is not true for the Harsanyi–Selten solution. It can easily be seen that X is the Harsanyi–Selten solution if $u > c-2$ and that Y is selected if $c-2 > u > 1$. Thus for all parameter constellations u, v, and c satisfying $c-2 > u = v > 1$ the solution is different for the two concepts. Whereas the ESBORA–solution is always X, the Harsanyi–Selten theory selects X as the solution if the payoff parameter c is rather small, and Y if it is rather large.

If c is positive and player 3 unilaterally deviates from X or Y players 1 and 2 suffer from it. Observe that the loss of both players is the same regardless whether player 3 deviates from X or Y. Nevertheless, the Harsanyi–Selten theory says that Y should be the solution if the deviation loss which is the same for X and Y is rather high whereas X should be the solution if this loss is rather low. Thus, if player 3 has an effective unbiased threat, his opponents are more inclined to concede the candidate which is best for player 3. The obvious intuition behind such a selection behavior is obviously that one should be generous with dangerous opponents.

4.1.4 An extensive game with chance moves

The following example is used to illustrate the effect of the weighting factors P_i in the definition of the resistance values $r(s^{k'},s^{k})$ for games with complete information. Consider the 2–person extensive game illustrated in Figure I.4.1.

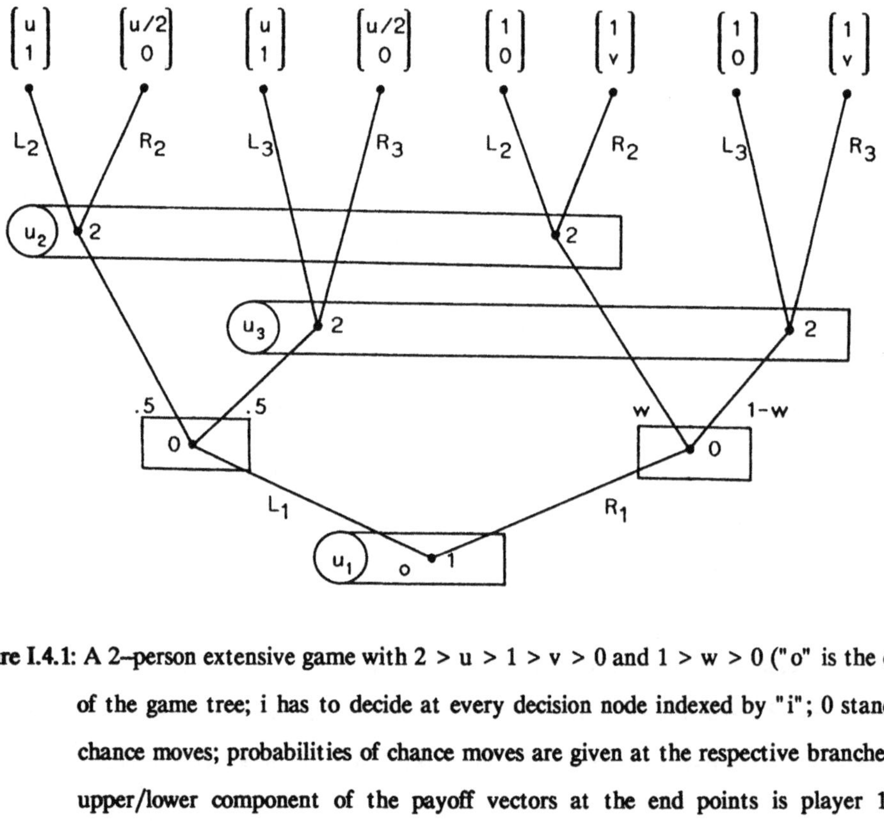

Figure I.4.1: A 2–person extensive game with $2 > u > 1 > v > 0$ and $1 > w > 0$ ("o" is the origin of the game tree; i has to decide at every decision node indexed by "i"; 0 stands for chance moves; probabilities of chance moves are given at the respective branches; the upper/lower component of the payoff vectors at the end points is player 1's/2's payoff; information sets are indicated by encircling the decision nodes belonging to the same information set; choice partitioning is defined by identifying all branches corresponding to the same move).

The complete (agent) normal form $G = (S_1,S_2,S_3;P;H)$ of this game is given by

$$S_i = \{L_i, R_i\} \qquad \text{for } i = 1, 2, 3 \qquad (I.4.33)$$

and

$$
(H(s);P(s)) = \begin{cases}
((u,1,1);(1,1/2,1/2)) & \text{for } s = (L_1,L_2,L_3) \\
((3u/4,1/2,1/2);(1,1/2,1/2)) & \text{for } s = (L_1,L_2,R_3) \\
((3u/4,1/2,1/2);(1,1/2,1/2)) & \text{for } s = (L_1,R_2,L_3) \\
((u/2,0,0);(1,1/2,1/2)) & \text{for } s = (L_1,R_2,R_3) \\
((1,0,0);(1,w,1-w)) & \text{for } s = (R_1,L_2,L_3) \\
((1,v(1-w),v(1-w));(1,w,1-w)) & \text{for } s = (R_1,L_2,R_3) \\
((1,vw,vw);(1,w,1-w)) & \text{for } s = (R_1,R_2,L_3) \\
((1,v,v);(1,w,1-w)) & \text{for } s = (R_1,R_2,R_3)
\end{cases} \qquad \text{(I.4.34)}
$$

where $2 > u > 1 > v > 0$, $1 > w > 0$ and $H(s) = (H_1(s),H_2(s),H_3(s))$ and $P(s) = (P_1(s),P_2(s),P_3(s))$ are the payoff vectors and the probability vectors, respectively. Player 1 is the only agent of player 1 in the extensive game, whereas player 2 in the extensive game has two agents, namely the players 2 and 3 in the agent normal form. It can be seen that the probabilities $P_2(s)$ and $P_3(s)$ depend on whether player 1 chooses L_1 or R_1. In case of L_1 both, $P_2(s)$ and $P_3(s)$, are .5. In case of R_1 the probability of player 2 is w and the one of player 3 is 1–w.

It is easy to see that $L = (L_1,L_2,L_3)$ and $R = (R_1,R_2,R_3)$ are the only strict equilibrium points. Considering

$$C = \{L, R\} \qquad \text{(I.4.35)}$$

as the set of solution candidates one has to compute

$$r_1(L,R) = \max\{z \in [0,1] \mid (1-z)^2 + \tfrac{3}{2}z(1-z) + \tfrac{1}{2}z^2 \geq 1/u\} \ . \qquad \text{(I.4.36)}$$

It follows that

$$\frac{r_1(L,R)}{r_1(R,L)} = \frac{2(u-1)}{2-u} \ . \qquad \text{(I.4.37)}$$

Similary, one derives

$$\frac{r_2(L,R)}{r_2(R,L)} = \frac{1}{2vw} \tag{I.4.38}$$

from

$$\begin{aligned} & r_2(L,R) \\ & = \max \{z \in [0,1] \mid (1-z)^2 + \tfrac{1}{2}z(1-z) + v(1-w)z^2 \geq \tfrac{1}{2}(1-z)^2 + vwz(1-z) + vz^2\}\,, \end{aligned} \tag{I.4.39}$$

and

$$\frac{r_3(L,R)}{r_3(R,L)} = \frac{1}{2v(1-w)} \tag{I.4.40}$$

from

$$\begin{aligned} & r_3(L,R) \\ & = \max \{z \in [0,1] \mid (1-z)^2 + \tfrac{1}{2}z(1-z) + vwz^2 \geq \tfrac{1}{2}(1-z)^2 + v(1-w)z(1-z) + vz^2\}\,. \end{aligned} \tag{I.4.41}$$

Since $P_1 = 1$, $P_2 = (1+2w)/4$ and $P_3 = (3-2w)/4$ it follows that

$$r(L,R) = r(R,L)^{-1} = w^{-\frac{1+2w}{4}} (1-w)^{-\frac{3-2w}{4}\frac{u-1}{(2-u)v}}\,. \tag{I.4.42}$$

Consequently, C^+ is equal to {L} if $r(L,R) > 1$ whereas in case of $r(L,R) < 1$ the set C^+ of resistance undominated solution candidates is given by {R}. Whether r(L,R) is greater or smaller than 1 depends on the specific values of the parameters u, v, and w within their possible range.

For a numerically specified vector (u,v,w) one can easily compute the resulting noise of resistance r(L,R) of L against R. But since r(L,R) depends on the parameters u, v, and w in a rather complicated way it is not easy to achieve a complete overview of all vectors (u,v,w) yielding C^+ = {L} or C^+ = {R}. Here we confine ourselves to the analysis whether L or R is the only resistance undominated solution candidate if some of the parameters approach the boundaries of their possible range. It is easy to see that $r(L,R) \to \infty$ if $w \to 0$ or $w \uparrow 1$ or $v \to 0$ and that $r(L,R) \to 0$ if $u \downarrow 1$. Consequently, one has $C^+ = \{L\}$ if w is either near to 0 or near to 1 and if v is close to 0 whereas $C^+ = \{R\}$ results if u is relatively close to 1.

The limiting results for $v \to 0$ and $u \downarrow 1$ can be explained easily: If $v \to 0$, players 2 and 3 have no incentive to choose their strategies R_2 and R_3, respectively. Similary, player 1 will prefer R if $u \downarrow 1$. If w approaches 0 player 2's decision matters only if 1 chooses L_1. Consequently, player 2 will play L_2. Similary $w \uparrow 1$ implies that player 3 will use his L_3–strategy. In both cases this is sufficient to make $L = (L_1,L_2,L_3)$ the only resistance undominated solution candidate. Observe that $w \to 0$ or $w \uparrow 1$ does not imply that player 2 or 3 become unimportant since the decisions of both players have important effects if 1 chooses L_1.

4.2 Games with incomplete information

Social conflicts in real life are nearly always decision problems under incomplete information. It is therefore very important to show how equilibrium selection theory can be applied to noncooperative games with incomplete information and to investigate whether it yields reasonable results. In the following we will explore the resistance dominance relationships for some specific games with incomplete information and partly compare our results with those of the Harsanyi–Selten theory.

4.2.1 Unanimity bargaining games with incomplete information

A finite $\bar{n}$–person unanimity bargaining game with incomplete information can be described by $\Delta = (I;T_1,\ldots,T_{\bar{n}};\mathcal{P};U)$ where

$$I = \{1,\dots,m\} \qquad \text{with } m \geq 2 \tag{I.4.43}$$

is a finite index set, which is each player's pure strategy set, and

$$T_i = \{t_i\} \qquad \text{with } 1 \leq |T_i| < \infty \tag{I.4.44}$$

for $i = 1,\dots,\bar{n}$ is player i's set of possible types. $\mathcal{P}$ is the probability distribution

$$\mathcal{P}: \begin{cases} T = T_1 \times \dots \times T_{\bar{n}} \longrightarrow (0,1] \\ t = (t_1,\dots,t_{\bar{n}}) \longmapsto \mathcal{P}(t) \end{cases} \tag{I.4.45}$$

which assigns to every possible type vector t the probability $\mathcal{P}(t)$ by which it is expected to result. The payoff function

$$h: \begin{cases} T \times I^{\bar{n}} \longrightarrow \mathbb{R}^{\bar{n}} \\ (t,s) \longmapsto h^t(s) = (h_1^{t_1}(s),\dots,h_{\bar{n}}^{t_{\bar{n}}}(s)) \end{cases} \tag{I.4.46}$$

assigns the vector $h^t(s)$ of utilities $h_i^{t_i}(s)$ to every possible type vector t and every strategy vector $s = (s_1,\dots,s_{\bar{n}}) \in I^{\bar{n}}$ where $h_i^{t_i}(s)$ is player i's evaluation of the play implied by s if he happens to be of type t_i. Now h is defined by the vector

$$U = ((u^j_{t_1})_{1 \leq j \leq m, t_1 \in T_1},\dots,(u^j_{t_{\bar{n}}})_{1 \leq j \leq m, t_{\bar{n}} \in T_{\bar{n}}}) \in \mathbb{R}_{>0}^{m|T_1|} \times \dots \times \mathbb{R}_{>0}^{m|T_{\bar{n}}|} \tag{I.4.47}$$

with positive components $u^j_{t_i}$ according to

$$h_i^{t_i}(s) = \begin{cases} u^j_{t_i} \ (> 0) & \text{if } s = (j,\dots,j) \in I^{\bar{n}}, \\ 0 & \text{otherwise} \ , \end{cases} \tag{I.4.48}$$

i.e. all players have to agree (choose the same index) in order to achieve a positive payoff.

The complete (agent) normal form $G(\Delta) = (S_1,...,S_n;P;H)$ of $\Delta = (I;T_1,...,T_{\bar{n}};\mathscr{P};U)$ is given by

$$S_i = I \qquad \text{for } i = 1,...,n \tag{I.4.49}$$

where $n = |T_1| + ... + |T_{\bar{n}}|$ is the number of types and thereby of players in the normal form game. For every strategy vector $s = (s_1,...,s_n) \in I^n$ the probabilities $P_{\pi(t_i)}(s) = \bar{P}_{\pi(t_i)}$ are given by

$$\bar{P}_{\pi(t_i)} = \sum_{t_{-i} \in T_{-i}} \mathscr{P}(t_i,t_{-i}) \ . \tag{I.4.50}$$

Here T_{-i} denotes the set $T_1 \times ... \times T_{i-1} \times T_{i+1} \times ... \times T_{\bar{n}}$ and (t_i,t_{-i}) the vector in T which results if $t_{-i} \in T_{-i}$ is completed by t_i as the i–th component. Furthermore, $\pi : \bigcup_{i=1}^{\bar{n}} T_i \longrightarrow \{1,...,n\}$ is the 1–1–mapping used to assign a player index $\pi(t_i) \in \{1,...,n\}$ to every type t_i of every original player $i = 1,...,\bar{n}$. For all $s \in I^n$ with $s_{\pi(t_i)} = j$ the payoffs $H_{\pi(t_i)}(s)$ are given by

$$H_{\pi(t_i)}(s) = (u^j_{t_i}/\bar{P}_{\pi(t_i)}) \sum_{\substack{t_{-i} \in T_{-i} \\ s(t_{-i})=(j,...,j)}} \mathscr{P}(t_i,t_{-i}) \ . \tag{I.4.51}$$

Here $s(t_{-i})$ is an abbreviation for the $(\bar{n}-1)$–vector $(s_{\pi(t_k)})_{k \neq i}$ of decisions of all players $\pi(t_k)$ with t_k being a component of $t_{-i} = (t_1,...,t_{i-1},t_{i+1},...,t_{\bar{n}}) \in T_{-i}$.

A unanimity bargaining game with incomplete information is called <u>regular</u> if there is an index $j^+ \in I$ such that

$$\prod_{i=1}^{\bar{n}} \prod_{t_i \in T_i} (u^{j^+}_{t_i})^{\bar{P}_{\pi(t_i)}} > \prod_{i=1}^{\bar{n}} \prod_{t_i \in T_i} (u^j_{t_i})^{\bar{P}_{\pi(t_i)}} \qquad \text{for all } j \in I-\{j^+\}. \tag{I.4.52}$$

The expression on the right–hand side of (I.4.52) is called the <u>generalized Nash–product</u> of j. In what follows, we only look at regular unanimity bargaining games.

Furthermore, we restrict our attention to those primitive formations of G arising from strict unanimous equilibrium points s = (j,...,j) with $j \in I$. We therefore consider

$$C = \{(1,...,1),...,(m,...,m)\} \tag{I.4.53}$$

as the set of solution candidates. An important property of resistance dominance is the following

Theorem 3:

In regular unanimity bargaining games with incomplete information and candidate sets $C = \{(1,...,1),...,(m,...,m)\}$ the set C^+ of resistance undominated solution candidates is given by $C^+ = \{(j^+,...,j^+)\}$ where j^+ is defined according to (I.4.52).

We will refer to the fact that $(j^+,...,j^+)$ is the only resistance undominated solution candidate in C by saying that the concept of resistance avoidance satisfies a (generalized) Nash–property. This is justified since $(j^+,...,j^+)$ is the cooperative Nash–solution of unanimity bargaining games if $|T_i| = 1$ for $i = 1,...,\bar{n}$ (NASH, 1953) and since it is the generalized cooperative Nash–solution of unanimity bargaining games with incomplete information (HARSANYI and SELTEN, 1972) whenever the generalized Nash–product of j^+ is greater than the generalized Nash–product of any convex combination of equilibrium points.

When developing the concept of resistance avoidance one decisive guideline was to satisfy this Nash–property. In his pioneering contribution NASH (1953) for the first time addressed very clearly the task to develop a theory of equilibrium selection. For the class of unanimity bargaining games he, furthermore, proposed an ad hoc–selection concept with a very convincing axiomatic characterization. This ad hoc–concept and its axiomatic characterization have been generalized to include unanimity bargaining games with incomplete information (HARSANYI and SELTEN, 1972). Therefore requiring this Nash–property when developing a theory of equilibrium selection amounts to generalizing the ad hoc–concept for unanimity bargaining situations to all noncooperative games.

MYERSON (1984) argues against the generalized Nash–property that it does not satisfy the axiom of <u>invariance of probabilities</u>. According to this axiom a change of probabilities and cardinal utilities which does not affect the expected utilities for all possible type constellations and all strategy vectors should not change the solution. This requires that the solution has to maximize a function depending on utilities <u>times</u> probabilities which illustrates that the generalized Nash–property and the axiom of invariance of probabilities are mutually inconsistent.

Let us now prove that the concept of resistance dominance satisfies the (generalized) Nash–property. Since $M = \{1,...,n\}$ is always the set of active players in the restricted game and

$$r_{\pi(t_i)}((j^+,...,j^+),(j,...,j))$$
$$= \max \{z \in [0,1] \mid u^{j^+}_{t_i}(1-z)^{\bar{n}-1} \geq u^j_{t_i} z^{\bar{n}-1}\} \tag{I.4.54}$$

it follows that

$$r((j^+,...,j^+),(j,...,j)) = \prod_{i=1}^{\bar{n}} \prod_{t_i \in T_i} \left[u^{j^+}_{t_i}/u^j_{t_i}\right]^{\frac{\bar{P}_{\pi(t_i)}}{\bar{n}-1}} > 1 \tag{I.4.55}$$

for all $j \in I$ with $j \neq j^+$. This shows that the first component of $R((j^+,...,j^+))$ is smaller than that of $R((j,...,j))$ for all $j \in I-\{j^+\}$ which proves Theorem 2 stated above.

We already mentioned that the Harsanyi–Selten theory has also been designed so that it selects for unanimity bargaining games with complete information the cooperative Nash–solution. But it does not necessarily select the strict equilibrium point $(j^+,...,j^+)$ in unanimity bargaining games with incomplete information.

SELTEN (1975b) has computed the generalized Nash–solution for the situation where two parties bargain about how to distribute a fixed amount of money. Because of the Nash–property this is also the solution implied by the concept of resistance dominance given that only unanimous equilibrium points are considered as initial solution candidates. For the special case of the game analysed by SELTEN, where one of the two players has only one type, HARSANYI (1980) has derived the solution which is determined by the Harsanyi–Selten theory of equilibrium selection.

We now consider a 2–person unanimity bargaining game with incomplete information on both sides that has three strict equilibria with only two of them being unanimous. Let $\Delta = (I;T_1,T_2;\mathscr{P};U)$ be determined by

$$I = \{1, 2\}, \qquad T_i = \{t_i^1, t_i^2\} \quad (i = 1, 2) \tag{I.4.56}$$

$$\mathscr{P}: \begin{cases} T = T_1 \times T_2 & \rightarrow (0,1] \\ t = (t_1, t_2) & \mapsto \mathscr{P}(t) = .25 \end{cases}, \tag{I.4.57}$$

and U by $u^j_{t_i}$ for i, j ∈ {1, 2} according to (I.4.47). The utility $u^j_{t_i}$ which type k of player i assigns to the agreement j is given in Table I.4.3.

	player 1		player 2	
	t_1^1	t_1^2	t_2^1	t_2^2
j = 1	3	1	4	1
j = 2	1	3	1	4

Table I.4.3: Utilities in a 2–person game with incomplete information on both sides ($u^j_{t_i}$ is given in the intersection of the j–th row and the column of type $t_i \in T_i$, for both players i = 1, 2 and for j = 1, 2).

The complete (agent) normal form $G(\Delta) = (S_1,\ldots,S_4;P;H)$ is then defined by

$$S_i = \{1, 2\} \quad \text{for } i = 1,\ldots,4, \tag{I.4.58}$$

$$\pi : \begin{cases} T_1 \cup T_2 \longrightarrow \{1, 2, 3, 4\} \\ t_i^k \longmapsto \pi(t_i^k) = 2(i-1) + k \end{cases}, \tag{I.4.59}$$

$$P_{\pi(t_i)}(s) = \bar{P}_{\pi(t_i)} = .5 \quad \text{for } t_i \in T_i\,,\; i = 1, 2\,, \text{ and } s \in S\ . \tag{I.4.60}$$

The last component of $G(\Delta)$, i.e. $H = (H_1,\dots,H_4) : S \longrightarrow \mathbb{R}^4$, is given by

$$H_{\pi(t_1)}(s) = \begin{cases} u^j_{t_1} & \text{for } s_{\pi(t_2^1)} = s_{\pi(t_2^2)} = j \\ .5\, u^j_{t_1} & \text{for } s_{\pi(t_2^1)} \neq s_{\pi(t_2^2)} \\ 0 & \text{otherwise} \end{cases} \tag{I.4.61}$$

for $t_1 \in T_1$ and $s \in S$, with $s_{\pi(t_1)} = j \in \{1, 2\}$, and by

$$H_{\pi(t_2)}(s) = \begin{cases} u^j_{t_2} & \text{for } s_{\pi(t_1^1)} = s_{\pi(t_1^2)} = j \\ .5\, u^j_{t_2} & \text{for } s_{\pi(t_1^1)} \neq s_{\pi(t_1^2)} \\ 0 & \text{otherwise} \end{cases} . \tag{I.4.62}$$

for $t_2 \in T_2$ and $s \in S$, with $s_{\pi(t_2)} = j \in \{1, 2\}$.

As can easily be shown there are exactly three strict equilibrium points, namely $s^1 = (1,1,1,1)$, $s^2 = (2,2,2,2)$, and $s^3 = (1,2,1,2)$. Let us now consider

$$C = \{s^1, s^2, s^3\} \tag{I.4.63}$$

to be the set of solution candidates. By aggregating the normalized individual resistances in the usual way, we get the following resistance values

$$r(s^1,s^2) = 1\ , \tag{I.4.64}$$

$$r(s^1,s^3) = r(s^2,s^3) = \sqrt{\frac{2\cdot 1}{3-1}\cdot\frac{2\cdot 1}{4-1}} = \sqrt{2/3} \quad . \tag{I.4.65}$$

Because of $r(s^i,s^j) = 1/r(s^j,s^i)$ for $i, j \in \{1, 2, 3\}$ and $i \neq j$ the resistance vectors

$$R(s^1) = (r(s^3,s^1),r(s^2,s^1)) = (\sqrt{3/2},1) \ , \tag{I.4.66}$$

$$R(s^2) = (r(s^3,s^2),r(s^1,s^2)) = (\sqrt{3/2},1) \ , \tag{I.4.67}$$

$$R(s^3) = (r(s^1,s^3),r(s^2,s^3)) = (\sqrt{2/3},\sqrt{2/3}) \ , \tag{I.4.68}$$

are derived. Obviously,

$$C^+ = \{s^3\} \ , \tag{I.4.69}$$

i.e. s^3 is the unique resistance undominated solution candidate. If we do not restrict ourselves to strict unanimous equilibrium points as solution candidates but accept all strict equilibrium points as candidates, a type–discriminating equilibrium point may be the only resistance undominated solution candidate.

The following two examples of bargaining situations require unanimous agreements for contracts to result but they are no unanimity bargaining situations with incomplete information as defined above since an equilibrium point does not imply positive payoffs for all possible types of all players, i.e. not all of the $u^j_{t_i}$–values are positive.

4.2.2 Wage bargaining with incomplete information

Consider the situation of an employer 1 who wants to hire an employee whose productivity p_i (≥ 0) is not completely known to him. Player 1 expects the employee to have productivity p_i with probability $\bar{P}_i$. There are n–1 possible productivity values/types p_i of the employee. The employee knows his own productivity and is aware of the employer's expectations. It is assumed that there is a smallest unit g (> 0) of money and that the expected productivity

$$\bar{I} = \sum_{i=2}^{n} \bar{P}_i p_i \quad (> 0) \qquad \text{with} \quad \sum_{i=2}^{n} \bar{P}_i = 1 \tag{I.4.70}$$

can be expressed in the form

$$\bar{I} = Kg \quad \text{with} \quad K \in 2\mathbb{N} \quad . \tag{I.4.71}$$

The complete (agent) normal form $G = (S_1,\dots,S_n;P;H)$ is defined as follows:

$$S_i = \{g,\, 2g, \dots,\, (K-1)g\} \qquad \text{for } i = 1,\dots,n\,, \tag{I.4.72}$$

$$P_i(s) = \begin{cases} 1 & \text{for } i = 1\,, \\ \bar{P}_i & \text{for } i \geq 2 \end{cases} \tag{I.4.73}$$

for all possible strategy vectors $s \in S$. The payoff function H is given by

$$H_i(s) = \begin{cases} \sum\limits_{\substack{j \geq 2 \\ s_j = s_1}} \bar{P}_j(p_j - s_1) & \text{for } i = 1\,, \\ s_1 & \text{for } i \geq 2 \text{ and } s_i = s_1\,, \\ 0 & \text{for } i \geq 2 \text{ and } s_i \neq s_1\,. \end{cases} \tag{I.4.74}$$

Both, the employer and the employee, choose a wage level kg with $k \in \{1,\dots,K\}$ and a contract results only if both have made the same proposal.

The solution candidates are the strict equilibrium points

$$C = \{U^k = (kg,...,kg) \mid k \in \{1,...,K\}\} \tag{I.4.75}$$

which has at least two different elements because of $K \geq 2$. From

$$r_1(U^{k'},U^k) = \max\{z \in [0,1] \mid (\bar{I}-k'g)(1-z) \geq (\bar{I}-kg)z\} \tag{I.4.76}$$

and

$$r_i(U^{k'},U^k) = \max\{z \in [0,1] \mid k'g(1-z) \geq kgz\} \tag{I.4.77}$$

for $i = 2,...,n$ follows that

$$r_1(U^{k'},U^k)/r_1(U^k,U^{k'}) = (K-k')/(K-k) \tag{I.4.78}$$

and

$$r_i(U^{k'},U^k)/r_i(U^k,U^{k'}) = k'/k \qquad \text{for all } i \geq 2 \ . \tag{I.4.79}$$

This implies

$$r(U^{k'},U^k) = \frac{K-k'}{K-k} \prod_{i=2}^{n} \left(\frac{k'}{k}\right)^{\bar{P}_i} = \frac{(K-k')k'}{(K-k)\,k} \tag{I.4.80}$$

and therefore

$$r(U^{k^+},U^k) > 1 \qquad \text{for } k^+ = K/2, \quad k \in \{1,...,K-1\}-\{k^+\} \ . \tag{I.4.81}$$

U^{k^+} is the only resistance undominated solution candidate, i.e.

$$C^+ = \{U^{k^+}\} \quad . \tag{I.4.82}$$

The same result is implied by the Harsanyi–Selten theory (SELTEN and LEOPOLD, 1982a). It is interesting to observe that the result is independent of the number n–1 of types for the employee, i.e. a change of n does not influence the wage level k^+g if it leaves the expected productivity $\bar{l}$ unchanged.

4.2.3 An art forgery situation

A buyer 3 wants to buy an object of art without having the necessary experience to judge whether it is an original or just an imitation. With probability $0 < w < 1$ player 3 expects the seller to be an art forger, i.e. player 1, with probability $1 - w$ he expects him to be an honest dealer, i.e. player 2. The complete (agent) normal form $G = (S_1,S_2,S_3;P;H)$ is given by

$$S_1 = S_2 = S_3 = \{1+g,\ 1+2g,\ldots,\ 1+(K-1)g\} \tag{I.4.83}$$

where

$$1+Kg = b = (1-w)h \qquad \text{with } K \geq 2 \quad . \tag{I.4.84}$$

Now let h be the value of the original for player 3 and let the value of an imitation be 0 for all players. b is therefore the expected value of the object of art for player 3. The value of the original is 1 for player 2, g (> 0) is the smallest unit of money.

The probability assignment is defined by

$$P(s) = (P_1(s),P_2(s),P_3(s)) = (w,1-w,1) \qquad \text{for all } s \in S \quad . \tag{I.4.85}$$

The payoffs are given by

$$H_1(s) = \begin{cases} s_3 & \text{if } s_1 = s_3 \\ 0 & \text{otherwise ,} \end{cases} \quad (I.4.86)$$

$$H_2(s) = \begin{cases} s_3 - 1 & \text{if } s_2 = s_3 \\ 0 & \text{otherwise ,} \end{cases} \quad (I.4.87)$$

$$H_3(s) = \begin{cases} -ws_3 & \text{if } s_1 = s_3, s_2 \neq s_3 \\ b - (1-w)s_3 & \text{if } s_1 \neq s_3, s_2 = s_3 \\ b - s_3 & \text{if } s_1 = s_2, s_2 = s_3 \\ 0 & \text{otherwise} \end{cases} \quad (I.4.88)$$

Both, the player and the art dealer, have to choose a price independently. A contract results only if both have proposed the same price.

The solution candidates are the strict equilibrium points

$$C = \{p^k = (1+kg, 1+kg, 1+kg) \mid k \in \{1,..,K\}\} \quad . \quad (I.4.89)$$

From

$$r_1(p^{k'},p^k) = \max \{z \in [0,1] \mid (1-z)(1+k'g) \geq z(1+kg)\} \quad , \quad (I.4.90)$$

$$r_2(p^{k'},p^k) = \max \{z \in [0,1] \mid (1-z)k'g \geq zkg\} \quad , \quad (I.4.91)$$

$$r_3(p^{k'},p^k) = \max \{z \in [0,1] \mid (1-z)(b-1-k'g) \geq z(b-1-kg)\} \quad (I.4.92)$$

follows that

$$r(p^{k'},p^k) = \left[\frac{1+k'g}{1+kg}\right]^w \left[\frac{k'}{k}\right]^{1-w} \frac{b-1-k'g}{b-1-kg} = \frac{f(k'g)}{f(kg)} \quad (I.4.93)$$

where $f(x) = (1+x)^w x^{1-w} (b-1-x)$. Now we try to find k^+ with $r(p^k,p^{k^+}) < r(p^{k^+},p^k)$ for all k

$\neq k^+$ which is true if $f(k^+g) < f(kg)$ for all $k \neq k^+$. Since f is a concave function in the range $[0,b-1]$, which is zero for $x = 0$ and for $x = b-1$, the global maximum x^+ of f in $[0,b-1]$ is the only local extremum of f in $(0,b-1)$. Differentiation yields

$$x^+ = \frac{1+b+w+\sqrt{(1+b+w)^2 - 8wb}}{4} - 1 \in (0,b-1) \quad . \tag{I.4.94}$$

In case there is $k^+ \in \mathbb{N}$ such that $x^+ = k^+g$ we obtain

$$C^+ = \{ (1+k^+g, 1+k^+g, 1+k^+g) \} \quad . \tag{I.4.95}$$

But in general this assumption will not be fulfilled. Since f is a concave function we know that

$$k^+ \in \{k_1, k_2\} \qquad \text{with } k_1 = [x^+/g], \quad k_2 = k_1 + 1 \quad , \tag{I.4.96}$$

where $[y]$ denotes the integer satisfying $y \leq [y] < y+1$. Then $k^+ = k_i$ if $r(p^{k_j}, p^{k_i}) < r(p^{k_i}, p^{k_j})$ for $j = 1, 2$ and $j \neq i$.

Here we do not want to determine the proper k^+ but confine ourselves to the above result because it already shows that

$$\lim_{g \to 0} p^{k^+(g)} = (1 + x^+, 1 + x^+, 1 + x^+) \tag{I.4.97}$$

where $p^{k^+(g)}$ denotes the solution of the game G with g being the smallest unit of money in G.

The Harsanyi–Selten solution (p^+,p^+,p^+) for G is given by

$$p^+ = \begin{cases} \frac{1+b}{2} + \frac{w}{4} & \text{if } 0 \leq w \leq 2(h-1)/(\sqrt{2}+2h) \quad , \\ b-g & \text{if } 2(h-1)/(\sqrt{2}+2h) < w < (h-1)/h \, . \end{cases} \tag{I.4.98}$$

The rather surprising discontinuity of p^+ at $\bar{w} = 2(h-1)/(\sqrt{2}+2h)$ results from the fact that for $w \leq \bar{w}$ and $w > \bar{w}$ different aspects of the Harsanyi–Selten theory are applied (SELTEN and GÜTH, 1982c). For all $0 < w < (h-1)/h$ the Harsanyi–Selten theory determines a solution price which is higher than the one implied by the concept of resistance avoidance.

Part II: Generating complete (agent) normal forms and candidate sets

In the following it will be described how the concept of resistance avoidance is used to define the ESBORA–theory of equilibrium selection. In doing so we often rely on procedures of the Harsanyi-Selten theory, sometimes by changing them slightly. When basing our theory on procedures of the Harsanyi–Selten theory we confine ourselves to a very brief description of these aspects. Furthermore, some mathematical statements, necessary to show that the ESBORA–solution is well–defined and unique, are not proved in full detail here. Some of them rely on well–known facts in game theory. Others, marked by "+", have not completely been proved yet and should therefore be considered only as reasonable conjectures. The mathematical difficulties, which will be discussed in more detail in KALKOFEN (1989), are related to the uniqueness of the ESBORA-solution in degenerate game situations.

It should be mentioned that the concept of resistance avoidance is also based on ideas of the Harsanyi–Selten theory. It has, for instance, been indicated that our resistance values $r_i(s^{k'},s^k)$ are closely related to the notion of bicentric priors in the Harsanyi–Selten theory (see also GÜTH, 1985).

Till now it has been shown how to determine for any pair $(G,\mathcal{C})$ the set $\mathcal{C}^+$ of resistance undominated solution candidates. Here $G = (S_1,...,S_n;P;H)$ is a finite game in complete (agent) normal form and $\mathcal{C}$ is a nonempty set of strict equilibrium points in G. In order to obtain a (uniformly) perfect equilibrium point as the solution of G, the solution procedure is not applied to G directly but to (every) ϵ–uniformly perturbed game G^ϵ. To obtain the solution for the unperturbed game G we take the limit $\epsilon \to 0$ which yields an equilibrium point in G being the limit of the solutions of the uniformly perturbed games as for the Harsanyi–Selten theory.

If the perturbed game G^ϵ has proper cells, i.e. if it is <u>decomposable</u>, the solution of G^ϵ is the composition of the solutions of its primitive cell games as well as of the residual game. After showing how the primitive cells and the residual game of a (uniformly) perturbed game in complete (agent) normal form are derived, we describe how to generate irreducible games in complete (agent) normal form. We then define the solutions for such games by applying the concepts of payoff dominance and resistance avoidance. Before considering various examples, which illustrate the different aspects of the constructive solution procedure, we show how the solution procedure can be simplified for nondegenerate game situations.

1. Uniformly perturbed (agent) normal forms

To assure the perfectness of the selected equilibrium point we first solve all ϵ–uniformly perturbed games G^ϵ of G, with $\epsilon > 0$ sufficiently small, and then determine the limit of the solutions of G^ϵ for ϵ approaching 0. Let $G = (S_1,...,S_n;P;H)$ be a game in complete (agent) normal form. The ϵ–uniformly perturbed games $G^\epsilon = (S_1^\epsilon,...,S_n^\epsilon;P;H)$ of G for $0 < \epsilon < \min \{1/|S_i| \mid i = 1,...,n\}$ are defined as follows.

Whereas player $i \in \{1,...,n\}$ can choose any probability distribution q_i over S_i in G he is now restricted to those probability distributions q_i over S_i satisfying

$$q_i(s_i) \geq \epsilon \qquad (s_i \in S_i) \ , \tag{II.1.1}$$

i.e. every player i in G^ϵ can only use completely mixed strategies which give at least the weight ϵ to every strategy in S_i.

With the help of the following notations we will reinterpret $G^\epsilon = (S_1^\epsilon,...,S_n^\epsilon;P;H)$ as a finite game in complete (agent) normal form. For $i = 1,...,n$ let S_i^ϵ denote the finite set of ϵ–extreme mixed strategies s_i^ϵ giving maximal weight to s_i and the minimal weight ϵ to all other strategies $\tilde{s}_i \neq s_i$ in S_i. Thus we have

$$s_i^\epsilon = [1-(|S_i|-1)\epsilon]s_i + \epsilon[\sum_{\tilde{s}_i \in S_i - \{s_i\}} \tilde{s}_i] \quad \text{and}$$

$$S_i^\epsilon = \{s_i^\epsilon | \ s_i \in S_i\} \quad , \tag{II.1.2}$$

The set of probability distributions over S_i^ϵ will sometimes be denoted by Q_i^ϵ, its elements by q_i^ϵ, i.e.

$$Q_i^\epsilon = \{q_i^\epsilon : S_i^\epsilon \rightarrow [0,1] \ | \sum_{s_i^\epsilon \in S_i^\epsilon} q_i^\epsilon(s_i^\epsilon) = 1\},$$

$$Q^\epsilon = Q_1^\epsilon \times \ldots \times Q_n^\epsilon \quad . \tag{II.1.3}$$

Furthermore, the probability assignment P of the game $G = (S_1,\ldots,S_n;P;H)$ can be naturally transferred to an ϵ–uniformly perturbed game G^ϵ of G by first extending P in the canonical way from the set S of pure strategy vectors s in G to the set Q of mixed strategy vectors q in G and then restricting P to the set Q^ϵ of completely mixed strategy vectors satisfying condition (II.1.1).

Thus from a technical point of view we need not distinguish between G and G^ϵ any longer since both are finite games in complete (agent) normal form and only differ by names. So all further procedures of our solution procedure can, without loss of generality, be described for an arbitrary finite game in complete (agent) normal form. This reinterpretation is also of practical importance since the procedures to be described below are sometimes adopted directly to the unperturbed game to simplify our calculations.

2. Cell composition

The cell composition, we are going to define now, is applied to the ϵ–uniformly perturbed games G^ϵ but will be described here for an arbitrary game G in complete (agent) normal form.

Let $G = (S_1,...,S_n;P;H)$ be a game in complete (agent) normal form. The first step when defining the solution of G is to observe important substructures of G which are closed with respect to the best reply correspondence of the game.

Let $C_1,...,C_k$, with $k \geq 1$, denote the primitive cells of G and take $C \in \{C_1,...,C_k\}$. Define

$$CH_i(s_C) = H_i(s_C,\bar{c}_{N-C}) \qquad \text{(II.2.1)}$$

for all $i \in C$, $s_C \in S_C := \underset{l \in C}{X} S_l$, and the vector $\bar{c}_{N-C}$ of centroid mixed strategies $\bar{c}_l$ of S_l for $l \in N-C$. The normal form game $CG = ((S_i)_{i\in C};CH)$, whose payoff function CH is defined by its components CH_i ($i \in C$), is called the cell game CG of G. It is obvious that the cell game CG resulting from a primitive cell C of G has no proper subcells.

Later on it will be shown how to solve a (finite) game in complete (agent) normal form without proper subcells. Suppose that $q^1,...,q^k$ are the solutions of the cell games $C_1G,...,C_kG$ of G, respectively. Anticipating that the players in C_j behave according to q^j ($j = 1,...,k$) the players in $\bar{C} = N-(C_1 \cup ... \cup C_k)$ find themselves in playing a normal form game $\bar{C}G = ((S_i)_{i\in\bar{C}};\bar{C}H)$. The definition of the residual game $\bar{C}G$ differs from the one of a cell game only with respect to the fact that the players $i \in N-\bar{C} = C_1 \cup ... \cup C_k$ are expected to use their cell solution strategies q_i^j (for $i \in C_j$) instead of their centroid mixed strategies $\bar{c}_i$.

Since the number of players is finite this amounts to solving a finite number of games without proper subcells. Suppose that $\bar{q}$ is the solution of $\bar{C}G$. The cell composition $q = (q_1,...,q_n)$ of the solutions of the cell games C_jG ($j = 1,...,k$) and the residual game is defined by

$$q_i = \begin{cases} q_i^j & \text{if there is } j \in \{1,...,k\} \text{ with } i \in C_j \text{ ,} \\ \bar{q}_i & \text{if } i \in \bar{C} \text{ .} \end{cases} \qquad \text{(II.2.2)}$$

for $i = 1,...,n$. If all cell solutions q^j are perfect equilibrium points in C_jG ($j = 1,...,k$) and if $\bar{q}$ is a perfect equilibrium point in $\bar{C}G$ the cell composition q of G is a perfect equilibrium point of G as well. The solution of the (finite) game G in complete (agent) normal form is defined as the cell composition q of G. In order to define a unique solution of G it is therefore necessary to show how to solve games in complete (agent) normal form without proper subcells.

3. Completing cell games and the residual game

Let $G = (S_1,\dots,S_n;P;H)$ be a game in complete (agent) normal form. If $q = (q_1,\dots,q_n)$ is a vector of mixed strategies q_i $(i = 1,\dots,n)$, the canonical way of extending P from S to Q, i.e. to define the probability vectors $P(q) = (P_1(q),\dots,P_n(q))$ implied by P for q, is given by

$$P_i(q) = \sum_{s \in S} [P_i(s) \prod_{j=1}^{n} q_j(s_j)] \qquad (i = 1,\dots,n) \ . \tag{II.3.1}$$

Let $C \subsetneq N = \{1,\dots,n\}$ and CG be a cell game as considered in Section 2. If C is a primitive cell of G the probability assignment $CP = (CP_1,\dots,CP_{|C|})$ of CG is prescribed by the probability assignment P of G according to

$$CP_i(s_C) = P_i(s_C,\bar{c}_{N-C}) \qquad (i \in C,\ s_C \in S_C) \ . \tag{II.3.2}$$

For the residual game $\bar{C}G$ the probability assignment $\bar{C}P = (\bar{C}P_1,\dots,\bar{C}P_{|\bar{C}|})$ is defined according to

$$\bar{C}P_i(s_{\bar{C}}) = P_i(s_{\bar{C}},q^1,\dots,q^k) \qquad (i \in \bar{C},\ s_{\bar{C}} \in S_{\bar{C}}) \tag{II.3.3}$$

where $q^1,\dots,q^k$ denote the solutions of the (complete) primitive cell games $C_1G,\dots,C_kG$ of G, respectively. Since the probability assignment of an ϵ–uniformly perturbed game is naturally determined by the one of the unperturbed game, the above description is complete.

4. Generating irreducible games

Contrary to HARSANYI and SELTEN we do not distinguish between duplicate and semi–duplicate strategies. Thus a strategy is called duplicate if it is either duplicate or semi–duplicate in the sense of HARSANYI and SELTEN (1988, Chapter 3), see also (I.1.8).

A game G in complete (agent) normal form without proper cells is called irreducible if there is no player with inferior or duplicate strategies. Except for the change in the definition of duplicate strategies we use the procedure of the Harsanyi–Selten theory to generate irreducible cell games in complete (agent) normal form for any reducible game. In Algorithm (1) we only give an abbreviated version of this procedure, the whole algorithm will be stated later on in the flow chart diagram of the constructive procedure to define the ESBORA–solution (see Figure II.6.1).

Algorithm (1):

Generating an irreducible game (starting with any game G in (agent) normal form one derives an irreducible cell game of G in (agent) normal form after finitely many steps).

i) START with a game G in (agent) normal form.

ii) If G is decomposable, select a primitive cell C of G and define G = CG.

iii) If there are inferior strategies in G eliminate them and go to ii).

iv) If there are duplicate strategies in G, substitute all sets of duplicate strategies by their centroids and go to ii).

v) G is irreducible, END.

The conceptual background of the reduction procedure of Algorithm (1) is that two games are considered as equivalent if their reduced forms are identical. Or in other words: The strategic aspects which do not appear in the reduced form do not influence the solution of the game. Imagine that the existence of duplicate or inferior strategies would affect the solution in an essential way. Then a player could argue to have or not to have duplicate or inferior strategies (for instance, by writing down the same decision with blue or black ink or by freely disposing utility).

This shows that practically it will be impossible to distinguish between games with identical reduced forms.

5. Generating candidate sets for irreducible games

Let $G = (S_1,...,S_n;P;H)$ be an irreducible game in complete (agent) normal form. The game $G^\delta = (S_1,...,S_n;P;H^\delta)$, with sufficiently small $\delta > 0$ and $H^\delta = (H_1^\delta,...,H_n^\delta)$ given by

$$H_i^\delta : \begin{cases} Q \longrightarrow \mathbb{R} \cup \{-\infty\} \\ q \longmapsto H_i(q) + \delta \sum\limits_{s_i \in S_i} \log(q_i(s_i)) \end{cases} \tag{II.5.1}$$

for all $i = 1,...,n$, will be called the <u>δ–perturbed game</u>. It is a game in complete (agent) normal form whose payoff function is changed according to (II.5.1) by adding a penalty term for choosing extreme strategies. Due to the logarithmic terms $\log(q_i(s_i))$ the perturbed payoff function is unbounded. In addition, for δ approaching 0 the penalty term vanishes and H^δ pointwise approaches H in the space of completely mixed strategies. During the solution procedure the δ–perturbations are applied to ϵ–uniformly perturbed games G^ϵ. The δ–perturbed ϵ–uniformly perturbed game will be called the <u>ϵ,δ–perturbed</u> game and will be denoted by $G^{\epsilon,\delta}$. The main reason for including the penalty term in the payoff function is to make sure that all δ–perturbed games contain only strict equilibrium points so that the concept of resistance avoidance can be applied. Without proof we state the following result.

Theorem$^+$ 4:

In almost all cases, a δ–perturbed game (of an irreducible game G in complete (agent) normal form) has finitely many equilibrium points which, in addition, are all strict.

Here the sense of "almost all" is the same as in Theorem 1 above. Consider a game G^δ as in Theorem 4 and let $q^1,...,q^m$ ($m \geq 1$) be the equilibrium points of G^δ. The set

$$\mathcal{C}_{0,0} = \{q^1,...,q^m\} \tag{II.5.2}$$

is called the <u>initial precandidate set</u>. Given a <u>precandidate set</u> $\mathcal{C}_{0,j}$ where $j \geq 0$ is an integer such that $0 < |\mathcal{C}_{0,j}| < +\infty$, it generates a <u>candidate set</u> $\mathcal{C}_{1,j}$ by eliminating all payoff dominated precandidates, i.e.

$$\mathcal{C}_{1,j} = \{\bar{q} \in \mathcal{C}_{0,j} | \text{ There is no } q' \in \mathcal{C}_{0,j} \text{ with } H_i^\delta(q') > H_i^\delta(\bar{q}) \text{ for all } i = 1,...,n\} \tag{II.5.3}$$

$\mathcal{C}_{1,0}$ is called the <u>initial candidate set</u> of G^δ. From what has been said so far it follows that the pair $(G^\delta, \mathcal{C}_{1,0})$ satisfies all the assumptions which are necessary to apply the concept of resistance avoidance. According to Theorem 1 the set $\mathcal{C}^+_{1,j}$ of <u>resistance undominated solution candidates</u> in $\mathcal{C}_{1,j}$ will almost always contain exactly one element, i.e. for almost all games G^δ the solution is already determined by the unique solution candidate in $\mathcal{C}^+_{1,j}$.

For the (degenerate) case $|\mathcal{C}^+_{1,j}| > 1$ it is impossible to select one solution candidate in $\mathcal{C}^+_{1,j}$ according to the concept of resistance avoidance because there are at least two solution candidates q^1, q^2 in $\mathcal{C}_{1,j}$ with $R(q^1) = R(q^2)$. Any such selection would be completely arbitrary in view of resistance dominance arguments. Since no reasonable choice is possible between the candidates in $\mathcal{C}^+_{1,0}$ none of these candidates should be selected as the solution of the game. As a consequence the elements in $\mathcal{C}^+_{1,j}$ are excluded from further considerations and the new precandidate set $\mathcal{C}_{0,j+1}$ is defined as $\mathcal{C}_{0,j} - \mathcal{C}^+_{1,j}$. Since we only apply this elimination step to irreducible games G we believe the set $\mathcal{C}_{0,j} - \mathcal{C}^+_{1,j}$ to be nonempty. The reasons are that the nonuniqueness of $\mathcal{C}^+_{1,j}$ will usually occur only in case of symmetric games and that, due to the generically odd number of equilibria, there is always a symmetry–invariant equilibrium point (NASH, 1951) whereas the set $\mathcal{C}^+_{1,j}$ contains an even number of elements. Therefore the set $\mathcal{C}_{0,j} - \mathcal{C}^+_{1,j}$ is generically nonempty. But till now we have not proved this formally. Now $\mathcal{C}_{0,j+1}$ replaces $\mathcal{C}_{0,j}$ and the same procedure starts again. All this is summarized in Algorithm (2).

Algorithm (2):

Generating precandidate and candidate sets.

i) START with a set of precandidates $C_0 \neq \emptyset$.

ii) Determine the set C_1 of payoff undominated candidates in C_0.

iii) Determine the set C_1^+ of resistance undominated candidates in C_1.

iv) If $|C_1^+| = 1$ the solution is $q \in C_1^+$, END.
Otherwise $C_0 = C_0 - C_1^+$.

v) If $C_0 = \emptyset$ the solution is not defined, END.
Otherwise, go to ii).

Since $C_{0,0}$ is finite and since neither $C_{1,j}$ nor $C_{1,j}^+$ can ever become empty, if $C_{0,j}$ is nonempty, Algorithm (2) stops after a finite number of steps either with $|C_1^+| = 1$ or with $C_0 = \emptyset$.

In what follows a pair of perturbance parameters (ϵ,δ) is called regular if Algorithm (2) applied to $G^{\epsilon,\delta}$, stops with $|C_1^+| = 1$.

Theorem$^+$ 5:

For any given $0 < \epsilon < \min\{1/|S_i| \mid i = 1,...,n\}$ almost all $\delta > 0$ yield a regular pair (ϵ,δ) of perturbance parameters.

When proving Theorem 5 one will rely on the regular oddness of the number of equilibrium points in $G^{\epsilon,\delta}$ which holds for almost all sufficiently small perturbance parameters $\delta > 0$. Furthermore, in case of $|C_1^+| > 1$ the game is characterized by a basic symmetry and there exists an equilibrium point in $G^{\epsilon,\delta}$ being invariant under this symmetry as described above.

Because of Theorem 5 we can find, for given $\epsilon > 0$, a sequence $(\epsilon,\delta_n)_{n\in\mathbb{N}}$ of regular pairs of perturbance parameters with $\delta_n \to 0$ for $n \to \infty$. The corresponding sequence $\left(q^{\epsilon,\delta_n}\right)_{n\in\mathbb{N}}$ of solutions of G^{ϵ,δ_n}, determined by Algorithm (2), consists of elements lying in the compact set Q^ϵ. Thus there must be at least one convergent subsequence with limit point in Q^ϵ.

If for all sequences $\left[q^{\epsilon,\delta_n}\right]_{n\in\mathbb{N}}$ of solutions of G^{ϵ,δ_n}, with fixed ϵ and (ϵ,δ_n) being regular ($n \in \mathbb{N}$), the limit $\lim_{n\to\infty} q^{\epsilon,\delta_n}$ exists and if, furthermore, the limits are all the same we define

$$q^{\epsilon} := \lim_{\delta\to 0} q^{\epsilon,\delta} := \lim_{n\to\infty} q^{\epsilon,\delta_n} \tag{II.5.4}$$

(with $(\epsilon,\delta_n)_{n\in\mathbb{N}}$ being an arbitrary sequence of regular pairs of perturbance parameters) as the <u>solution of G^{ϵ}</u>.

At first one might think that in the Harsanyi–Selten theory similar problems do not occur since the tracing path, being defined by a piecewise algebraic curve, guarantees that the solution of an ϵ–uniformly perturbed game exists. However, the tracing procedure is only one of many tools which have to be applied when solving a uniformly perturbed game.

We think that future research will show that, at least for all reasonable games, the existence of the limit q^{ϵ} is always guaranteed. For the time being we have not proved it but we have good reasons to believe that our conjecture is true. A way to prove it is to show that for all sequences $(\delta_n > 0)_{n\in\mathbb{N}}$ converging to 0 the limit $\lim_{n\to\infty} q^{\epsilon,\delta_n}$ exists.

6. The limit solution for the unperturbed game

Up to now we have described the main steps to determine the solution of an ϵ–uniformly perturbed game G^{ϵ}. Assume now that all these games have been solved and that q^{ϵ} is the solution of G^{ϵ}. Once again we face the problem whether the limit $\lim_{\epsilon\to 0} q^{\epsilon}$ exists. Remember that this problem is also present in the Harsanyi–Selten theory. In case the above limit does not exist we consider the underlying unperturbed game G as badly modelled since for any reasonable game the limit should exist. For games which we have analysed so far such problems of existence did never occour.

We think the whole algorithm determining the ESBORA–solution of a game in complete (agent) normal form is best described by the flow chart diagrams of Figure II.6.1. To understand how the ESBORA–concept works one should simply take several examples and follow the various steps of the algorithm in the flow charts below.

The reader will find out that in the subroutines SOLUTION and DOM some kind of error–exits exist. In case they are reached only finitely many times, this will have no impact on other parts of the algorithm. But if the limit to be taken in the Main Program does not exist the game should be considered as badly modelled.

a) Main Program

Input: $G = (S_1,\ldots,S_n;P;H)$ game in complete (agent) normal form

Output: q, solution of G

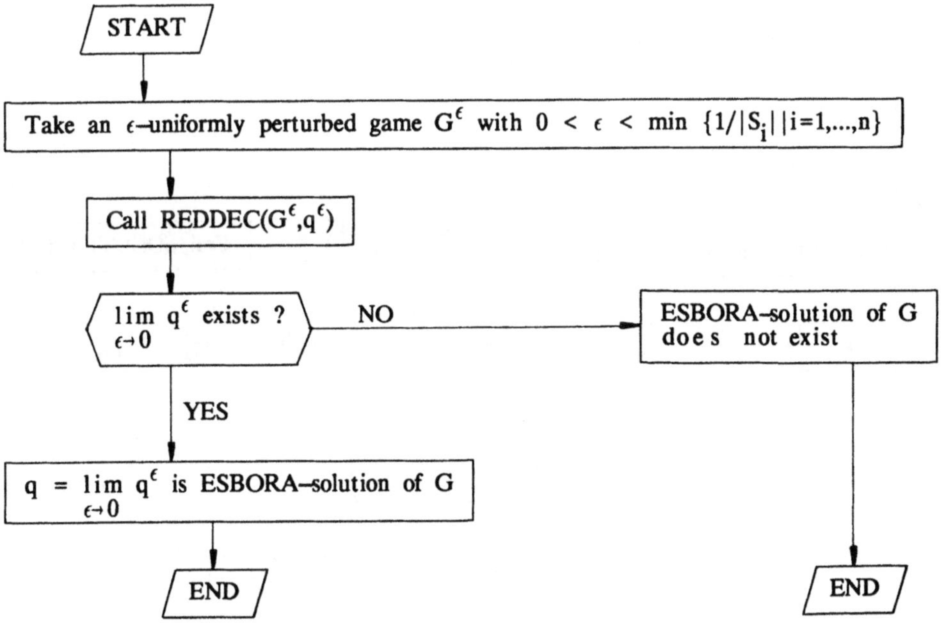

b) Subroutine REDDEC(G^ϵ,q^ϵ)

Input: G^ϵ, ϵ–uniformly perturbed game in complete (agent) normal form

Output: q^ϵ, solution of G^ϵ

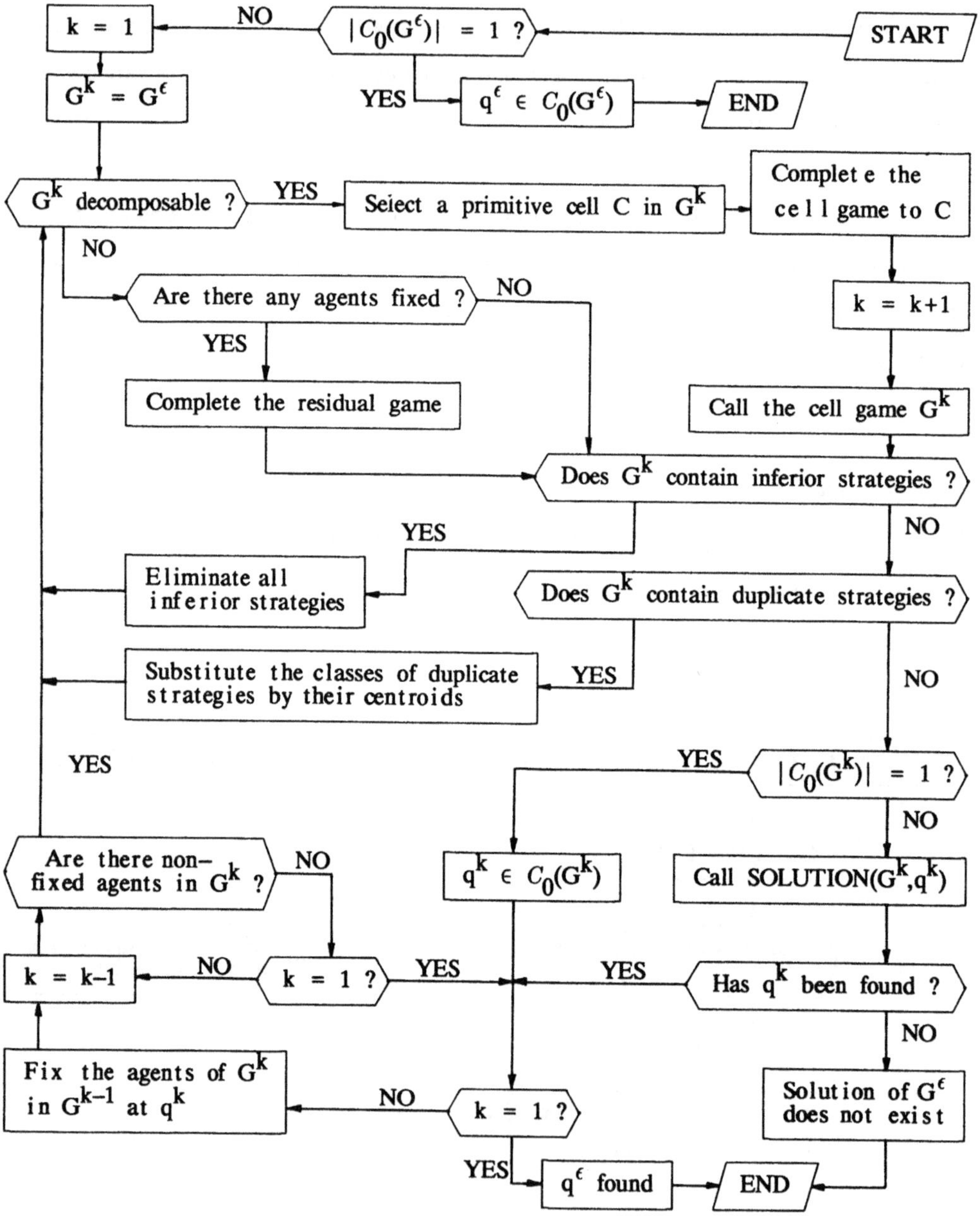

c) Subroutine SOLUTION(G^ϵ,q^ϵ)

Input: G^ϵ, irreducible uniformly perturbed game in complete (agent) normal form

Output: q^ϵ, solution of G^ϵ (in case it is defined)

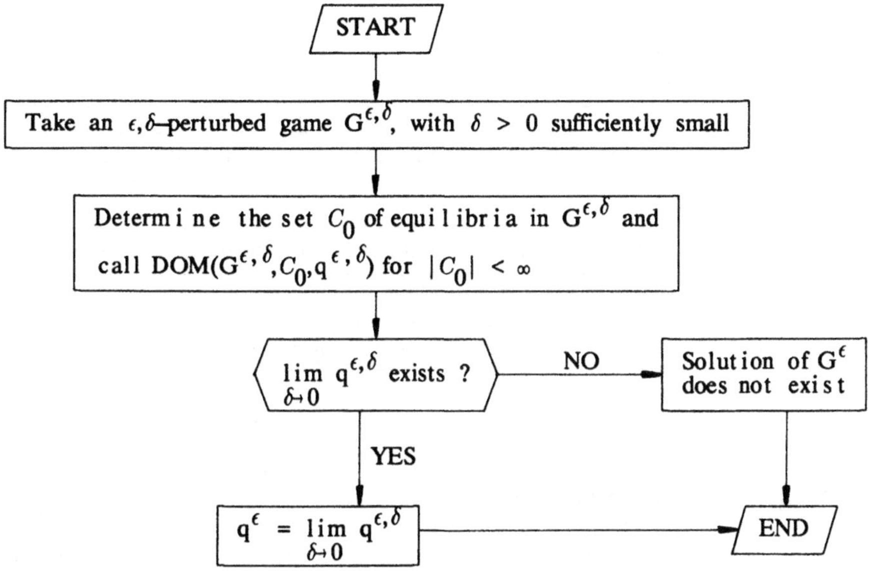

d) Subroutine DOM(G, C_0, q)

Input: G, irreducible double–perturbed game in complete (agent) normal form

C_0, the set of strict equilibrium points in G

Output: q, solution of G (in case it exists)

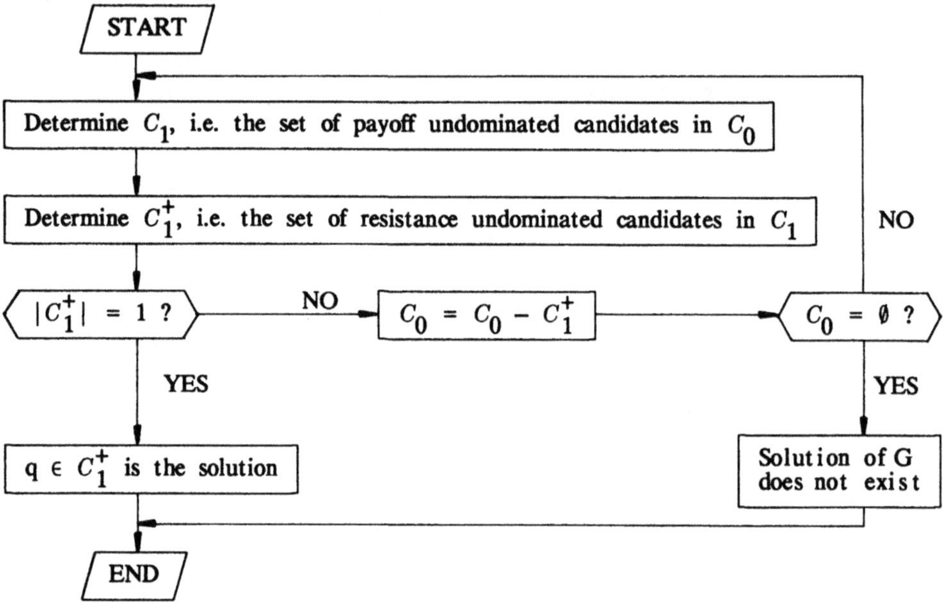

Figure II.6.1: The solution procedure of the ESBORA–concept, given in algorithmic form by flow chart diagrams, and consisting of a Main Program, where the algorithm starts and finally ends, and three subroutines being called up in the course of the procedure:

a) Main Program

b) Subroutine REDDEC (being the reduction and decomposition program),

c) Subroutine SOLUTION (being the "proper" solution procedure),

d) Subroutine DOM (being the selection procedure with respect to payoff and resistance dominance).

7. Simplifications of the solution procedure in nondegenerate games

A game is called indecomposable if it has no proper subcells. Let $G = (S_1,...,S_n;P;H)$ be an irreducible, hence indecomposable, game in complete (agent) normal form. We say that G is uniformly irreducible if there exists a positive perturbance parameter $\bar{\epsilon}$ such that for all ϵ with $0 \leq \epsilon \leq \bar{\epsilon}$ the ϵ–uniformly perturbed games G^{ϵ} of G are irreducible.

When considering specific examples it is often not necessary to consider a whole sequence of ϵ–uniformly perturbed games G^{ϵ} of the given game G since Algorithm (2) can be directly applied to the game G itself. The following Lemma 6 is therefore a very helpful result when applying the ESBORA–theory of equilibrium selection. By $R_1(q)$ we denote the first component of the vector R(q), i.e. the loudest resistance by any other solution candidate against q. If $R_1(q^+) < R_1(q)$, we will say that q^+ resistance dominates q in the first place.

Lemma 6:

Let $G = (S_1,...,S_n;P;H)$ be a uniformly irreducible game in complete (agent) normal form, C_0 its nonempty set of perfect equilibrium points and C_1 the set of payoff undominated equilibrium points in C_0, which in case of $|C_1| > 1$ all lie in different primitive formations of G. Assume, furthermore, that $|C_1^+| = 1$. Then $q^+ \in C_1^+$ is the ESBORA–solution of G if

(i) $|C_1| = 1$ or

(ii) $R_1(q^+) < R_1(q)$ for all $q \in C_1 - \{q^+\}$,

i.e. q^+ resistance dominates every other candidate q in C_1 in the first place.

The fact that q^+ either payoff dominates any other equilibrium point of G or resistance dominates any other solution candidate in C_1 is a consequence of a finite number of strict inequalities which still holds if the perturbance parameter $\epsilon > 0$ is chosen sufficiently small. Lemma 6 is therefore implied by the continuity of a finite number of functions in ϵ in the range $\bar{\epsilon} > \epsilon > 0$. For very small values of the perturbance parameter $\epsilon > 0$ the ϵ–uniformly perturbed games G^{ϵ} of G will have initial candidate sets $C_{1,0}$ which correspond to C_1. Furthermore, the set $C_{1,0}^+$ in G^{ϵ} will correspond to the set C_1^+ of resistance undominated candidates in G.

Another helpful result refers to examples G where we can neglect the penalty term of the payoff function, i.e. we need not consider double–perturbed games but can restrict ourselves to ϵ–uniformly perturbed games.

Let $G^{\epsilon} = (S_1^{\epsilon},...,S_n^{\epsilon};P;H)$ be an ϵ–uniformly perturbed game of a game G in complete (agent) normal form. By $C_{0,0}(G^{\epsilon})$ we denote the set of equilibrium points in G^{ϵ} and by $C_{1,0}(G^{\epsilon})$ the set of candidates in $C_{0,0}(G^{\epsilon})$ which are not payoff dominated by another precandidate in $C_{0,0}(G^{\epsilon})$. Furthermore, denote by $C_{1,0}^{+}(G^{\epsilon})$ the set of candidates in $C_{1,0}(G^{\epsilon})$ which are not resistance dominated by another candidate.

Lemma 7:

Let $G = (S_1,...,S_n;P;H)$ be a uniformly irreducible game in complete (agent) normal form. Assume that there exists an $\bar{\epsilon} > 0$ such that for all $0 < \epsilon < \bar{\epsilon}$ the candidate sets $C_{1,0}(G^{\epsilon})$ of the ϵ–uniformly perturbed games G^{ϵ} consist of strict equilibrium points only. Furthermore assume that these games can be solved in the sense of

$$|C_{1,0}^{+}(G^{\epsilon})| = 1 \text{ because of } |C_{1,0}(G^{\epsilon})| = 1 \text{ or}$$

since there exists $q^{\epsilon} \in C_{1,0}(G^{\epsilon})$ such that

$$R_1(q^{\epsilon}) < R_1(q) \quad \text{for all } q \in C_{1,0}(G^{\epsilon})-\{q^{\epsilon}\} .$$

The ESBORA–solution of G is then given by

$$q^{+} = \lim_{\epsilon \to 0} q^{\epsilon} ,$$

with $q^{\epsilon} \in C_{1,0}^{+}(G^{\epsilon}) \quad (0 < \epsilon < \bar{\epsilon})$.

Remember that for $\delta \to 0$ the penalty term in the payoff function (II.5.1) approaches 0. This implies that for sufficiently small $\delta \to 0$ a strict equilibrium point in $G^{\epsilon,\delta}$ will correspond to a strict equilibrium point in G^{ϵ}. The games $G^{\epsilon,\delta}$ may have more (strict) equilibrium points (corresponding to nonstrict ones in G^{ϵ}), but for every strict equilibrium point q^{ϵ} in G^{ϵ} there will always be a unique sequence of equilibrium points $q^{\epsilon,\delta}$ in $G^{\epsilon,\delta}$ converging to q^{ϵ} for $\delta \to 0$.

8. Examples

For our previous examples 4.1.1–4, 4.2.1–3 in Section 4 of Part I it can be shown that all pure strategy equilibrium points are strict and that all mixed strategy equilibrium points are payoff dominated by strict equilibrium points. Except for the examples 4.1.1, 4.1.4, and (sometimes also) 4.1.3 none of the strict equilibrium points payoff dominates another strict equilibrium point. In all examples resistance dominance appeared in the form of resistance dominance in the first place. Thus in all previous examples the conditions of Lemma 6 are given. Except for 4.1.1, 4.1.3, and 4.1.4 the solutions, which have been derived by simply applying the concept of resistance dominance, are therefore the ESBORA–solutions. This demonstrates again that the concept of resistance avoidance is the central idea of our theory of equilibrium selection.

An important consequence of example 4.2.1 is that the ESBORA–theory of equilibrium selection has the Nash–property as it has been defined above. In 4.1.1 the solution of G is obviously $X = (X_1,X_2)$ which is the only payoff undcminated solution candidate.

For the class of games in 4.1.3 it has been shown that the relation of resistance dominance is independent of the parameter c. The same is not true for the ESBORA–solution. If $c = 0$, players 1 and 2 form a primitive cell. Composing the cell solutions one gets X as the ESBORA–solution if $c = 0$. For $c \neq 0$ the games G in 4.1.3 have no proper primitive cell. For $v < 1$ candidate X is the ESBORA–solution since X payoff dominates Y. So only for $c \neq 0$ and $v \geq 1$ the solution has to be determined by considering the resistance dominance between X and Y. For all v with $u^4 > v \geq 1$ the ESBORA–solution is X whereas it is Y if both, $c \geq 0$ and $v > u^4$.

In example 4.1.4 there is a unique strict equilibrium point which is not payoff dominated. According to Lemma 6 the strict equilibrium point $L = (L_1,L_2,L_3)$ is the ESBORA–solution of the game even when R resistance dominates L. This shows that the principle of payoff dominance is of higher priority than the one of resistance dominance. Only if payoff dominance does not yield a unique selection, considerations of resistance avoidance become important.

In the following we will discuss some examples illustrating different aspects of the constructive solution procedure as it has been described in Section 6.

8.1 A degenerate unanimity bargaining game

Let us look again at the symmetric 2–person games with two strict equilibrium points X and Y described in Table I.2.1 and completed by $P_i(s) = 1$ for $s \in S$ and $i = 1, 2$. Here we will restrict ourselves to the special case $u = 1$ given by Table II.8.1.

	X_2	Y_2
X_1	1 \ 1	0 \ 0
Y_1	0 \ 0	1 \ 1

Table II.8.1: A degenerate 'battle of sexes'–game (player 1 (2) is the row (column) player, 1's (2's) payoff is given in the upper left (lower right) corner).

Obviously there are three equilibrium points, namely $X = (X_1,X_2)$, $Y = (Y_1,Y_2)$, and $q = (q_1,q_2)$, being the one in mixed strategies. The latter is determined by

$$q_1(X_1) = q_1(Y_1) = q_2(X_2) = q_2(Y_2) = .5 \quad . \tag{II.8.1}$$

We first consider the ϵ–uniformly perturbed games G^ϵ, $0 < \epsilon < .5$. Let H_i denote the payoff in G and H_i^ϵ the payoff in G^ϵ. By using the positive linear utility transformation

$$H_i^\epsilon = \frac{H_i - 2\epsilon(1-\epsilon)}{1 - 4\epsilon + 4\epsilon^2} \tag{II.8.2}$$

for both players, G^ϵ is also given by Table II.8.1, with X_i^ϵ (Y_i^ϵ) instead of X_i (Y_i), $i = 1, 2$.

Due to the obvious symmetry of G (and all G^ϵ) neither X (X^ϵ) resistance dominates Y (Y^ϵ) in the first place nor vice versa. Since, furthermore, $q^\epsilon = (.5X_1^\epsilon+.5Y_1^\epsilon,.5X_2^\epsilon+.5Y_2^\epsilon)$ is payoff dominated by X^ϵ and Y^ϵ this shows that Lemma 6 and 7 are of no help for the game at hand. Of course, one could simply rely on symmetry invariance. But here we want to demonstrate how to use the algorithm described in Figure II.6.1.

For convenience, we describe the mixed strategy $q_i \in Q_i^\epsilon$ by the probability it assigns to X_i^ϵ. For sufficiently small $\delta > 0$ we introduce the perturbed payoff function $H^\delta = (H_1^\delta, H_2^\delta)$ which due to (II.5.1) is given by

$$H_i^\delta(q) = q_1 q_2 + (1-q_1)(1-q_2) + \delta \log(q_i(1-q_i)) \tag{II.8.3}$$

for all $q = (q_1,q_2) \in [0,1]^2$ and $i = 1, 2$. Our next task is to determine all equilibrium points of the double-perturbed game $G^{\epsilon,\delta}$. Since we have

$$\frac{\partial H_i^\delta}{\partial q_i}(q_1,q_2) = q_j - (1-q_j) + \frac{\delta(1-2q_i)}{q_i(1-q_i)} \quad (i, j \in \{1, 2\}, j \neq i) \tag{II.8.4}$$

we get

$$(2q_1-1) + \frac{\delta(1-2q_2)}{q_2(1-q_2)} = 0 \ , \tag{II.8.5}$$

$$(2q_2-1) + \frac{\delta(1-2q_1)}{q_1(1-q_1)} = 0 \tag{II.8.6}$$

as necessary conditions for an interior equilibrium point $q \in (0,1)^2$.

In general, a system of nonlinear equations, as given by (II.8.5) and (II.8.6), cannot be solved directly. But here a few preliminary considerations will simplify this task drastically. Observe first of all that

$$q_1^0 = q_2^0 = .5 \tag{II.8.7}$$

is a solution and that combinations (q_1,q_2) of the form $(0 < q_2 < .5 < q_1 < 1)$ or $(0 < q_1 < .5 < q_2 < 1)$ can never solve (II.8.5) or (II.8.6). Hence we restrict ourselves to the cases $0 < q_1, q_2 < .5$ or $.5 < q_1, q_2 < 1$. Since the assumption of $q_1 \neq q_2$ leads to a contradiction a necessary requirement for a solution is

$$0 < q_1 = q_2 < 1 \ . \tag{II.8.8}$$

Because of (II.8.8) we have reduced the nonlinear system with two unknowns to one equation with one unknown, namely

$$(2q_1 - 1)(1 - \frac{\delta}{q_1(1-q_1)}) = 0 \ . \tag{II.8.9}$$

One solution of (II.8.9) is given by (II.8.7), the other solutions are

$$q_1 = (1 - \sqrt{1-4\delta})/2 \ , \tag{II.8.10}$$

$$q_1 = (1 + \sqrt{1-4\delta})/2 \ . \tag{II.8.11}$$

For $0 < \delta < .25$, the right–hand side of (II.8.10) and the one of (II.8.11) are in (0,1).

Since for i = 1, 2

$$H_i^\delta(q) = -\infty \qquad \text{for } q_i \in \{0, 1\} \ , \tag{II.8.12}$$

no equilibrium point exists on the boundary of $[0,1]^2$.

Thus we have shown the existence of exactly three equilibrium points in the double–perturbed games $G^{\epsilon,\delta}$, i.e.

$$q^1 = (q_1^1, q_2^1) = ((1 - \sqrt{1-4\delta})/2, (1 - \sqrt{1-4\delta})/2) \quad , \tag{II.8.13}$$

$$q^2 = (q_1^2, q_2^2) = ((1 + \sqrt{1-4\delta})/2, (1 + \sqrt{1-4\delta})/2) \quad , \tag{II.8.14}$$

$$q^0 = (q_1^0, q_2^0) = (1/2, 1/2) \quad . \tag{II.8.15}$$

Here it is important to remember that a mixed strategy $q_i \in Q_i^\epsilon$ is described by the probability it assigns to X_i^ϵ, $i = 1, 2$.

Thus we get

$$\mathcal{C}_{0,0} = \{q^0, q^1, q^2\} \tag{II.8.16}$$

as the initial precandidate set in $G^{\epsilon,\delta}$ for given $0 < \epsilon < .5$ and $\delta < .25$. When q^0 or q^j $(j = 1, 2)$ is played player i's payoff is given by

$$H_i^\delta(q^0) = .5 + \delta \log(.25) \quad , \tag{II.8.17}$$

or

$$H_i^\delta(q^j) = 1 - 2\delta + \delta \log(\delta) \qquad (j = 1, 2) \quad , \tag{II.8.18}$$

for $i = 1, 2$.

With the help of a few elementary calculations it can be shown that for sufficiently small $\delta > 0$, especially for

$$\delta \leq .125 \tag{I.8.19}$$

q^0 is payoff dominated by both other equilibria q^1 and q^2. Hence, our initial candidate set consists of q^1 and q^2:

$$C_{1,0} = \{q^1, q^2\} \ . \tag{II.8.20}$$

Our next task is to determine the resistance value of q^1 against q^2 and vice versa. This is possible since by construction q^1 and q^2 are strict equilibrium points in $G^{\epsilon,\delta}$.

As can easily be seen the restricted game for the resistance comparison of q^1 and q^2 is a symmetric game which can, once again, be reduced to the game given in Table II.8.1 with q_i^1 and q_i^2 instead of X_i and Y_i, respectively, i = 1, 2. This is done with the help of the positive linear utility transformation $H_i' = m \cdot H_i + b$ for both players i, where $m = 1/(2-6\delta) > 0$ and $b = -\delta/(1-3\delta)$.

Since due to their symmetry, neither q^1 can resistance dominate q^2 nor vice versa, we obtain

$$C_{1,0}^{+} = \{q^1, q^2\} \tag{II.8.21}$$

and therefore

$$C_{0,1} = C_{0,0} - C_{1,0}^{+} = \{q^0\} \ . \tag{II.8.22}$$

The solution of the ϵ,δ–perturbed game is therefore given by

$$q^0 = (.5X_1^\epsilon + .5Y_1^\epsilon, .5X_2^\epsilon + .5Y_2^\epsilon) \ . \tag{II.8.23}$$

For δ approaching 0 we get

$$\lim_{\delta \to 0} q^0 = q^0 \tag{II.8.24}$$

and

$$\lim_{\delta\to 0} H_i^{\delta}(q^0) = \lim_{\delta\to 0} (.5 + \delta \log(.25)) = .5 \quad . \tag{II.8.25}$$

The ESBORA–solution of G is determined by taking the limit $\epsilon \to 0$:

$$\lim_{\epsilon\to 0} q^0 = (.5X_1 + .5Y_1, .5X_2 + .5Y_2) \quad . \tag{II.8.26}$$

With (II.8.26) we have derived the ESBORA–solution of the degenerate unanimity bargaining game in Table II.8.1. The only symmetry–invariant equilibrium point

$$q_1(X_1) = q_1(Y_1) = q_2(X_2) = q_2(Y_2) = .5 \tag{II.8.27}$$

is the ESBORA–solution of G. This illustrates that the ESBORA–concept has the desired property of selecting the symmetry–invariant equilibrium point.

Observe that due to their specific assumptions Lemmas 6 and 7 could not be applied here. Nevertheless, we could have used the fact that the given game is uniformly irreducible and has three (perfect) equilibrium points, two strict ones and one in completely mixed strategies which is payoff dominated. The two strict equilibria lie in different primitive formations. Therefore, there are only the two possibilities that one of the two solutions candidates resistance dominates the other or that none resistance dominates the other. In the first case, the resistance dominating candidate is the solution and in the second case, the solution is the unique candidate in $C_{0,0} - C^+_{1,0}$, i.e. the equilibrium in completely mixed strategies. Hence for all 2×2–bimatrix games with two strict equilibria and a payoff dominated mixed equilibrium point the solution can be determined directly without considering ϵ–uniformly or even double–perturbed games.

8.2 An extensive game

The following example is used to illustrate how starting from a game in extensive form one first derives the complete (agent) normal form for which one has to investigate whether it is reducible or not. Given the irreducible game one can then determine its ESBORA–solution.

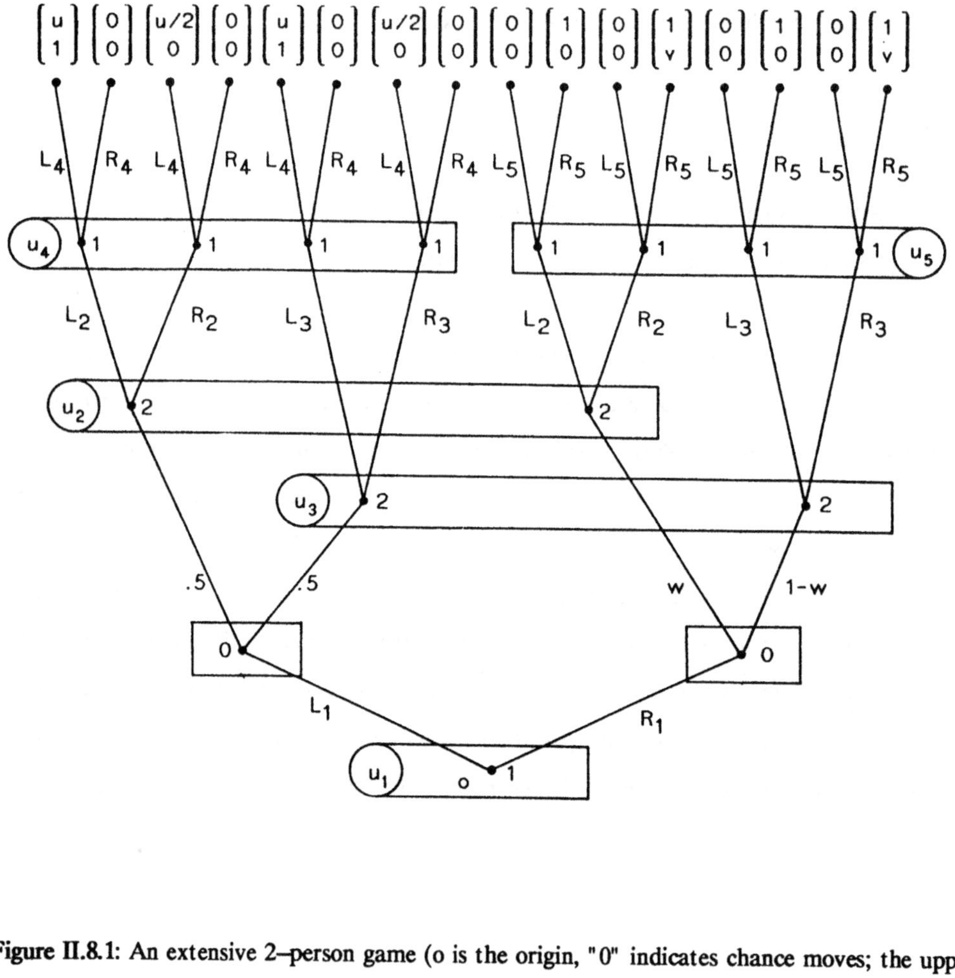

Figure II.8.1: An extensive 2–person game (o is the origin, "0" indicates chance moves; the upper (lower) component of a payoff vector is player 1's (2's) payoff; $1 > w > 0$, $1 > v > 0$, $2 > u > 1$).

Consider the extensive game whose game tree is described in Figure II.8.1 where o is the origin of the game tree. The player partition is defined by indicating the player who has to decide at the given decision node ("0" stands for chance moves); the probabilities of chance moves are given at the respective branches; the upper (lower) component of the payoff vectors at the end points is player 1's (2's) payoff; information sets are indicated by encircling the decision nodes belonging to the same information set; the choice partition is illustrated by identifying all the branches belonging to the same choice.

For the complete agent normal form $G = (S_1,...,S_5;P;H)$ let player $i = 1,...,5$ be the agent who has to decide in the information set u_i; i.e. 1, 4, and 5 are the agents of player 1 in the extensive game, whereas 2 and 3 are the agents of player 2. The probability assignment P of G is given by

$$P_i(s) = \begin{cases} 1 & \text{for } i = 1 \\ 1 & \text{for } i = 4 \quad \text{if } s_1 = L_1 \\ 1 & \text{for } i = 5 \quad \text{if } s_1 = R_1 \\ .5 & \text{for } i = 2 \quad \text{if } s_1 = L_1 \\ .5 & \text{for } i = 3 \quad \text{if } s_1 = L_1 \\ w & \text{for } i = 2 \quad \text{if } s_1 = R_1 \\ 1-w & \text{for } i = 3 \quad \text{if } s_1 = R_1 \\ 0 & \text{otherwise.} \end{cases} \tag{II.8.28}$$

The payoff function $H(s) = (H_1(s),...,H_5(s))$ is defined according to

$$H(s) = \begin{cases} (u,1,1,u,u) & \text{if } s_i=L_i \ (i=1,2,3,4) \\ (\frac{3u}{4},\frac{1}{2},\frac{1}{2},\frac{3u}{4},\frac{3u}{4}) & \text{if } s_i=L_i \ (i=1,4), \quad s_2=L_2,\ s_3=R_3 \text{ or} \\ & \text{if } s_i=L_i \ (i=1,4), \quad s_2=R_2,\ s_3=L_3 \\ (\frac{u}{2},0,0,\frac{u}{2},\frac{u}{2}) & \text{if } s_i=L_i \ (i=1,4), \quad s_2=R_2,\ s_3=R_3 \\ (1,v,v,1,1) & \text{if } s_i=R_i \ (i=1,2,3,5) \\ (1,wv,wv,1,1) & \text{if } s_i=R_i \ (i=1,5), \quad s_2=R_2,\ s_3=L_3 \\ (1,v(1-w),v(1-w),1,1) & \text{if } s_i=R_i \ (i=1,5), \quad s_2=L_2,\ s_3=R_3 \\ (1,0,0,1,1) & \text{if } s_i=R_i \ (i=1,5), \quad s_2=L_2,\ s_3=L_3 \\ (0,0,0,0,0) & \text{otherwise} \end{cases} \tag{II.8.29}$$

Since L_4 (R_5) is player 4's (5's) best strategy regardless of the behavior of all other players, the strategies R_4 and L_5 are inferior. The sets $C_1 = \{4\}$ and $C_2 = \{5\}$ are therefore primitive cells. Since player 2's and 3's best replies depend on player 1's decision and vice versa, C_1 and C_2 are, furthermore, the only primitive cells. The cell solutions of C_1G and C_2G are obviously $q^1 = (L_4)$ and $q^2 = (R_5)$. It is easy to see that the residual game $\check{C}G$ is irreducible.

This shows that the resulting residual game $\check{C}G$ in complete agent normal form is the game which has been analysed in 4.1.4 of Part I. According to what has been said at the beginning of this chapter, the ESBORA–solution of the original game $G = (S_1,...,S_5;P;H)$ is therefore $s^+ = (L_1,L_2,L_3,L_4,R_5)$.

It is interesting to analyse the reduction procedure if the payoff parameter u is restricted to $u > 2$ instead of $2 > u > 1$. In the residual game $\check{C}G$ the strategy $s_1 = R_1$ of player 1 is then inferior since by using $s_1 = L_1$ player 1 is sure to receive at least $u/2$ (> 1) whereas $s_1 = R_1$ yields the payoff level 1. Therefore the residual game $\check{C}G^\epsilon$ of G^ϵ with $\epsilon > 0$ has the only primitive cell $\{1\}$ whose cell game solution is (L_1). By elimination of R_1 the strategies R_2 and R_3 in turn become inferior. This shows that for $u > 2$ the ESBORA–solution is also the strategy vector (L_1,L_2,L_3,L_4,R_5).

8.3 The Condorcet Paradox

The following game, related to one analysed by GÜTH and SELTEN (1988) with the help of the Harsanyi–Selten theory, illustrates how to study the limit of the q^ϵ–solutions of the ϵ–uniformly perturbed games if the assumptions of Lemma 6 do not hold, but if Lemma 7 can still be applied.

The complete (agent) normal form of the game, which we will simply call the Condorcet Paradox (game), is given by $G = (S_1,S_2,S_3;P;H)$ where

$$S_i = \{A, B, C\} \qquad \text{for } i=1, 2, 3 \ , \tag{II.8.30}$$

$$P(s) = (P_1(s),P_2(s),P_3(s)) = (1,1,1) \tag{II.8.31}$$

for all $s \in S = S_1 \times S_2 \times S_3$. The von Neumann–Morgenstern utilities, as given by

$$H(s) = \begin{cases} (H_1^a, H_2^a, H_3^a) & \text{if } |\{i \in N|\ s_i = A\}| \geq 2\ , \\ (H_1^b, H_2^b, H_3^b) & \text{if } |\{i \in N|\ s_i = B\}| \geq 2\ , \\ (H_1^c, H_2^c, H_3^c) & \text{if } |\{i \in N|\ s_i = C\}| \geq 2\ , \\ (0,0,0) & \text{otherwise}, \end{cases} \tag{II.8.32}$$

are assumed to satisfy

$$\begin{aligned} H_1^a &= 1 > H_1^b > H_1^c > .5\ , \\ H_2^c &= 1 > H_2^a > H_2^b > .5\ , \\ H_3^b &= 1 > H_3^c > H_3^a > .5\ . \end{aligned} \tag{II.8.33}$$

Players 1 and 2 prefer A to B, players 1 and 3 prefer B to C, and players 2 and 3 prefer C to A. Furthermore, all players consider any of the alternatives A, B, or C to be better than a nonmajority result. The assumption that any alternative must yield more than .5 for every player has been imposed to avoid a complicated case distinction. To avoid border cases we assume that the utilities of the second best for two different players are not the same, i.e. $H_1^b \neq H_2^a$, $H_1^b \neq H_3^c$, and $H_2^a \neq H_3^c$.

Game G has infinitely many equilibrium points which are all nonstrict. Let q_3 be a mixed strategy for player 3 with carrier in {A, B}. All strategy vectors (A,A,q_3) are equilibrium points of G implying a majority result for the alternative A. It is obvious how to construct similar classes of equilibrium points yielding a majority for B and C, respectively. Observe that there is no equilibrium point which implies the conflict result (0,0,0) with probability 1.

It is a typical result that, although the game G has infinitely many equilibrium points, in its ϵ–uniformly perturbed games G^ϵ, with $\epsilon > 0$, the number of equilibrium points is finite. The strict equilibria, furthermore, payoff dominate all nonpure equilibrium points if ϵ is sufficiently small.

Consider a perturbance parameter ϵ with $1/3 > \epsilon > 0$ and the strategy vector A^ϵ, B^ϵ, C^ϵ in G^ϵ according to which <u>all</u> players choose A, B, C, respectively, with maximal probability in G. The condition for A^ϵ to be a strict equilibrium point in G^ϵ is

$$\min\{H_2^a, H_3^a\} > \frac{1}{2} + \frac{\epsilon}{2(1-2\epsilon)} \quad , \tag{II.8.34}$$

The similar conditions for B^ϵ and C^ϵ to be strict equilibrium points in G^ϵ are

$$\min\{H_1^b, H_2^b\} > \frac{1}{2} + \frac{\epsilon}{2(1-2\epsilon)} \tag{II.8.35}$$

and

$$\min\{H_1^c, H_3^c\} > \frac{1}{2} + \frac{\epsilon}{2(1-2\epsilon)} \quad , \tag{II.8.36}$$

respectively. Because of (II.8.33) to (II.8.36) there exists a perturbance parameter $\bar{\epsilon}$ with $1/3 > \bar{\epsilon}$ such that for all ϵ with $\bar{\epsilon} \geq \epsilon > 0$ the strategy vectors A^ϵ, B^ϵ, and C^ϵ are the only strict equilibrium points of the ϵ–uniformly perturbed games G^ϵ. In the following we will restrict our attention to perturbance parameters ϵ in the range $\bar{\epsilon} \geq \epsilon > 0$. In view of Lemma 7 we can therefore confine ourselves to determining the solutions q^ϵ of the ϵ–uniformly perturbed games G^ϵ for $\epsilon \to 0$. Up to now we have not shown that all conditions of Lemma 7 are fulfilled. But we suppose the requirements to be true and prove later on that this assumption is true.

In the following G^ϵ is always an ϵ–uniformly perturbed game of G satisfying $\bar{\epsilon} \geq \epsilon > 0$. Because of what has been said above, $C_{0,0} = \{A^\epsilon, B^\epsilon, C^\epsilon\}$ is the initial precandidate set of G^ϵ. Since none of the precandidates payoff dominates another, we obtain

$$C_{1,0} = \{A^\epsilon, B^\epsilon, C^\epsilon\} \quad . \tag{II.8.37}$$

According to Algorithm (2) one has to determine the resistance vectors $R(A^\epsilon)$, $R(B^\epsilon)$, and $R(C^\epsilon)$ to solve the ϵ–uniformly perturbed games G^ϵ of G. Obviously, the set M of essential players in the restricted games for the resistance comparison of two candidates in $C_{1,0}$ is always the set $N = \{1,$

2, 3} of players in G.

Let X^ϵ, $Y^\epsilon \in \mathcal{C}_{1,0}$ and $X^\epsilon \neq Y^\epsilon$. We take $i \in N$ and assume that the players j ($\neq i$) use X_j^ϵ in G^ϵ with probability $1-z$ and their strategy Y_j^ϵ in G with probability z. Choosing X_i with maximal probability in G^ϵ is player i's best reply against this expectation if

$$\frac{N_i(X^\epsilon,Y^\epsilon)}{D_i(X^\epsilon,Y^\epsilon)} \geq \frac{z}{1-z} \tag{II.8.38}$$

where

$$N_i(X^\epsilon,Y^\epsilon) = \sqrt{[H_i^x-H_i^y]^2C_3^2 - [(H_i^x)^2+(H_i^y)^2]C_1C_2 + H_i^xH_i^y[C_1^2+C_2^2]} - [H_i^x-H_i^y]C_3 , \tag{II.8.39}$$

$$D_i(X^\epsilon,Y^\epsilon) = H_i^x C_1 - H_i^y C_2 , \tag{II.8.40}$$

$$C_1 = -(1-3\epsilon)(1-\epsilon)2\epsilon , \tag{II.8.41}$$

$$C_2 = -(1-3\epsilon)(1-2\epsilon)4\epsilon , \tag{II.8.42}$$

$$C_3 = -(1-3\epsilon)(1-3\epsilon+4\epsilon^2) . \tag{II.8.43}$$

With the help of this notation the noise of resistance $r(X^\epsilon,Y^\epsilon)$ of X^ϵ against Y^ϵ can be expressed as follows

$$r(X^\epsilon,Y^\epsilon) = \prod_{i=1}^{3} N_i(X^\epsilon,Y^\epsilon)/D_i(X^\epsilon,Y^\epsilon) . \tag{II.8.44}$$

Observe that

$$\lim_{\epsilon \to 0} N_i(X^\epsilon,Y^\epsilon)/D_i(X^\epsilon,Y^\epsilon) = \begin{cases} +\infty & \text{for } H_i^x > H_i^y , \\ 0 & \text{otherwise} . \end{cases} \qquad \text{(II.8.45)}$$

This means that in the limit those two players, who prefer X to Y, will ultimately resist against Y whereas the third player, who prefers Y to X, will cause no resistance at all against Y. The Condorcet cycle of majority voting is therefore reflected by a corresponding cycle of resistance majorities.

Using de l'Hospital's Rule (de l'HOSPITAL, 1696, BRONSHTEIN and SEMENDYAYEV, 1985) it can be shown that for sufficienctly small $\epsilon > 0$

$$r(X^\epsilon,Y^\epsilon) > r(Z^\epsilon,Y^\epsilon) \qquad \text{(II.8.46)}$$

is equivalent to

$$|\{i \in \{1, 2, 3\} |\ H_i^x > H_i^y\}| = 2 , \ |\{i \in \{1, 2, 3\} |\ H_i^z > H_i^y\}| = 1 , \qquad \text{(II.8.47)}$$

i.e. in the limit the louder resistance against Y^ϵ is caused by the alternative which is preferred to Y^ϵ by a majority. This implies that for sufficiently small $\epsilon > 0$, the resistance vectors $R(Y^\epsilon)$ of the initial candidates $Y^\epsilon \in \{A^\epsilon, B^\epsilon, C^\epsilon\}$ are as follows:

$$R(A^\epsilon) = (r(C^\epsilon,A^\epsilon),r(B^\epsilon,A^\epsilon)) , \qquad \text{(II.8.48)}$$

$$R(B^\epsilon) = (r(A^\epsilon,B^\epsilon),r(C^\epsilon,B^\epsilon)) , \qquad \text{(II.8.49)}$$

$$R(C^\epsilon) = (r(B^\epsilon,C^\epsilon),r(A^\epsilon,C^\epsilon)) . \qquad \text{(II.8.50)}$$

Assume that

$$|\{i \in \{1, 2, 3\} |\ H_i^x > H_i^y\}| = |\{i \in \{1, 2, 3\} |\ H_i^z > H_i^v\}| = 2 , \qquad \text{(II.8.51)}$$

i.e. there is a majority of voters who prefer X to Y and another preferring Z to V. By using de l'Hospital's Rule again we can show that for sufficiently small $\epsilon > 0$

$$r(X^\epsilon,Y^\epsilon) < r(Z^\epsilon,V^\epsilon) \tag{II.8.52}$$

is equivalent to

$$T(X,Y) < T(Z,V) \tag{II.8.53}$$

with

$$T(X,Y) = \frac{(2H_i^x - H_i^y) \prod_{j \neq i} (H_j^x - H_j^y)}{(H_i^y - H_i^x) \prod_{j \neq i} (2H_j^y - H_j^x)} \ . \tag{II.8.54}$$

Here player i is the unique player who does not prefer X to Y. Together with our observations this implies the following result.

Theorem 6:

The ESBORA–solution of the Condorcet Paradox as described above is the unique equilibrium point in $C^+_{1,0}(G) = \lim_{\epsilon \to 0} C^+_{1,0}(G^\epsilon)$ where

$$C^+_{1,0}(G) = \begin{cases} \{A\} & \text{for } T(C,A) < \min\{T(A,B), T(B,C)\} \ , \\ \{B\} & \text{for } T(A,B) < \min\{T(C,A), T(B,C)\} \ , \\ \{C\} & \text{for } T(B,C) < \min\{T(A,B), T(C,A)\} \ . \end{cases} \tag{II.8.55}$$

To illustrate how the solution of G depends on the parameters of the game we give the values T(C,A), T(A,B), and T(B,C) according to (II.8.54):

$$T(C,A) = \frac{(1-H_2^a)(H_3^c-H_3^a)(2H_1^c-1)}{(2H_2^a-1)(2H_3^a-H_3^c)(1-H_1^c)} \ , \tag{II.8.56}$$

$$T(A,B) = \frac{(1-H_1^b)(H_2^a-H_2^b)(2H_3^a-1)}{(2H_1^b-1)(2H_2^b-H_2^a)(1-H_3^a)} , \tag{II.8.57}$$

$$T(B,C) = \frac{(1-H_3^c)(H_1^b-H_1^c)(2H_2^b-1)}{(2H_3^c-1)(2H_1^c-H_1^b)(1-H_2^b)} . \tag{II.8.58}$$

The values (II.8.56) to (II.8.58) are all positive since all cardinal utilities H_i^x appearing as parameters on the right–hand side in (II.8.56) to (II.8.58) satisfy the condition $1 > H_i^x > .5$.

According to Theorem 6 for almost all parameter constellations satisfying conditions (II.8.33) the result of G is a unanimous majority for one of the three alternatives. The resulting alternative depends in a rather complicated way on the cardinal utilities of all players. It seems that especially the cardinal utilities of the least preferred alternatives, i.e. the parameters H_3^a, H_2^b, and H_1^c are of crucial importance. Let player i be the player not preferring X to Y. Equation (II.8.54) then reveals a decrease of T(X,Y) with increasing cardinal utilities H_j^y $(j \neq i)$ or with decreasing H_i^x. For all possible pairs X and Y of two different candidates two of these three payoff parameters are utilities of least preferred alternatives.

It could be argued that the utilities of the least preferred alternatives are connected to aspects of resistance avoidance. If an alternative treats one player rather badly, we have to expect loud resistance against this alternative as solution.

According to the Harsanyi–Selten theory of equilibrium selection the special situation (II.8.33) requires an extremely complicated case distinction which makes it very difficult to compare the results implied by the two different selection theories.

8.4 A 2–person bargaining game with a nonbargaining strategy on one side

In this section we will show that solving a game in complete (agent) normal form by considering its ϵ–uniformly perturbed games strongly influences the solution of the unperturbed game. The game model is a bilateral bargaining situation where both parties 1 and 2 can agree on two different proposals X and Y and where party 1 has the additional possibility W_1 not to bargain at all. We will present a class of games with two strict equilibria and a continuum of mixed strategy equilibrium points which, except for degenerate cases, all collapse into one mixed strategy equilibrium when perturbing the game uniformly. Thus we show that, as for the Condorcet Pardox, the number of ϵ–uniformly perfect equilibria is generically odd even if this is not true for the unperturbed game. The model is then changed by allowing player 1 to decide first whether he wants to bargain at all and then, in case he has chosen to bargain, which proposal he wants to make. This model with a sequential move structure results if the original player 1 with the three moves X_1, Y_1, and W_1 is split up into an agent deciding whether to use W_1 or not and an agent who, after the initial choice not to use W_1, decides between the two possible bargaining proposals X_1 and Y_1. In the terminology of HARSANYI and SELTEN (1988, Section 3.12) the second model results from the first one by sequential agent splitting where it is, of course, essential that the sequential move structure between X_1, Y_1, and W_1 is common knowledge. Although HARSANYI and SELTEN show that, due to the agent normal form, one cannot expect results to be immune against sequential agent splitting, we are nevertheless interested in comparing the solutions of the two game models. The sequential model will demonstrate how relevant uniform perturbations can be for detecting the generic substructure of a game.

8.4.1 The case of simultaneous decisions

We consider the bargaining game G in complete (agent) normal form given by Table II.8.2 where $P_i \equiv 1$ and where player i has the two bargaining strategies X_i and Y_i (i = 1, 2) and player 1, furthermore, the nonbargaining strategy W_1, i.e. $S_1 = \{X_1, Y_1, W_1\}$ and $S_2 = \{X_2, Y_2\}$. A more general situation of this kind is analysed by HARSANYI and SELTEN (1988, Chapter 6).

	X_2		Y_2	
X_1	x	1–x	0	0
Y_1	0	0	y	1–y
W_1	c	0	c	0

Table II.8.2: A 2–person bargaining game with the nonbargaining strategy W_1 where $0 \leq c < y < x < 1$ (player 1 (2) is the row (column) player whose payoff appears in the upper left (lower right) corner).

Because of the parameter restrictions

$$0 \leq c < y < x < 1 \tag{II.8.59}$$

game G has two strict equilibrium points, $X = (X_1,X_2)$ and $Y = (Y_1,Y_2)$. For further considerations it is important whether the nonbargaining profit c, which player 1 can assure himself by using W_1, is greater than half of the harmonic mean of x and y or not. If $c \leq \frac{xy}{x+y}$, the nonbargaining strategy W_1 of player 1 is inferior to X_1 and Y_1 in G^ϵ for $\epsilon \geq 0$. As a consequence, G^ϵ is then reduced to a 2×2–unanimity bargaining game with the pure strategy sets $\{X_i, Y_i\}$ for i = 1, 2. This reduced game has the three equilibrium points X^ϵ, Y^ϵ, and $q^\epsilon = (q_1^\epsilon,q_2^\epsilon)$ with

$$(q_1^\epsilon(X_1),q_1^\epsilon(Y_1),q_1^\epsilon(W_1)) = (\frac{1-y}{2-x-y},\frac{1-x}{2-x-y},\epsilon) ,$$

$$(q_2(X_2),q_2(Y_2)) = (\frac{x}{x+y},\frac{y}{x+y}) \qquad \text{(II.8.60)}$$

if ϵ is sufficiently small. Because of the Nash–property and the computations in Section 8.1 the ESBORA–solution s^+ of G is given by

$$s^+ = \begin{cases} X & \text{if } x(1-x) > y(1-y) \text{ and } c \le \frac{xy}{x+y} , \\ Y & \text{if } x(1-x) < y(1-y) \text{ and } c \le \frac{xy}{x+y} , \\ (q_1,q_2) & \text{if } x+y = 1 \quad \text{and } c \le \frac{xy}{x+y} . \end{cases} \qquad \text{(II.8.61)}$$

If the sure nonbargaining profit c exceeds player 1's expected profit $\frac{xy}{x+y}$ for the mixed strategy equilibrium point q, there are no inferior strategies and the game is irreducible. Remember that an equilibrium point (of G) is called <u>uniformly perfect</u> if it is the limit of a sequence of equilibria q^ϵ of ϵ–uniformly perturbed games G^ϵ of G for $\epsilon \to 0$. Although, in case of $c > \frac{xy}{x+y}$, game G has a continuum of mixed equilibrium points of the form $(W_1,\hat{q}_2)$ with $\hat{q}_2$ such that W_1 is 1's best choice, it has exactly three uniformly perfect equilibrium points, namely X, Y, and (W_1,q_2) where q_2 is determined by (II.8.60). Since $c < y < x$, the incompletely mixed equilibrium point is payoff dominated by X and Y. Therefore we get the following case distinctions for the ESBORA–solution of G:

$$s^+ = \begin{cases} X & \text{if } x(1-x) > y(1-y) \text{ and } c > \frac{xy}{x+y} \\ Y & \text{if } x(1-x) < y(1-y) \text{ and } c > \frac{xy}{x+y} \\ (W_1,q_2) & \text{if } x+y = 1 \quad \text{and } c > \frac{xy}{x+y} . \end{cases} \qquad \text{(II.8.62)}$$

Thus we have shown that

$$s^+ = \begin{cases} X & \text{if } x(1-x) > y(1-y) \\ Y & \text{if } x(1-x) < y(1-y) \\ (q_1,q_2) & \text{if } x+y = 1 \quad \text{and } c \le \frac{xy}{x+y} \\ (W_1,q_2) & \text{if } x+y = 1 \quad \text{and } c > \frac{xy}{x+y} \end{cases} \qquad \text{(II.8.63)}$$

is the ESBORA–solution s^+ of G.

8.4.2 Sequential agent splitting

Now imagine the situation that player 1 can first decide whether he wants to bargain with player 2 ($\bar{W}$) or not (W) and that player 2 is informed about 1's move. In case player 1 has chosen W the game is over. In case of $\bar{W}$ players 1 and 2 play the 2×2–unanimity bargaining game with the possible agreements X and Y. As before we refer to the parameter restrictions given in (II.8.59). The extensive form of game G is illustrated in Figure II.8.2 and given by Table II.8.3 in complete agent normal form.

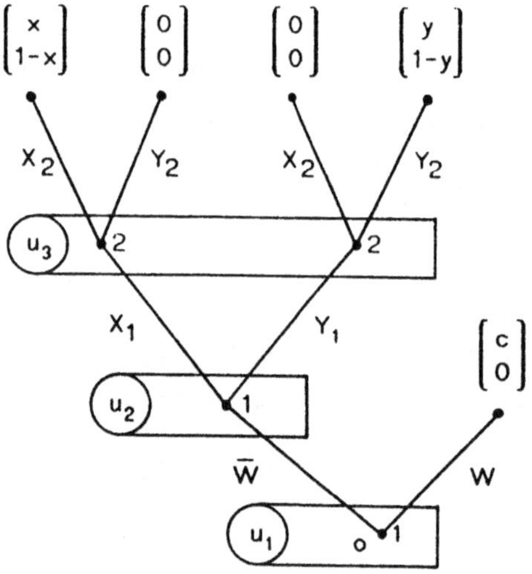

Figure II.8.2: An extensive 2–person game (o is the origin, the upper (lower) component of each payoff vector is player 1's (2's) payoff, $0 \leq c < y < x < 1$).

For the complete agent normal form of G we attach a player index $\pi(u)$ to every information set u according to (I.1.2), i.e.

$$\pi(u_1) = 3,\ \pi(u_2) = 1,\ \pi(u_3) = 2 \qquad \text{(II.8.64)}$$

implying the pure strategy sets $S_1 = \{X_1, Y_1\}$, $S_2 = \{X_2, Y_2\}$, and $S_3 = \{W, \bar{W}\}$. As can easily be seen, the probability distribution is given by $P_3 \equiv 1$, $P_1(s) = P_2(s) = 1$ for $s_3 = \bar{W}$, and $P_1(s) = P_2(s) = 0$ for $s_3 = W$.

c, 0, c	W / $\bar{W}$	X_2	Y_2	c, 0, c
	X_1	x, 1–x, x	0, 0, 0	
	Y_1	0, 0, 0	y, 1–y, y	
c, 0, c				c, 0, c

Table II.8.3: A 3–person game in normal form with $0 \leq c < y < x < 1$ being the agent normal form representation of the extensive form game in Figure II.8.2 (player 1 (2) is the row (column) player, player 3 chooses between 'inside' and 'outside'; 1's (3's) payoff appears in the upper left (lower right) corner, 2's payoff stands in between).

Since – loosely speaking – any subgame in an extensive game yields a cell game in the corresponding agent normal form game we would expect {1, 2} to be a cell. But this is not true in the unperturbed game since there are no positive linear utility transformations to map the subgame starting in u_2 with agent 3 fixed on $\bar{W}$ into the subgame starting in u_2 with agent 3 fixed on W.

In the ϵ–uniformly perturbed game $G^\epsilon = (S_1^\epsilon, S_2^\epsilon, S_3^\epsilon; P; H)$ the payoff function H is given by

$$H(s_1^\epsilon,s_2^\epsilon,s_3^\epsilon) = \eta^3 H(s_1,s_2,s_3) + \epsilon^3 H(t_1,t_2,t_3)$$
$$+ \epsilon\eta^2[H(t_1,s_2,s_3) + H(s_1,t_2,s_3) + H(s_1,s_2,t_3)]$$
$$+ \epsilon^2\eta[H(s_1,t_2,t_3) + H(t_1,s_2,t_3) + H(t_1,t_2,s_3)] \quad . \tag{II.8.65}$$

where $\eta = 1 - \epsilon > 0$, $t_i \neq s_i$, and s_i^ϵ is defined according to (II.1.2), $i = 1, 2, 3$. For the first component of H we then get

$$H_1(s_1^\epsilon,s_2^\epsilon,s_3^\epsilon) = (\eta-\epsilon)f_1(s_1) + \epsilon \sum_{\sigma_1 \in S_1} f_1(\sigma_1) \tag{II.8.66}$$

where, for given s_1^ϵ, s_2^ϵ, s_3^ϵ, the function f_1 is defined by

$$f_1(\sigma_1) = \eta^2 H_1(\sigma_1,s_2,s_3)$$
$$+ \epsilon\eta[H_1(\sigma_1,t_2,s_3) + H_1(\sigma_1,s_2,t_3)] + \epsilon^2 H_1(\sigma_1,t_2,t_3) \tag{II.8.67}$$

for $\sigma_1 \in S_1$. Since the sum $\sum_{\sigma_1 \in S_1} f_1(\sigma_1)$ is independent of the choice made by player 1, it can be neglected for all further strategic considerations (see also LEOPOLD–WILDBURGER (1982, p. 12) who has proved for the 2–person case that the sets of pure best replies do not change when truncating the payoff function in this way). Division of $(\eta-\epsilon)f_1(s_1)$ by $(\eta-\epsilon)\eta^2$ yields

$$\bar{H}_1(s_1^\epsilon,s_2^\epsilon,s_3^\epsilon) \tag{II.8.68}$$
$$= H_1(s_1,s_2,s_3) + \epsilon'[H_1(s_1,t_2,s_3) + H_1(s_1,s_2,t_3)] + (\epsilon')^2 H_1(s_1,t_2,t_3)$$

with $\epsilon' = \epsilon/\eta$. The game $\bar{G}^\epsilon = (S_1^\epsilon,S_2^\epsilon,S_3^\epsilon;P;\bar{H})$ is called the <u>modified ϵ–uniformly perturbed</u> game of G where the other components of $\bar{H}$ are given by

$$\bar{H}_2(s_1^\epsilon,s_2^\epsilon,s_3^\epsilon) \tag{II.8.69}$$
$$= H_2(s_1,s_2,s_3) + \epsilon'[H_2(t_1,s_2,s_3) + H_2(s_1,s_2,t_3)] + (\epsilon')^2 H_2(t_1,s_2,t_3)$$

and

$$\bar{H}_3(s_1^\epsilon, s_2^\epsilon, s_3^\epsilon) \tag{II.8.70}$$
$$= H_3(s_1,s_2,s_3) + \epsilon'[H_3(t_1,s_2,s_3) + H_3(s_1,t_2,s_3)] + (\epsilon')^2 H_3(t_1,t_2,s_3) \quad .$$

$\bar{H}$ is summarized in Table II.8.4 where for

$$2c\epsilon' < y-c \tag{II.8.71}$$

the best replies of players 1 and 2 do not depend on player 3's decision, i.e. $\{1, 2\}$ is a cell in $\bar{G}^\epsilon$. This is due to the fact that there are $\alpha_i > 0$, $\beta_i \in \mathbb{R}$ $(i = 1, 2)$ such that for all $s_i^\epsilon \in S_i^\epsilon$ the equations

$$H_i(s_1^\epsilon, s_2^\epsilon, W^\epsilon) = \alpha_i H_i(s_1^\epsilon, s_2^\epsilon, \bar{W}^\epsilon) + \beta_i \tag{II.8.72}$$

hold, e.g. for $\alpha_1 = \alpha_2 = \epsilon' > 0$, $\beta_1 = c[1+\epsilon'-(\epsilon')^2-(\epsilon')^3]$, and $\beta_2 = 0$.

$c+\epsilon'(c+x)$ $\epsilon'^2(1-x)$ $c(1+\epsilon')^2$	W^ϵ / $\bar{W}^\epsilon$ X_2^ϵ	Y_2^ϵ	$c+\epsilon'(c+\epsilon' x)$ $\epsilon'^2(1-y)$ $c(1+\epsilon')^2$
X_1^ϵ	$x+\epsilon' c(1+\epsilon')$ $1-x$ $x+\epsilon'^2 y$	$\epsilon'(x+c+\epsilon' c)$ $\epsilon'(1-y)$ $\epsilon'(x+y)$	
Y_1^ϵ	$\epsilon'(y+c+\epsilon' c)$ $\epsilon'(1-x)$ $\epsilon'(x+y)$	$y+\epsilon' c(1+\epsilon')$ $1-y$ $y+\epsilon'^2 x$	
$c+\epsilon'(c+\epsilon' y)$ $\epsilon'^2(1-x)$ $c(1+\epsilon')^2$			$c+\epsilon'(c+y)$ $\epsilon'(1-y)$ $c(1+\epsilon')^2$

Table II.8.4: The modified ϵ–uniformly perturbed 3–person game of the game given in Table II.8.3 where player 1 (2) is the row (column) player and player 3 chooses between 'inside' and 'outside' (1's (3's) payoff is in the upper left (lower right) corner, 2's payoff stands in between).

In the following we solve the ϵ–uniformly perturbed games illustrated in Table II.8.4. First of all we have to solve the cell game G^1 where 1 and 2 are the only active players which is summarized in Table II.8.5. By shifting the origin of player 1's utility function we get G^2.

G^1	X_2^ϵ	Y_2^ϵ
X_1^ϵ	$x+\epsilon'c(1+\epsilon')$ $1-x$	$\epsilon'x+\epsilon'c(1+\epsilon')$ $\epsilon'(1-y)$
Y_1^ϵ	$\epsilon'y+\epsilon'c(1+\epsilon')$ $\epsilon'(1-x)$	$y+\epsilon'c(1+\epsilon')$ $1-y$

G^2	X_2^ϵ	Y_2^ϵ
X_1^ϵ	x $1-x$	$\epsilon'x$ $\epsilon'(1-y)$
Y_1^ϵ	$\epsilon'y$ $\epsilon'(1-x)$	y $1-y$

Table II.8.5: Two equivalent 2–person games describing the cell game to the cell {1, 2} of the game in Table II.8.4 (player 1 (2) is the row (column) player, 1's (2's) payoff appears in the upper left (lower right) corner).

Game G^2 is exactly the modified ϵ–uniformly perturbed game for the resistance comparison of X and Y analysed in Section 8.4.1. $(X_1^\epsilon, X_2^\epsilon)$ is the solution of G^2 if

$$(x-\epsilon'y)(1-x-\epsilon'(1-y)) > (y-\epsilon'x)(1-y-\epsilon'(1-x)) \tag{II.8.73}$$

which is equivalent to

$$x(1-x) - y(1-y) > 0 \ . \tag{II.8.74}$$

$Y^\epsilon = (Y_1^\epsilon, Y_2^\epsilon)$ is the solution of the cell game for the reversed inequality sign in (II.8.74) and the equilibrium point $q^\epsilon = (q_1^\epsilon, q_2^\epsilon)$, given by

$$q_1^\epsilon(X_1^\epsilon) = \frac{1-y}{2-x-y}, \quad q_2^\epsilon(X_2^\epsilon) = \frac{y-\epsilon'x}{(x+y)(1-\epsilon')}, \tag{II.8.75}$$

is the solution if the left–hand side of (II.8.74) equals zero. Obviously $q_2^\epsilon(X_2^\epsilon) \to \frac{y}{x+y}$ for $\epsilon \to 0$.

For solving the residual game we have to take into account the different cell solutions. The games G^+, G^-, or G^0 in Table II.8.6 denote the residual games in case the left–hand side of (II.8.74) is positive, negative, or equals zero, respectively. For convenience the payoffs of the inactive players in the residual game, i.e. players 1 and 2, are dropped in Table II.8.6.

G^+

W^ϵ	$(1+\epsilon')c$
$\bar{W}^\epsilon$	$x+\epsilon' y$

G^-

W^ϵ	$(1+\epsilon')c$
$\bar{W}^\epsilon$	$y+\epsilon' x$

G^0

W^ϵ	$(1+\epsilon')c$
$\bar{W}^\epsilon$	$\frac{xy(1+\epsilon')}{x+y}$

Table II.8.6: Three 1–person residual games of the game in Table II.8.4 with player 3 as the only active player.

For all $\epsilon' > 0$ the solution of G^+ and of G^- is $\bar{W}^\epsilon$ and the solution of G^0 is W^ϵ, $\bar{W}^\epsilon$ or $q = .5\, W^\epsilon + .5\, \bar{W}^\epsilon$ if $c > \frac{xy}{x+y}$, $c < \frac{xy}{x+y}$ or $c = \frac{xy}{x+y}$, respectively.

Thus we have shown that the ESBORA–solution s^+ of G is

$$s^+ = \begin{cases} (X_1, X_2, \bar{W}) & \text{for } x(1-x) > y(1-y) \\ (Y_1, Y_2, \bar{W}) & \text{for } x(1-x) < y(1-y) \\ (q_1, q_2, W) & \text{for } x+y=1 \text{ and } c > \frac{xy}{x+y} \\ (q_1, q_2, \bar{W}) & \text{for } x+y=1 \text{ and } c < \frac{xy}{x+y} \\ (q_1, q_2, .5W + .5\bar{W}) & \text{for } x+y=1 \text{ and } c = \frac{xy}{x+y} \end{cases} \tag{II.8.76}$$

where $q_1 = \frac{1-y}{2-x-y} X_1 + \frac{1-x}{2-x-y} Y_1$ and $q_2 = \frac{y}{x+y} X_2 + \frac{x}{x+y} Y_2$.

Since the cell game is a 2×2–bimatrix game with two strict equilibrium points and a payoff dominated equilibrium point in mixed strategies the Harsanyi–Selten solution and the ESBORA–solution of the game at hand are identical.

A comparison with the results obtained in Section 8.4.1 shows that only for the very special case that $x+y = 1$ and $c = \frac{xy}{x+y}$ the ESBORA–solution depends on the fact whether a sequential agent splitting is carried out or not. As the above calculations have demonstrated neither X nor Y can be selected as the solution of the game for $x+y = 1$. If in this case the sure nonbargaining profit c is greater than the expected profit $\frac{xy}{x+y}$ of player 1 for the bargaining solution q, he will naturally choose the nonbargaining strategy. When for $x+y = 1$ he is indifferent between bargaining and nonbargaining, i.e. $c = \frac{xy}{x+y}$, he obviously gives equal weights to both possibilities. In the complete normal form game of Section 8.4.1 player 1 cannot do this kind of weighting but is forced to decide between q_1 and W_1 as shown in (II.8.63).

8.5 A 2–person bargaining game with a nonbargaining strategy on both sides

Whereas in the example analysed in the preceding section only player 1 had a nonbargaining strategy giving him a sure profit of $c \geq 0$, we now examine a game in normal form where both players get a payoff of 1 unit only if they both agree to nonbargaining. If player i demonstrates that he does not want to bargain by choosing W_i and if his opponent $j \neq i$ chooses to bargain, both players will get a payoff of zero. We furthermore assume that both players have to make their choices simultaneously. This means that we are dealing with $G = (S_1, S_2; P; H)$ where $S_i = \{X_i, Y_i, W_i\}$, $P_i \equiv 1$ $(i = 1, 2)$, and H is given in Table II.8.7.

	X_2	Y_2	W_2
X_1	1, 1	a, 0	0, 0
Y_1	0, b	c, d	0, 0
W_1	0, 0	0, 0	1, 1

Table II.8.7: A 2–person game with parameter restrictions $a > c > 0$ and $b > d > 0$ (player 1 (2) is the row (column) player, 1's (2's) payoff is given in the upper left (lower right) corner).

Because of the parameter restrictions there are two strict equilibrium points, namely $X = (X_1, X_2)$ and $W = (W_1, W_2)$, giving a payoff of 1 unit to both players and there is another payoff dominated equilibrium point in mixed strategies. The payoff or resistance comparison of X and W in the unperturbed game would not yield X as the solution of the game although due to a > 0 and b > 0 candidate X is the intuitively more convincing solution candidate. However these considerations mainly suffer from one shortcoming, i.e. they do not take into account the ϵ–uniformly perturbed games revealing the "true" structure of the game at hand.

Let $\epsilon < 1/3$ be a given perturbance parameter. Using the abbreviations $\eta = 1 - 2\epsilon$ and $\epsilon' = \epsilon/\eta$ the game $G^\epsilon = (S_1^\epsilon, S_2^\epsilon; P; H)$ in complete normal form with $P_i \equiv 1$ for i = 1, 2 is defined in Table II.8.8.

	X_2^ϵ	Y_2^ϵ	W_2^ϵ
X_1^ϵ	$1+\epsilon' a+\epsilon'^2(c+1)$ $1+\epsilon' b+\epsilon'^2(d+1)$	$a+\epsilon'(1+c)+\epsilon'^2$ $\epsilon'(1+d)+\epsilon'^2(b+1)$	$\epsilon'(2+a)+\epsilon'^2 c$ $2\epsilon'+\epsilon'^2(b+d)$
Y_1^ϵ	$\epsilon'(c+1)+\epsilon'^2(a+1)$ $b+\epsilon'(1+d)+\epsilon'^2$	$c+\epsilon' a+2\epsilon'^2$ $d+\epsilon' b+2\epsilon'^2$	$\epsilon'(c+1)+\epsilon'^2(a+1)$ $\epsilon'(1+b+d)+\epsilon'^2$
W_1^ϵ	$2\epsilon'+\epsilon'^2(a+c)$ $\epsilon'(2+b)+\epsilon'^2 d$	$\epsilon'(a+c+1)+\epsilon'^2$ $\epsilon'(d+1)+\epsilon'^2(b+1)$	$1+\epsilon'^2(1+a+c)$ $1+\epsilon'^2(1+b+d)$

Table II.8.8: The ϵ–uniformly perturbed 2–person game of the game in Table II.8.7.

For sufficiently small $\epsilon > 0$ there are two strict equilibrium points in G^ϵ, namely $X^\epsilon = (X_1^\epsilon, X_2^\epsilon)$ and $W^\epsilon = (W_1^\epsilon, W_2^\epsilon)$, and another equilibrium point q^ϵ in mixed strategies. A comparison of the payoff vectors $H(X^\epsilon)$ and $H(W^\epsilon)$ shows that X^ϵ payoff dominates W^ϵ and therefore also q^ϵ for all $\epsilon > 0$.

Thus X is the ESBORA–solution of G since X^ϵ payoff dominates all other equilibrium points in G^ϵ and $\lim_{\epsilon \to 0} X^\epsilon = X$. Obviously, the Harsanyi–Selten solution of G is also X.

Part III: Generalizing the weights for normalized individual resistances

In the following we will first illustrate by an example that weighting the normalized individual resistance levels $r_i(s^{k'},s^k)/r_i(s^k,s^{k'})$ simply by P_i according to (I.2.9) may yield counterintuitive results. This will inspire us to define generalized weights for the individual resistance levels. Since not all other players necessarily suffer if a player deviates from a given solution candidate these generalized weights take into account whether a deviation of a given player is harmful for his opponents or not. Again we will analyse several examples to illustrate the selection properties of the generalized ESBORA–concept as well as the differences between the preliminary and the generalized concept of resistance avoidance.

1. The 'one seller and n–1 buyers'–problem

This section will report on the results of GÜTH and STEPHAN (1984). Consider the game G = $(S_1,\ldots,S_n;P;H)$ in complete (agent) normal form where the pure strategy sets

$$S_i = \{g, 2g,\ldots, Kg\} \qquad \text{with } K, (K-1)/n \in \mathbb{N}, (K-1)g = 100 \tag{III.1.1}$$

are the same for all players i = 1,...,n and g (> 0) is the smallest unit of money. We will refer to a strategy kg, with $g \leq kg \leq 100 - g$ and $k \in \mathbb{N}$, as the price kg suggested by player i. The probability assignment P of G is given by

$$P_i(s) = 1 \qquad \text{for all } s \in S_1\times\ldots\times S_n \text{ and } i = 1,\ldots,n \ . \tag{III.1.2}$$

Player 1 is the only seller of one unit of an indivisible commodity which all players 2,...,n (the potential buyers) are interested to buy. Define by

$$m(s) = |\{j \in \{2,...,n\} | s_j = s_1\}| \tag{III.1.3}$$

the number of buyers who, according to s, have named the same price as the seller. With the help of this notation every buyer j's payoff function (j = 2,...,n) can be expressed as

$$H_j(s) = \begin{cases} (100-s_j)/m(s) & \text{if } s_j = s_1, \\ 0 & \text{otherwise} . \end{cases} \tag{III.1.4}$$

If m(s) is greater than 1 each of the m(s) buyers, whose price coincides with seller 1's proposal, has the same chance to get the commodity at the price s_1. For the seller the payoff is given by

$$H_1(s) = \begin{cases} s_1 & \text{if } m(s) \geq 1 , \\ 0 & \text{otherwise} . \end{cases} \tag{III.1.5}$$

Thus seller 1's utility for the commodity is 0, whereas every buyer evaluates it by 100.

For any $k \in \mathbb{N}$ with $k \leq K$ let $s^k = (s_1,...,s_n)$ denote the strategy vector with $s_i = kg$ for i = 1,...,n. It can easily be seen that the set $C_{1,0}$ of strict and in $C_{0,0}$ payoff undominated equilibrium points is the set

$$\{s^k \mid 1 \leq k \leq K\} \tag{III.1.6}$$

of unanimous price vectors s^k. Let s^k and $s^{k'}$ be two different price vectors in $C_{1,0}$. Obviously, M = {1,...,n} is the set of active players in the restricted game for the resistance comparison of $s^{k'}$ and s^k. When investigating a player's individual resistance of $s^{k'}$ against s^k, one derives

$$r_1(s^{k'},s^k) = \max \{z \in [0,1] \mid k'[1-z^{n-1}] \geq k[1-(1-z)^{n-1}]\} \tag{III.1.7}$$

and

$$r_j(s^{k'},s^k) \tag{III.1.8}$$
$$= \max \{z \in [0,1] \mid (K+1-k')[1-z^{n-1}] \geq (K+1-k)[1-(1-z)^{n-1}] \}$$

for all buyers $j = 2,...,n$. Define

$$u_i^{(')} = \begin{cases} k^{(')} & \text{for } i = 1 \quad , \\ K+1-k^{(')} & \text{for } i = 2,...,n \, , \end{cases} \tag{III.1.9}$$

and

$$d_i(z) = u_i[1-(1-z)^{n-1}] - u_i'[1-z^{n-1}] \tag{III.1.10}$$

for $i = 1,...,n$. With the help of this notation (III.1.7) and (III.1.8) can be written as

$$r_1(s^{k'},s^k) = \max \{z \in [0,1] \mid 0 \geq d_1(z)\} \tag{III.1.11}$$

and

$$r_j(s^{k'},s^k) = \max \{z \in [0,1] \mid 0 \geq d_j(z)\} \tag{III.1.12}$$

for all $j = 2,...,n$. Since for all players $i = 1,...,n$ we have $d_i(0) = -u_i'$ (< 0) and $d_i(1) = u_i$ (> 0) and since d_i is strictly increasing and continuous on $[0,1]$ the maximal z_i, with $d_i(z_i) \leq 0$, is unique and satisfies $0 < z_i < 1$ for all $i = 1,...,n$. Thus for $Z_i = z_i/(1-z_i)$ we get

$$Z_i = r_i(s^{k'},s^k)/r_i(s^k,s^{k'}) \qquad \text{III.1.13)}$$

for all $i = 1,...,n$. It can be shown that player i's normalized individual resistance Z_i, $i = 1,...,n$, can be computed by solving the following equation in Z_i:

$$u_i Z_i^{n-1} - u_i' + (u_i - u_i') \sum_{m=1}^{n-2} \binom{n-1}{m} Z_i^m = 0 \quad . \tag{III.1.14}$$

Equation (III.1.14) illustrates that for large values of n it will be very difficult to determine the individual resistance values Z_i for all possible pairs $s^{k'}$ and s^k and thus the ESBORA–solution. For $n \leq 4$ the ESBORA–solution can still be computed directly, being the strict equilibrium point

s^k with $kg = 100/n$. Because of the assumption $(K-1)/n \in \mathbb{N}$ the solution price $100/n$ can be expressed as an integer multiple of the smallest money unit g. Numerical computations have shown that for increasing $n > 4$ the solution price decreases further.

The fact that the ESBORA–solution price decreases with an increasing number n–1 of identical potential buyers makes the 'one seller and n–1 buyers'–problem an important test for the ESBORA–concept. For the Harsanyi–Selten theory (see HARSANYI, 1982) the solution price is $100(2^{n-1}-1)/(2^{n-1}+n-2)$, i.e. it increases with an increasing number n–1 of indentical buyers. Here the solution price is the limit $g \to 0$ of the solution prices for the (finite) games with smallest unit of money g. Although we do not face a cooperative game it is worthwhile mentioning that also the Shapley–value prescribes a price which increases with the number of identical buyers, namely $100(n-1)/n$ (see HARSANYI, 1982). Of course, the Shapley–value is the same for all agent normal forms with characteristic functions v satisfying $v(\bar{M}) = 100$ if $1 \in \bar{M}$ and $|\bar{M}| \geq 2$, and $v(\bar{M}) = 0$ otherwise. One can vary the agent normal form of the 'one seller and n–1 buyers'-problem in many and strategically different ways without changing its characteristic function. Nevertheless, both results indicate that the seller does not become less powerful in case of more potential buyers.

That the ESBORA–solution price decreases with an increasing number n–1 of identical buyers is mainly due to the fact that for any comparison $s^{k'}$ against s^k all players $i = 1,\ldots,n$ have the weight $P_i = 1$ when determining $r(s^{k'},s^k)$ according to (I.2.10). This means that the total weight of all buyers increases with the number n–1 of identical potential buyers. Now the weight of a potential buyer should decrease when n–1 increases since intuitively he becomes less powerful if more buyers compete for a contract with player 1. That the counterintuitive results of the ESBORA–concept are due to the weights P_i used in (I.2.10) is supported by the fact that for $k' > k$ the individual resistance levels $r_j(s^{k'},s^k)$ of all buyers $j = 2,\ldots,n$ approach 0 whereas $r_1(s^{k'},s^k)$ approaches 1 if n–1 goes to infinity. If there are many competing potential buyers, the seller will ultimately resist against a lower price. But although a potential buyer prefers a lower price he will not really resist against a higher price if he faces many competitors. This clearly indicates that the individual resistance levels according to (I.2.8) are in line with our intuitive expectations how an individual player will argue for or against a higher solution price. It is our simple weighting approach which causes the apparently counterintuitive results for the 'one seller and n–1 buyers'-problem.

2. The generalized ESBORA–concept

The counterintuitive result is no real surprise. From the very beginning we considered the weights P_i preliminary and planned to develop more sophisticated weights. In the following we will define $\tilde{\varepsilon}$–perturbed generalized weights which avoid the counterintuitive results for the 'one seller and n–1 buyers'–problem. But since other examples might bring about other shortcomings, also this approach might appear to be preliminary in the light of new experiences. That is why we have started with our preliminary version. The naive weights P_i can serve as a starting point for various approaches to improve the ESBORA–concept – see Part IV –. Of course, we will require that these improvements do not endanger important properties of the ESBORA–concept like, for instance, the Nash–property. The generalized ESBORA–concept avoids the counterintuitive results for the 'one seller and n–1 buyers'–problem without questioning the Nash–property of the ESBORA–concept or other important properties discussed in Part I.

Consider a game $G = (S_1,\ldots,S_n;P;H)$ in complete (agent) normal form with at least two different strict equilibrium points $s^{k'}$ and s^k. Define by

$$M_i(s^{k'},s^k) = \{j \in M-\{i\} \mid H_j(s^k) > H_j(s_i^{k'},s_{-i}^k)\} \tag{III.2.1}$$

the set of active players $j \neq i$ in the restricted game for the resistance comparison of $s^{k'}$ and s^k who suffer from player i's deviation from s^k. When measuring how player i contributes to the total resistance $r(s^{k'},s^k)$ of $s^{k'}$ against s^k, it is important to observe that only the players in $M_i(s^{k'},s^k)$ have reasons to listen to player i's objections. By our concept of generalized weights we want to take into account whether player i's deviation is harmful for his opponents or not. Instead of the weights P_i which are used to aggregate the normalized individual resistances $r_i(s^{k'},s^k)/r_i(s^k,s^{k'})$

according to (I.2.10) we propose to use the following generalized weights

$$P_i(s^{k'},s^k) = P_i \sum_{j \in M_i(s^{k'},s^k)} P_j \tag{III.2.2}$$

for $i \in M$ when aggregating the normalized individual resistance of $s^{k'}$ against s^k according to

$$r(s^{k'},s^k) = \prod_{i \in M} \left[r_i(s^{k'},s^k)/r_i(s^k,s^{k'})\right]^{P_i(s^{k'},s^k)} \quad . \tag{II.2.3}$$

Since the set $M_i(s^{k'},s^k)$ may be empty all generalized weights $P_i(s^{k'},s^k)$ may be zero. By our concept of $\tilde{\epsilon}$–perturbed generalized weights, $\tilde{\epsilon} > 0$, we will later on exclude zero–weights for all ϵ,δ–perturbed games $G^{\epsilon,\delta}$ which have to be considered according to the constructive solution procedure described in Figure II.6.1.

Observe that for the generalized resistance $r(s^{k'},s^k)$ of $s^{k'}$ against s^k it is no longer true that $r(s^k,s^{k'}) = 1/r(s^{k'},s^k)$. The reason is that in general $P_i(s^{k'},s^k) \neq P_i(s^k,s^{k'})$. Consider, for instance, example 4.1.2 of Part I with the two strict equilibrium points $X = (X_1,X_2,X_3)$ and $Y = (Y_1,Y_2,Y_3)$. The weights for the resistance comparison of X and Y are as follows:

$$P_1(X,Y) = P_2(X,Y) = 1\,, \quad P_3(X,Y) = 0 \tag{III.2.4}$$

and

$$P_1(Y,X) = P_2(Y,X) = 1\,, \quad P_3(Y,X) = 2\,. \tag{III.2.5}$$

Although player 3 has the highest weight when measuring the resistance of Y against X, his resistance in view of X against Y will not be taken into account. Since player 3 does not harm any opponent if he deviates from Y, no one listens to his objections against Y. The example demonstrates that the new concept of resistance avoidance does not only take into account how strongly a player objects against a given solution candidate but also how much reason the other players have to listen to his objections.

Thus for example 4.1.2 of Part I the generalized resistances of X against Y and vice versa are

$$r(Y,X) = (1 + \sqrt{3})^2/(1 + x) \tag{III.2.6}$$

and

$$r(X,Y) = 1/(1 + \sqrt{3})^2 \ , \tag{III.2.7}$$

respectively. Although the generalized resistances are very different from the resistances with preliminary weights the condition for X to be the ESBORA–solution is surprisingly the same as before, namely:

$$1.25 < X < (1 + \sqrt{3})^4 - 1 \ . \tag{III.2.8}$$

Y is the ESBORA–solution in case of

$$x > (1 + \sqrt{3})^4 - 1 = 27 + 16\sqrt{3} \ . \tag{III.2.9}$$

The generalized weights can be zero for many games. As a consequence Theorem 1, saying that generically there is a unique resistance undominated strict equilibrium point, does not hold for a concept of resistance avoidance relying on generalized weights. We want to illustrate this by a 3–person game in (agent) normal form completed by $P_i(s) = 1$ for all strategy vectors s and players i = 1, 2, and 3 (see Table III.2.1). It is easy to see that $X = (X_1,X_2,X_3)$ and $Y = (Y_1,Y_2,Y_3)$ are the only strict equilibrium points. We will neglect nonpure equilibrium points even if they are not payoff dominated. Because of the other parameter restrictions we, furthermore, obtain

$$P_i(X,Y) = P_i(Y,X) = 0 \tag{III.2.10}$$

for all three players i = 1, 2, and 3. In all games satisfying the parameter restrictions a deviation by a single player from one of the two strict equilibrium points does not harm any of his opponents. Since the sets $M_i(X,Y)$ and $M_i(Y,X)$ are empty for i = 1, 2, and 3 all generalized weights are zero. The example demonstrates that for games of a given size the class of those games, for which all generalized weights are zero, is of positive Lebesgue–measure in the sense of Theorem 1. This implies that the generic uniqueness of the resistance undominated strict equilibrium point is no longer true.

a_1 a_2 v_3	Y_3 / X_3 X_2	Y_2	0 b_2 b_3
X_1	x_1 x_2 x_3	c_1 v_2 c_3	
Y_1	v_1 d_2 d_3	e_1 e_2 0	
f_1 0 f_3			y_1 y_2 y_3

Table III.2.1: A 3–person game in (agent) normal form with payoff parameters $x_i > v_i$, $y_i > 0$ for $i = 1, 2, 3$; $a_i \geq x_i$ and $e_i \geq y_i$ for $i = 1, 2$; $c_i \geq x_i$ and $f_i \geq y_i$ for $i = 1, 3$; $d_i \geq x_i$ and $b_i \geq y_i$ for $i = 2, 3$.

The example of Table III.2.1 illustrates that the considerations of resistance avoidance will be neglected if all generalized weights are zero. Depending on the specific values of the payoff parameters the two candidates X and Y will, nevertheless, have to face serious objections by the three players. To have a certain example in mind consider Table III.2.2 which is a special case of Table III.2.1.

1 1 0	Y_3 / X_3 X_2	Y_2	0 100 100
X_1	1 1 2	1 .99 2	
Y_1	.99 1 2	100 100 0	
100 0 100			2 2 1

Table III.2.2: A special 3–person game in the class of games illustrated by Table III.2.1.

If player i = 1 or i = 2 chooses Y_i, he can be sure to receive at least .99 which is nearly as much as the highest payoff level 1 for his strategy X_i. Thus players 1 and 2 do not face a serious risk when they object against X and push for Y which they both prefer to X.

To avoid that resistance considerations are completely neglected if all the generalized weights are zero, we will exclude generalized weights of zero in all ϵ,δ–perturbed games $G^{\epsilon,\delta}$. For sufficiently small $\tilde{\epsilon} > 0$ we define

$$P_i^{\tilde{\epsilon}}(s^{k'},s^k) = \max\,\{P_i(s^{k'},s^k),\ \tilde{\epsilon}\}\ . \tag{III.2.11}$$

$P_i^{\tilde{\epsilon}}(s^{k'},s^k)$ is called the <u>$\tilde{\epsilon}$–perturbed generalized weight</u> for the resistance comparison of $s^{k'}$ against s^k. When solving an ϵ,δ–perturbed game $G^{\epsilon,\delta}$ and applying Algorithm (2) according to the constructive solution procedure illustrated in Figure II.6.1, the $\tilde{\epsilon}$–perturbed generalized weights are used instead of P_i and the limit $\tilde{\epsilon} \to 0$ is taken. Thus in any essentially perturbed game all generalized weights are positive which implies that considerations of resistance avoidance are always taken into account. Only in the limit the normalized resistances $r_i(s^{k'},s^k)/r_i(s^k,s^{k'})$ of players i with $P_i(s^{k'},s^k) = 0$ will be completely dominated by the corresponding resistance values of those players j for whom $P_j(s^{k'},s^k)$ is positive. If, as in Table III.2.1, all generalized weights $P_i(s^{k'},s^k)$ are zero, the normalized resistances $r_i(s^{k'},s^k)/r_i(s^k,s^{k'})$ are, of course, of crucial importance even in the limit. This consequence is the essential reason for introducing $\tilde{\epsilon}$–perturbed generalized weights. On the one hand, like generalized weights $\tilde{\epsilon}$–perturbed generalized weights consider whether the opponents of a given player have reasons to listen to his objections. On the other hand, like the simple weights P_i, $\tilde{\epsilon}$–perturbed generalized weights avoid that considerations of resistance dominance are completely neglected.

We will speak of the generalized ESBORA–concept when instead of the simple weights P_i the the $\tilde{\epsilon}$–perturbed generalized weights are used to aggregate the normalized individual resistance values $r_i(s^{k'},s^k)/r_i(s^k,s^{k'})$ to the resistance $r(s^{k'},s^k)$ of $s^{k'}$ against s^k for every ϵ,δ–perturbed game $G^{\epsilon,\delta}$.

Similarly to Lemma 6 and Lemma 7 the generalized ESBORA–concept can be applied directly to the game or its ϵ–uniformly perturbed games if the respective assumptions are satisfied. An important simplification for applying the generalized ESBORA–concept is

Lemma 8:

If according to the generalized weights there is a unique resistance undominated solution candidate in $C_{1,0}$, the generalized ESBORA–solution can be determined by using the generalized weights instead of the $\tilde{\epsilon}$–perturbed generalized weights.

Since in the limit only the normalized resistances of players with positive generalized weights are important, Lemma 8 is obvious. Furthermore, Lemma 8 is helpful when analysing how the results of our previous examples will change when using the generalized ESBORA–concept.

As the preliminary ESBORA–concept the generalized ESBORA–concept also satisfies the generalized Nash–property as described in Theorem 3. Consider a regular unanimity bargaining game with incomplete information and the two different unanimous strategy vectors $(j^+,...,j^+)$ and $(j,...,j)$ as in equations (I.4.54) and (I.4.55). If agent $\pi(t_i)$ deviates from $(j,...,j)$, all agents $\pi(t_j)$ with $j \neq i$ suffer a loss while the payoff of agents $\pi(t_i')$ with $t_i' \neq t_i$ is not affected. Since for all $i = 1,...,n$ we have

$$\sum_{\substack{j=1 \\ j\neq i}}^{n} \sum_{t_j \in T_j} \bar{P}_{\pi(t_j)} = n-1 \qquad \text{(III.2.12)}$$

the generalized weights are

$$P_{\pi(t_i)}((j^+,\dots,j^+),(j,\dots,j)) = (n-1)\,\bar{P}_{\pi(t_i)} \tag{III.2.13}$$

for all agents $\pi(t_i)$ with $t_i \in T_i$. Observe that because of $\bar{P}_{\pi(t_i)} > 0$ for all $t_i \in T_i$ and $i = 1,\dots,n$ all generalized weights are positive. Similar to (I.4.55) follows that the generalized resistance $r((j^+,\dots,j^+),(j,\dots,j))$ is greater than 1 and that $r((j,\dots,j), (j^+,\dots,j^+))$ is smaller than 1 for all $j \neq j^+$. Thus also the generalized ESBORA–concept satisfies our generalized Nash–property.

3. Examples

By the following examples we want to illustrate the consequence of substituting the weights P_i by the generalized weights $P_i(s^{k'},s^k)$. This will clarify the differences between the preliminary and the generalized ESBORA–concept. It is probably needless to say that for many classes of games the preliminary and the generalized ESBORA–concept will determine the same solution. To simplify our analysis we will restrict ourselves, as before, to games or, respectively, to parameter constellations where all nonpure equilibrium points are payoff dominated.

3.1 The 'one seller and n–1 buyers'–problem reconsidered

Let us consider the 'one seller and n–1 buyers'–problem in the light of the generalized ESBORA-concept. If we consider two different strategy vectors s^k and $s^{k'}$ in $C_{1,0}$, we have the weights

$$P_j(s^{k'},s^k) = \begin{cases} 0 & \text{if } n > 2\,, \\ 1 & \text{if } n = 2 \end{cases} \tag{III.3.1}$$

for all potential buyers j = 2,...,n. For the seller the generalized weight is

$$P_1(s^{k'},s^k) = n-1 . \tag{III.3.2}$$

Thus generalized weights imply that the resistance of any potential buyer is completely neglected whenever there exist at least two of them. The generalized ESBORA–solution of the 'one seller and n–1 buyers'–problem is therefore the unanimous price vector $p^+ = (p_1^+,...,p_n^+)$ with proposals

$$p_i^+ = \begin{cases} 50 & \text{for } n = 2, \\ 100 - g & \text{for } n > 2 \end{cases} \tag{III.3.3}$$

for all players i = 1,...,n. The result for n = 2 is a simple consequence of the Nash–property. For n > 2 the result can easily be seen by considering equation (II.1.7). For $k' > k$ we obtain $r_1(s^{k'},s^k) > 1/2$ and $r_1(s^{k'},s^k)/r_1(s^k,s^{k'}) > 1$. Since only player 1's normalized resistance $r_1(s^{k'},s^k)/r_1(s^k,s^{k'})$ is relevant s^K resistance dominates all other unanimous price vectors s^k with $1 \leq k < K$.

For n > 2 the solution price Kg = 100–g is the competitive price in the 'one seller and n–1 buyers'–situation. At a lower price there would always be a potential buyer preferring to buy the commodity with certainty at a higher price. It is probably needless to say that for n > 2 the price 100–g is also the only price in the core of the game. This shows that the generalized ESBORA-solution is clearly in line with our economic intuitions. Already two potential buyers are enough for competition since for any price below the competitive price there will always be one potential buyer willing to attract the seller by a higher price offer. It is, in our view, a weakness of the Harsanyi–Selten theory that its solution price does not reflect the sharp increase in the competitiveness of the market when switching from n = 2 to n > 2 (HARSANYI, 1982).

3.2 A class of 3–person games with three solution candidates

Let us consider a class of 3–person games with three strict equilibrium points to illustrate the difference between the preliminary and the generalized ESBORA–concept. Consider the games $G = (S_1,S_2,S_3;P;H)$ in complete (agent) normal form with

$$S_i = \{X_i, Y_i, Z_i\} \tag{III.3.4}$$

for i=1, 2, and 3 and $P_i \equiv 1$ for i=1, 2, and 3. The payoff function H of G is illustrated in Table III.3.1 in the usual way. Only $X = (X_1,X_2,X_3)$, $Y = (Y_1,Y_2,Y_3)$, and $Z = (Z_1,Z_2,Z_3)$ are strict equilibrium points. Furthermore, because of the parameter restrictions none of the three strict equilibrium points payoff dominates another. Without stating the exact conditions for the parameters of the game we restrict ourselves to those parameter constellations where every nonpure equilibrium point is payoff dominated by a strict equilibrium point.

X_3	X_2	Y_2	Z_2
X_1	1; 1; 1	$1+d_2$; 0; $f_2+c_3-f_0$	a_2; 0; c_2
Y_1	0; e_0; f_0	1; $1+e_0-b_2$; 0	0; e_2; f_1
Z_1	0; b_6; i_0	0; 1; i_1	1; 0; 0

Y_3	X_2	Y_2	Z_2
X_1	0; 1; 0	0; b_2; c_3	1; 0; c_4
Y_1	d_2; 0; f_2	d_3; e_3; f_3	d_4; 0; f_4
Z_1	1; 0; i_2	0; h_4; $i_5+f_6-f_4$	0; 1; 0

Z_3	X_2	Y_2	Z_2
X_1	1; 0; 0	0; 1; c_5	0; b_6; $c_2+i_0-i_4$
Y_1	0; e_4; f_5	1; e_5; 0	0; e_5+h_4-1; f_6
Z_1	a_2; 0; i_4	$1+d_4$; 0; i_5	g_6; h_6; i_6

Table III.3.1: A 3–person game in (agent) normal form (player 1/ 2/ 3 chooses between rows/ columns/ boxes; player 1's (3's) payoff is in the upper left (lower right) corner, player 2's payoff stands in between; $1 > d_3 > g_6 > 0$; $e_3 > h_6 > 1$; $i_6 > 1 > f_3 > 0$; $d_3e_3f_3 \neq g_6h_6i_6$, $d_3e_3f_3 \neq 1$, $g_6h_6i_6 \neq 1$).

The class of games has been constructed such that the normalized individual resistances $r_i(s^{k'},s^k)/r_i(s^k,s^{k'})$ are easy to calculate. One derives

$$r_1(Y,X)/r_1(X,Y) = \sqrt{d_3} \tag{III.3.5}$$

$$r_2(Y,X)/r_2(X,Y) = \sqrt{e_3} \tag{III.3.6}$$

$$r_3(Y,X)/r_3(X,Y) = \sqrt{f_3} \tag{III.3.7}$$

$$r_1(Z,X)/r_1(X,Z) = \sqrt{g_6} \tag{III.3.8}$$

$$r_2(Z,X)/r_2(X,Z) = \sqrt{h_6} \tag{III.3.9}$$

$$r_3(Z,X)/r_3(X,Z) = \sqrt{i_6} \tag{III.3.10}$$

$$r_1(Z,Y)/r_1(Y,Z) = \sqrt{g_6/d_3} \tag{III.3.11}$$

$$r_2(Z,Y)/r_2(Y,Z) = \sqrt{h_6/e_3} \tag{III.3.12}$$

$$r_3(Z,Y)/r_3(Y,Z) = \sqrt{i_6/f_3}\,. \tag{III.3.13}$$

To express the generalized weights $P_i(s^{k'},s^k)$ we will use the following notation. Let r and r' be two real numbers. We define the value $\lambda(r,r')$ by

$$\lambda(r,r') = \begin{cases} 2 & \text{if } \max\{r, r'\} < 0\ , \\ 1 & \text{if } \max\{r, r'\} \geq 0 > \min\{r, r'\}\,, \\ 0 & \text{otherwise}\,. \end{cases} \tag{III.3.14}$$

With the help of this notation the generalized weights can be written as follows:

$$P_1(Y,X) = \lambda(e_0-1,f_0-1) \tag{III.3.15}$$

$$P_2(Y,X) = \lambda(d_2,f_2+c_3-f_0-1) \tag{III.3.16}$$

$$P_3(Y,X) = 1 \tag{III.3.17}$$

$$P_1(X,Y) = \lambda(b_2-e_3,c_3-f_3) \tag{III.3.18}$$

$$P_2(X,Y) = \lambda(d_2-d_3,f_2-f_3) \tag{III.3.19}$$

$$P_3(X,Y) = \lambda(1-d_3,1+e_0-b_2-e_3), \tag{III.3.20}$$

$$P_1(Z,X) = \lambda(b_6-1,i_0-1) \tag{III.3.21}$$

$$P_2(Z,X) = \lambda(a_2-1,c_2-1) \tag{III.3.22}$$

$$P_3(Z,X) = 1 \tag{III.3.23}$$

$$P_1(X,Z) = \lambda(b_6-h_6,c_2+i_0-i_4-i_6) \tag{III.3.24}$$

$$P_2(X,Z) = \lambda(a_2-g_6,i_4-i_6) \tag{III.3.25}$$

$$P_3(X,Z) = 1 \tag{III.3.26}$$

$$P_1(Y,Z) = \lambda(e_5+h_4-1-h_6, f_6-i_6) \tag{III.3.27}$$

$$P_2(Y,Z) = \lambda(1+d_4-g_6, i_5-i_6) \tag{III.3.28}$$

$$P_3(Y,Z) = 2 \tag{III.3.29}$$

$$P_1(Z,Y) = \lambda(h_4-e_3, i_5+f_6-f_4-f_3) \tag{III.3.30}$$

$$P_2(Z,Y) = \lambda(d_4-d_3, f_4-f_3) \tag{III.3.31}$$

$$P_3(Z,Y) = \lambda(1-d_3, e_5-e_3)\,. \tag{III.3.32}$$

Because of $d_3 < 1$, $P_3(X,Y)$ and $P_3(Z,Y)$ are not smaller than 1. According to the preliminary ESBORA–concept X is the solution if

$$1 > \max\,\{d_3e_3f_3,\ g_6h_6i_6\}\ . \tag{III.3.33}$$

Similarly, Y or Z is the solution if

$$d_3e_3f_3 > \max\,\{1,\ g_6h_6i_6\} \tag{III.3.34}$$

or

$$g_6h_6i_6 > \max\,\{1,\ d_3e_3f_3\} \tag{III.3.35}$$

holds, respectively. For the generalized ESBORA–concept the same conditions for the solution X, Y, and Z will be true if for all possible pairs $s^{k'}$ and s^k of strict equilibrium points the generalized weights $P_i(s^{k'},s^k)$ are all equal and positive. But according to equations (III.3.15) to (III.3.32) this is only one of several possibilities. As for the preliminary concept the payoff parameters d_3, e_3, f_3,

g_6, h_6, and i_6 are of crucial importance also for the generalized ESBORA–concept. But different to the preliminary ESBORA–concept other payoff parameters are relevant, too. These other payoff parameters influence the generalized weights so that several subclasses of games with identical generalized weights have to be considered. In each subclass the result depends on d_3, e_3, f_3, g_6, h_6, and i_6 only. But in general the mathematical form, by which these parameters determine the solution, will be different for different subclasses. This clearly demonstrates that the generalized ESBORA–concept is more reactive to the payoff structure of the game. It tries to consider not only the resistance of a given player, but also whether this player's resistance is relevant for the others.

3.3 Decentralized or centralized bargaining ?

The following example is closely related to a situation which has been analysed in SELTEN and GÜTH (1978) with the help of the Harsanyi–Selten theory. Player 1 has to bargain with players 2 and 3 who beforehand can merge into one bargaining party (centralized bargaining) or not (decentralized bargaining). In the case of decentralized bargaining player 1 has to offer both opponents the same contract, i.e. he cannot discriminate between the two.

In the decentralized case the game $G = (S_1,S_2,S_3;P;H)$ in complete normal form is given by

$$S_i = \{b+g,...,b+Kg\} \qquad \text{with } b/g \in \mathbb{N},\quad b + Kg = 100 - g \tag{III.3.36}$$

where g (> 0) is the smallest unit of money, and $P_i(s) = 1$ for all $s \in S_1{\times}S_2{\times}S_3$ and $i=1, 2$, and 3. The payoff function is defined according to

$$H(s) = \begin{cases} (200\text{-}2x, x, x) & \text{if } s = (x,x,x)\ , \\ (100\text{-}x, x, b) & \text{if } s = (x,x,y) \text{ with } y \neq x\ , \\ (100\text{-}x, 0, x) & \text{if } s = (x,y,x) \text{ with } y \neq x\ , \\ (0, 0, b) & \text{otherwise}\ . \end{cases} \tag{III.3.37}$$

Player 3's conflict payoff b is restricted to $0 \leq b \leq 100-g$. For players 1 and 2 the conflict payoff is zero.

Obviously, all strict equilibrium points are of the form $s^k = (kg,kg,kg)$ with $k \in \mathbb{N}$ and $b+g \leq kg \leq b+Kg$. Furthermore, none of the strict equilibrium points s^k payoff dominates another and every nonpure equilibrium point is payoff dominated by a strict equilibrium point. Let $s^{k'}$ and s^k be two different strict equilibrium points. Because of

$$\frac{r_1(s^{k'},s^k)}{r_1(s^k,s^{k'})} = \frac{100 - k'g}{100 - k\,g} \tag{III.3.38}$$

$$\frac{r_2(s^{k'},s^k)}{r_2(s^k,s^{k'})} = \frac{k'}{k} \tag{III.3.39}$$

$$\frac{r_3(s^{k'},s^k)}{r_3(s^k,s^{k'})} = \frac{k'g - b}{k\,g - b} \tag{III.3.40}$$

and

$$P_i(s^{k'},s^k) = \begin{cases} 2 & \text{for } i = 1\ , \\ 1 & \text{for } i = 2, 3\ . \end{cases} \tag{III.3.41}$$

one derives

$$r(s^{k'},s^k) = \frac{k'(k'g - b)(100 - k'g)^2}{k\,(k\,g - b)(100 - k\,g)^2}\ . \tag{III.3.42}$$

It can be seen easily that the function

$$f(x) = x(x-b)(100-x)^2, \qquad (b < x < 100) \tag{III.3.43}$$

has a unique maximum

$$x^+ = \frac{200+3b+\sqrt{40000 - 400b + 9b^2}}{8}. \qquad \text{(III.3.44)}$$

In general $x^+ \notin S_i$ $(i = 1, 2, 3)$. But it can be shown that the solution must be either $b + k^*g$ or $b + (k^* + 1)g$ where $k^*g \leq x^+ - b < (k^* + 1)g$. As we are only interested in the limit for $g \to 0$ it is sufficient to know that the solution $s^{k^+} = (k^+g, k^+g, k^+g)$ converges to x^+ for $g \to 0$.

Since $r(s^{k^+}, s^k) > 1$ and $r(s^k, s^{k^+}) < 1$ for all $k \neq k^+$, it follows that $s^{k^+} = (k^+g, k^+g, k^+g)$ is the generalized ESBORA–solution in the decentralized case. The corresponding result for the preliminary ESBORA–concept is

$$x_p^+ = \frac{100 + b + \sqrt{10000 - 100b + b^2}}{3} \qquad \text{(III.3.45)}$$

maximizing $x(x - b)(100 - x)$ in the range $b < x < 100$. For all b with $0 \leq b < 100$ one has $x_p^+ > x^+$, for $b \to 100$ both solution prices converge to 100. Because of their relatively higher weights according to the preliminary ESBORA–concept players 2 and 3 succeed in refusing contracts which are rather unfavorable for them. By taking into account for whom the resistances of player 2 and 3 really matter, one derives relatively lower weights for players 2 and 3 who therefore are less successful in resisting unfavorable contracts.

Consider now the case that players 2 and 3 have merged into player 2 before bargaining begins. Assuming that the new player 2's payoff is the sum of the payoffs for the original players 2 and 3 the game $G = (S_1,S_2;P;H)$ is defined by

$$S_i = \{b+g,\dots,b+Kg\} \quad \text{with } b/g \in \mathbb{N},\ b + Kg = 100 - g \qquad \text{(III.3.46)}$$

and $P_i(s) = 1$ for all $s \in S_1{\times}S_2$, $i = 1, 2$ and

$$H(s) = \begin{cases} (200-2x, 2x) & \text{if } s = (x,x)\,, \\ (0,b) & \text{otherwise}\ . \end{cases} \qquad \text{(III.3.47)}$$

Again all strict equilibrium points are unanimous agreements. Furthermore, no strict equilibrium point payoff dominates another and every nonpure equilibrium point is payoff dominated by a strict equilibrium point. For any two different strict equilibrium points all generalized weights are 1 so that the preliminary and the generalized solution are the same. Assuming that

$$x_z^+ = 50 + \frac{b}{4} \;, \tag{III.3.48}$$

which maximizes the polynomial (200–2x)(2x–b) in the range $b < x < 100$, can be expressed in the form $x_z^+ = b + kg$ with $k \in \mathbb{N}$ one derives $s^+ = (x_z^+, x_z^+)$ as the ESBORA–solution in the case of centralized bargaining. In Figure III.3.1 we have illustrated how the three solutions x^+, x_p^+, and x_z^+ depend on the opportunity costs b.

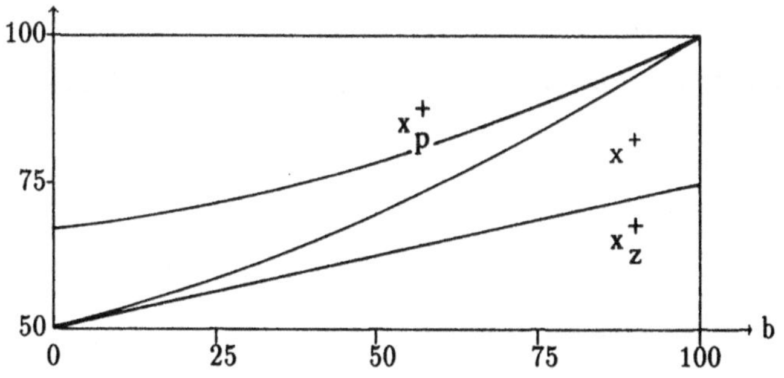

Figure III.3.1: Agreement levels according to the preliminary and the generalized ESBORA –concept for the case of decentralized (x^+, x_p^+) and centralized (x_z^+) bargaining as functions of the opportunity costs b.

For $b = 0$ the agreement level according to the generalized ESBORA–concept is the same for centralized and decentralized bargaining. For all $b > 0$ it pays for players 2 and 3 to bargain separately with player 1. According to the preliminary ESBORA–concept the agreement level for decentralization is always higher, i.e. decentralization also pays for $b = 0$.

It is a surprising result that according to the preliminary ESBORA–concept the agreement depends on the centralization level even if both opponents of player 1 are identical, i.e. if $b = 0$. The intuitive reason for decentralization in the range of $b > 0$ is that player 3 will be especially tough because of his higher opportunity costs. Compared to player 3, who only looses x–b, the cartel of both, players 2 and 3, (i.e. player 2 in the centralized case) has to face a more serious loss of 2x–b if it refuses a contract x. But this argument does not support the decentralization advantage for b = 0 according to the preliminary concept. The reason for this result is that in the decentralized case players 2 and 3 in total have a higher weight. Similarly to the 'one seller and n–1 buyers'–problem our generalized weights avoid that one bargaining side can gain simply by splitting into identical players.

3.4 Market entry games

SELTEN and GÜTH (1977 and 1982a) have analysed a class of games $G = (S_1,...,S_n;P;H)$ with

$$S_i = \{0, 1\} \qquad \text{for } i = 1,...,n \quad , \tag{III.3.49}$$

$$P_i \equiv 1 , \tag{III.3.50}$$

and

$$H_i(s) = \begin{cases} R_{m(s)} - C_i^* & \text{if } s_i = 1 , \\ S^*_{m(s)} & \text{if } s_i = 0 , \end{cases} \tag{III.3.51}$$

for all $s \in S = S_1 \times ... \times S_n$ and $i = 1,...,n$ where $m(s)$ is defined by

$$m(s) = \sum_{i=1}^{n} s_i \quad . \tag{III.3.52}$$

To have something specific in mind think of $s_i = 1$ as a potential seller i's decision to enter a market whereas $s_i = 0$ means that the potential seller i refrains from market entry. Correspondingly, $R_{m(s)}$ are the market revenues if m(s) sellers are on the market and C_i^* are the costs of market entry. If a potential seller does not enter the market, his payoff $S_{m(s)}^*$ may as well depend on the number m(s) of actual sellers in the market. It is assumed that the n potential sellers are ordered in such a way that

$$C_1^* < C_2^* < \ldots. < C_n^* \qquad \text{(III.3.53)}$$

and that the incentive $A_{m(s)} = R_{m(s)} - S_{m(s)-1}^*$ for market entry does not increase with m(s). To avoid border cases we, furthermore, require that $A_{m(s)} \neq C_i^*$ for all $s \in S$ and all $i = 1,\ldots,n$.

In SELTEN and GÜTH (1982a) it has been shown that there exists a unique integer $\bar{m} \in \{0, 1,\ldots,n\}$ satisfying

$$C_j^* < A_j \qquad \text{for } 1 \leq j \leq \bar{m} \text{ or } \bar{m} = 0 \quad , \qquad \text{(III.3.54)}$$

and

$$C_j^* > A_j \qquad \text{for } \bar{m} + 1 \leq j \leq n \text{ or } \bar{m} = n \quad , \qquad \text{(III.3.55)}$$

and that the strategy vector $s^+ = (s_1^+,\ldots,s_n^+)$ with

$$s_i^+ = \begin{cases} 1 & \text{for } i = 1, \ldots, \bar{m} \quad , \\ 0 & \text{for } i = \bar{m}+1,\ldots,n \quad . \end{cases} \qquad \text{(III.3.56)}$$

is a strict equilibrium point. Furthermore, for every other strict equilibrium point $s = (s_1,\ldots,s_n)$ it must be true that

$$m(s) = \bar{m} \quad . \qquad \text{(II.3.57)}$$

In the following we will restrict our attention to situations with $C_n^* < A_1$ and $C_1^* > A_n$ which implies that $0 < \bar{m} < n$ and that no player will enter or will not enter the market regardless what the others decide to do, i.e. no player has an inferior strategy. Furthermore, we assume that all nonpure equilibrium points are payoff dominated by strict ones. If $\bar{m} = 0$ or $\bar{m} = n$ only one strict equilibrium point exists.

Market entry games are important since any reasonable selection theory should determine the strategy vector s^+ defined in (III.3.56) to be the solution of the game. In SELTEN and GÜTH (1977 and 1982a) it has been shown that the Harsanyi–Selten theory satisfies this necessary requirement for a theory of equilibrium selection.

To show that also the relation of resistance dominance selects s^+ as the solution, we will prove that $r(s^+,s) > r(s,s^+)$ for all strict equilibrium points s with $s \neq s^+$ regardless whether we use the preliminary or the generalized ESBORA–concept. Consider a strict equilibrium point $s \neq s^+$ and observe first of all that there must exist players i and j with $i \neq j$ such that $s_i \neq s_i^+$ and $s_j \neq s_j^+$. Then we obtain

$$\frac{H_j(s) - H_j(s_i^+,s_{-i})}{H_j(s) - H_j(s_j^+,s_{-j})} = \begin{cases} (S^*_{\bar{m}} - S^*_{\bar{m}+1})/(C^*_j - A_{\bar{m}+1}) & \text{if } s_j = 0,\ s_i = 0, \\ (S^*_{\bar{m}} - S^*_{\bar{m}-1})/(C^*_j - A_{\bar{m}+1}) & \text{if } s_j = 0,\ s_i = 1, \\ (R_{\bar{m}} - R_{\bar{m}+1})/(A_{\bar{m}} - C^*_j) & \text{if } s_j = 1,\ s_i = 0, \\ (R_{\bar{m}} - R_{\bar{m}-1})/(A_{\bar{m}} - C_j) & \text{if } s_j = 1,\ s_i = 1. \end{cases} \tag{III.3.58}$$

Since $C^*_j - A_{\bar{m}+1} \geq C^*_j - A_j > 0$ $(j \leq \bar{m})$ and $C^*_j - A_{\bar{m}} \leq C^*_j - A_j < 0$ $(j \geq \bar{m}+1)$ all denominators on the right–hand side of (III.3.58) are positive. So if $S_{\bar{m}+1} \neq S_{\bar{m}}$, $S_{\bar{m}} \neq S_{\bar{m}-1}$ and $R_{\bar{m}+1} \neq R_{\bar{m}}$, $R_{\bar{m}} \neq R_{\bar{m}-1}$, this relation of utility differences will be either positive or negative. Since according to both strict equilibria s^+ and s the number of actual sellers on the market is $\bar{m}$, there exists a permutation π on $N = \{1,\dots,n\}$ such that

$$\pi: \begin{cases} \bar{M} = \{i \in N \mid s_i^+ = 1, s_i = 0\} \longrightarrow \{i \in N \mid s_i^+ = 0, s_i = 1\} \\ \qquad\qquad\qquad\qquad i \longmapsto \pi(i) \end{cases} \tag{III.3.59}$$

Assumption (III.3.53) together with the definition of s^+ given in (III.3.56) implies that $C^*_i < C^*_{\pi(i)}$ for all $i \in \bar{M}$. This implies that

$$r_i(s^+,s)/r_i(s,s^+) > r_{\pi(i)}(s,s^+)/r_{\pi(i)}(s^+,s) \tag{III.3.60}$$

for all $i \in \bar{M}$. The reason for (III.3.60) is that, when comparing s^+ to s in view of player i and s to s^+ in view of player $\pi(i)$, both players are confronted with the same payoff incentives on and off the market except for the higher entry costs of player $\pi(i)$. Since

$$\prod_{i \in M} \frac{r_i(s^+, s)}{r_i(s, s^+)} = \prod_{i \in \bar{M}} \frac{r_i(s^+, s)\, r_{\pi(i)}(s^+, s)}{r_i(s, s^+)\, r_{\pi(i)}(s, s^+)} > 1 \tag{III.3.61}$$

we have $r(s^+,s) > r(s,s^+)$, and the preliminary ESBORA–solution is s^+.

For the generalized ESBORA–concept it follows from (III.3.58) that $P_i(s^+,s) = P_{\pi(i)}(s,s^+)$ for all $i \in \bar{M}$. Observe that it does not depend on C_i^* or C_j^* whether the relation of utility differences in (III.3.58) is positive, negative, or zero. Thus one can associate any opponent j of i, for whom this relation is positive (negative or zero), with an opponent j of $\pi(i)$, for whom this relation is also positive (negative or zero) and vice versa. This shows that $P_i(s^+,s) = P_{\pi(i)}(s,s^+)$ is true. It is, of course, possible, that the weights $P_i(s^+,s)$ for $i \in \bar{M}$ are not positive. In this case one has to use the $\tilde{\varepsilon}$–perturbed generalized weights which also satisfy $P_i(s^+,s) = P_{\pi(i)}(s,s^+) = \tilde{\varepsilon}$ for all $i \in \bar{M}$. Since in any case players i and $\pi(i)$ will have the same ($\tilde{\varepsilon}$–perturbed) generalized weight, the same argument as for the preliminary ESBORA–concept implies that s^+ is the solution.

Part IV: Further perspectives for improving the ESBORA–concept

In the following we will shortly describe and investigate some possibilities to improve the ESBORA–concept. One way will be to define continuous weights $P_i(s^{k'},s^k)$ which depend continuously on the payoff parameters of the other players j ($\neq$ i). Till now we did not follow this approach because it will seriously complicate the computation of the ESBORA–solution for many games. The other possibility, which we will consider, is to substitute our definition of the restricted game for the resistance comparison between $s^{k'}$ and s^k by the one of HARSANYI and SELTEN (1988). Whereas according to our definition the players i in M can only choose between $s_i^{k'}$ and s_i^k, the pure strategy sets according to HARSANYI and SELTEN are enlarged to the smallest formation $\underset{i \in M}{X} F_i$ such that $\{s_i^{k'}, s_i^k\} \subseteq F_i$ for all active players i in M. It will be illustrated by an example that due to our definition of the restricted game strategies may be neglected which are serious threats. It could be said that our definition of the restricted game assumes <u>independence of irrelevant alternatives</u>. For a theory of resistance avoidance it might be less important to include all possible threats than for a theory of risk dominance. But a final definition would be premature. More examples have to be analysed before one can judge whether better selection results justify the more complicated definition and computation of the ESBORA–solution which is implied by the Harsanyi–Selten definition of the restricted game. In the final section we will give an example to illustrate that the ESBORA–solution can be a mixed strategy equilibrium point in spite of the fact that the game has a strict equilibrium point which payoff or resistance dominates all other strict equilibrium points.

1. Continuous weights

According to the definition (III.2.2) of generalized weights $P_i(s^{k'},s^k)$ one only considers whether another player j ($\neq$ i) suffers from a deviation of player i but not how serious this loss is. Player j is a member of $M_i(s^{k'},s^k)$ if $H_j(s^k)$ is greater than $H_j(s_i^{k'},s_{-i}^k)$. Whether a positive payoff difference

$H_j(s^k) - H_j(s_i^{k'}, s_{-i}^k)$ is more or less important is completely neglected. In other words: We have only asked whether player j has reasons to listen to player i's objections or not. What we did not ask is how much reason player j has to do so.

1.1 New weights

It is, of course, possible to have weights which depend continuously on the utility losses $H_j(s^k) - H_j(s_i^{k'}, s_{-i}^k)$. Naturally these new weights should also be independent of positive linear transformations of the players' utility functions and the ESBORA–concept, based on the new weights, should also satisfy our generalized Nash–property. Both requirements are obviously fulfilled if we define the new weights $P_i(s^{k'}, s^k)$ according to

$$P_i(s^{k'}, s^k) = P_i \sum_{j \in M_i(s^{k'}, s^k)} P_j \frac{H_j(s^k) - H_j(s_i^{k'}, s_{-i}^k)}{H_j(s^k) - H_j(s_j^{k'}, s_{-j}^k)} \tag{IV.1.1}$$

for all players i in M and all pairs of different candidates $s^{k'}$ and s^k. Since s^k is a strict equilibrium point and since $M_i(s^{k'}, s^k) \subseteq M$, the 'new weights' $P_i(s^{k'}, s^k)$ are well–defined. To measure whether j's loss $H_j(s^k) - H_j(s_i^{k'}, s_{-i}^k)$ is serious or not, we compare it to the loss $H_j(s^k) - H_j(s_j^{k'}, s_{-j}^k)$ caused by his own deviation.

That the new weights are not influenced by positive linear transformations of the payoff functions H_j is a well–known property of cardinal utilities. Relations of utility differences are invariant under positive linear transformations. To see that the new weights do not question the Nash-property of the ESBORA–concept, observe that in unanimity bargaining games one has

$$\frac{H_{\pi(t_j)}(s^k) - H_{\pi(t_j)}(s_{\pi(t_i)}^{k'}, s_{-\pi(t_i)}^k)}{H_{\pi(t_j)}(s^k) - H_{\pi(t_j)}(s_{\pi(t_j)}^{k'}, s_{-\pi(t_j)}^k)} = 1 \qquad \text{for } j \neq i\,. \tag{IV.1.2}$$

Thus for unanimity bargaining games with complete or incomplete information the new weights do not differ from the generalized weights which were defined in Part III and which were shown to be in line with the Nash–property.

Similarly to the $\tilde{\epsilon}$–perturbed generalized weights one can define $\tilde{\epsilon}$–perturbed new weights to avoid that considerations of resistance avoidance are completely neglected in games with pairs $s^{k'}$ and s^k and $P_i(s^{k'},s^k) = 0$ for all i in M. It is probably needless to say that the ESBORA–theory based on $\tilde{\epsilon}$–perturbed new weights will react in a more subtle way to the payoff structure of the game. Small changes in the utilities for the strategy vectors appearing on the right–hand side of (IV.1.1) will cause small changes in the new weights. For the generalized weights such changes in the payoff structure either did not cause any change or implied discontinuous jumps of the generalized weights. The <u>new ESBORA–concept</u> is the ESBORA–concept which results if we substitute the preliminary weights P_i by the <u>$\tilde{\epsilon}$–perturbed new weights</u> for every ϵ,δ–perturbed game $G^{\epsilon,\delta}$ which has to be considered according to Figure II.6.1 during the solution procedure. For the ESBORA-concept a statement analogous to Lemma 8 is true saying that one can rely on the new weights instead of the $\tilde{\epsilon}$–perturbed new weights if there is a unique candidate which is not resistance dominated according to the new weights.

From our point of view the new ESBORA–concept is more convincing. Unfortunately, computing the new ESBORA–solution will be far more difficult than computing the preliminary ESBORA-solution or even the generalized ESBORA–solution. Because of the new weights the exponents appearing on the right–hand side of (I.2.10) will usually make it rather difficult to solve games which are not numerically specified. Except for classes of rather simple games like, for instance, unanimity bargaining games, one will not be able to solve whole classes of games.

1.2 Alternative weights

Looking at the definition (IV.1.1) of new weights $P_i(s^{k'},s^k)$ it is an obvious idea that players j with $H_j(s_i^{k'},s_{-i}^k) \geq H_j(s^k)$ should also contribute to $P_i(s^{k'},s^k)$. This can be accomplished by defining '<u>alternative weights</u>' $P_i(s^{k'},s^k)$, $i \in M$, according to

$$P_i(s^{k'},s^k) = P_i \sum_{j \in M-\{i\}} P_j \frac{H_j(s^k)-H_j(s_i^{k'},s_{-i}^k)}{H_j(s^k)-H_j(s_j^{k'},s_{-j}^k)} \quad . \qquad \text{(IV.1.3)}$$

Observe that the alternative weights can be negative. For instance, for nearly all games described in Table III.2.1 all weights $P_i(s^{k'},s^k)$ are negative which means that player i's normalized individual resistance $r_i(s^{k'},s^k)/r_i(s^k,s^{k'})$ will be reversed. Of course, it is not necessary to perturb alternative weights. The obvious interpretation of alternative weights is that players j fearing a deviation of player i from s^k can be counterbalanced by those players j who are not afraid of player i's threat. Thus the resistance of player i against s^k will be heard according to the 'differences in weight' of those who fear him and those who do not mind if he deviates from s_i^k to $s_i^{k'}$. In this sense alternative weights $P_i(s^{k'},s^k)$ take into account all payoff effects which are implied by player i's deviation from s_i^k to $s_i^{k'}$. Of course, also the alternative ESBORA–concept satisfies the Nash–property since no player can gain by a deviation of another player in unanimity bargaining games.

Here we do not investigate the <u>alternative ESBORA–concept</u> in more detail which results from substituting the preliminary weights by the alternative weights $P_i(s^{k'},s^k)$. Till now we did not find examples with counterintuitive results which could be avoided by using alternative weights. But more experiences with ESBORA might make it necessary to consider the alternative ESBORA–concept more seriously.

1.3 A 3–person game in the light of the various weighting approaches

Consider game $G = (S_1,S_2,S_3;P;H)$ in complete (agent) normal form illustrated by Table IV.1.1 and completed according to $P_i(s)=1$ for all $s \in S_1{\times}S_2{\times}S_3$ and $i = 1, 2, 3$.

1 1 0	Y_3 / X_3	X_2	Y_2	0 2 c
	X_1	1 1 1	1 0 c	
	Y_1	0 1 c	0 0 0	
2 0 c				u u v

Table IV.1.1: A 3–person game in agent normal form with parameters u, v, and c satisfying $v > 1 > u > 0$, $u^2v > 1$ and $c \in \mathbb{R}$.

The only strict equilibrium points of G are $X = (X_1,X_2,X_3)$ and $Y = (Y_1,Y_2,Y_3)$. Neither X nor Y payoff dominates the other. We restrict ourselves to situations where the nonpure equilibrium point is payoff dominated by at least one of the two strict equilibria. Since $r_i(X,Y)/r_i(Y,X) = 1/\sqrt{u}$ for $i = 1, 2$ and $r_3(X,Y)/r_3(Y,X)=1/\sqrt{v}$ and because of $u^2v > 1$ the strict equilibrium point Y is the preliminary ESBORA–solution for all games G satisfying the parameter conditions.

Now players 1 and 2 both prefer X to Y since $u < 1$. Furthermore, if player 1 or 2 chooses his X–strategy, a deviation of one of his opponents would not harm him. Only if both opponents deviate from X, player 1 or 2 would suffer a loss. Whereas players 1 and 2, if they both expect X as the solution, do not have to fear a deviation of player 3, the opposite is true for the solution candidate Y. This indicates that basing their decisions on their preferred solution candidate X seems less risky for players 2 and 3 than relying on Y as determined by the preliminary ESBORA-concept.

We want to see now whether and how the different weighting approaches change the result of the game. The generalized weights are

$$P_1(Y,X) = P_2(Y,X) = \begin{cases} 1 & \text{for } c < 1\,, \\ 0 & \text{otherwise}\,, \end{cases} \tag{IV.1.4}$$

$$P_1(X,Y) = P_2(X,Y) = \begin{cases} 1 & \text{for } c < v\,, \\ 0 & \text{otherwise}\,, \end{cases} \tag{IV.1.5}$$

$$P_3(Y,X) = 0 \text{ and } P_3(X,Y) = 2\,. \tag{IV.1.6}$$

For all possible values of c the generalized weights imply that $r(X,Y) < r(Y,X)$. This shows that Y is the generalized ESBORA–solution for all games which satisfy our parameter restrictions.

For the new weights one derives

$$P_1(Y,X) = P_2(Y,X) = \begin{cases} 1-c & \text{for } c < 1\,, \\ 0 & \text{otherwise}\,, \end{cases} \tag{IV.1.7}$$

$$P_1(X,Y) = P_2(X,Y) = \begin{cases} (v-c)/u & \text{for } c < v\,, \\ 0 & \text{otherwise}\,, \end{cases} \tag{IV.1.8}$$

$$P_3(Y,X) = 0 \text{ and } P_3(X,Y) = 2u/v\,. \tag{IV.1.9}$$

Here the condition for Y to be the (new ESBORA–)solution depends on the range of the parameter c. Y resistance dominates X if

$$vu^{\frac{v}{u}(\frac{v-c}{u} + 1-c)} > 1 \tag{IV.1.10}$$

for $c < 1$ and if condition

$$vu^{\frac{v(v-c)}{u^2}} > 1 \tag{IV.1.11}$$

is satisfied in the range $1 \leq c < v$. For $c \geq v$, Y always resistance dominates X.

For our example the alternative weights are

$$P_1(Y,X) = P_2(Y,X) = 1 - c \ , \tag{IV.1.12}$$

$$P_1(X,Y) = P_2(X,Y) = (v - c + u - 2)/u \ , \tag{IV.1.13}$$

$$P_3(Y,X) = 0 \text{ and } P_3(X,Y) = 2u/v \ . \tag{IV.1.14}$$

According to these weights the alternative ESBORA–solution will be Y if

$$vu^{\frac{v}{u}(\frac{v-c+u-2}{u} + 1-c)} > 1 \ . \tag{IV.1.15}$$

The example demonstrates the drastic changes in the selection behavior which are caused by our various weighting approaches. Whereas for the preliminary and for the generalized weights Y is always the solution, X can also be the solution according to the continuous weighting approaches. Since $u < 1$, the left–hand side of (IV.1.15) is greater than the one of (IV.1.11) for $c \geq 1$. If therefore Y is the new ESBORA–solution, it is also the alternative ESBORA–solution. Since the reverse implication does not hold, the most favorable concept for X to be the solution is the new weighting approach. The more one considers the incentives of all players fearing a deviation of the opposing player when aggregating the normalized individual resistances, the better are the chances for Y to become the solution.

The example also indicates that among the continuous approaches the alternative ESBORA-concept is sometimes more comfortable since the formula to be considered is independent of whether $H_j(s^k) - H_j(s_i^{k'}, s_{-i}^k)$ is positive or negative for $j \neq i$. Of course, the classes of situations with different results for the various weighting approaches might diminish if we consider the condition that the mixed strategy equilibrium is payoff dominated by a strict one.

1.4 The 'one seller and n–1 buyers'–problem once again

Let us shortly analyse the results the continuous weighting approaches imply for the 'one seller and n–1 buyers'–problem. For n = 2 we have a unanimity game with complete information so that all versions of the ESBORA–concept imply the same solution price of 50. Let us therefore restrict our attention to 'one seller and n–1 buyers'–games with $n \geq 3$. For two different unanimous price vectors s^k and $s^{k'}$ and $i, j \in \{1,...,n\}$, with $j \neq i$, one has

$$\frac{H_j(s^k) - H_j(s_i^{k'}, s_{-i}^k)}{H_j(s^k) - H_j(s_j^{k'}, s_{-j}^k)} = \begin{cases} 0 & \text{for } j \neq 1, \\ 1 & \text{for } j \neq 1,\ i = 1\,, \\ -\frac{1}{n-2} & \text{for } j \neq 1,\ i \neq 1\,. \end{cases} \tag{IV.1.16}$$

This implies that for k' > k the new weights are given by

$$P_1(s^{k'}, s^k) = n - 1 \quad ,$$

$$P_j(s^{k'}, s^k) = 0 \qquad \text{for } j = 2,...,n \;. \tag{IV.1.17}$$

As for the generalized weights the solution price is therefore 100–g. According to (IV.1.16) and for k' > k the alternative weights are

$$P_1(s^{k'}, s^k) = n - 1 \quad , \tag{IV.1.18}$$

$$P_j(s^{k'}, s^k) = -1 \qquad \text{for } j = 2,...,n \;. \tag{IV.1.19}$$

Since

$$\frac{r_1(s^{k'}, s^k)}{r_1(s^k, s^{k'})} > 1 \quad , \tag{IV.1.20}$$

because of (III.1.7), and since

$$\frac{r_j(s^{k'},s^k)}{r_j(s^k,s^{k'})} < 1 \qquad \text{for } j = 2,\ldots,n\,, \tag{IV.1.21}$$

because of (III.1.8), it follows that

$$r(s^{k'},s^k) > 1 \qquad \text{for all } 1 \leq k < k' \leq K\;. \tag{IV.1.22}$$

This shows that also the alternative weights select the competitive price 100–g as the solution price in the 'one seller and n–1 buyers'–problem.

1.5 A 3–person bargaining game with an unbiased threat reconsidered

In the following we want to look again at the 3–person bargaining game introduced in Section 4.1.3 of Part I where we now restrict our attention to the special situation $v = u > 1$ and $c \geq 0$. Recall that according to the preliminary weights the ESBORA–solution is the strict equilibrium point X being preferred by (the identical) players 1 and 2. Player 3 who has an unbiased threat prefers Y to X. Since the generalized weights are given by

$$P_i(X,Y) = P_i(Y,X) = 2 \qquad \text{for } i = 1, 2 \tag{IV.1.23}$$

and

$$P_3(X,Y) = P_3(Y,X) = \begin{cases} 2 & \text{for } c > 0\,, \\ 0 & \text{otherwise}\,, \end{cases} \tag{IV.1.24}$$

the generalized ESBORA–solution is also always X.

The new and the alternative weights for players 1 and 2 are identical with their generalized weights. For player 3 the new weights and the alternative weights are

$$P_3(X,Y) = 2c \quad , \tag{IV.1.25}$$

and

$$P_3(Y,X) = \frac{c}{u} \quad . \tag{IV.1.26}$$

It is easy to see that for all $c > 0$ the inequality

$$r(X,Y) = \frac{u^4}{u^c} < \frac{u^{c/u}}{u^4} = r(Y,X) \quad , \tag{IV.1.27}$$

or equivalently,

$$8 - c(1 + \frac{1}{u}) < 0 \quad , \tag{IV.1.28}$$

can be fulfilled for all $u > 1$ in case of

$$c \geq 8 \quad . \tag{IV.1.29}$$

Thus Y is the new and the alternative ESBORA–solution if (IV.1.28) holds and X is the solution if the reverse inequality is true. This implies that for a deviation loss $c \geq 8$ candidate Y is the solution whereas X is the solution for $c \leq 4$.

It is interesting to observe that on the one hand, the preliminary and the generalized ESBORA-solution are identical, independent of c, and equal to X and that, on the other hand, the new and the alternative ESBORA–solution are identical but depend considerably on the deviation loss c. As for the Harsanyi–Selten theory the solution now changes from X to Y (see Section 4.1.3 of Part I). Where the change exactly takes place relies on u and c. But a necessary restriction is that $c \in (4,8)$.

2. Defining restricted games by the formation structure

The restricted game for the resistance comparison of $s^{k'}$ against s^k as defined by (I.2.5) and (I.2.6) may not be closed with respect to the best reply correspondence of the game. In other words: Even if all the other players $j \neq i$ restrict themselves to the choice of mixed strategies which give positive probability only to $s_j^{k'}$ and s_j^k, player i's best replies must not be mixed strategies with carrier $\{s_i^{k'}, s_i^k\}$, i.e. it is possible that a pure strategy, different from $s_i^{k'}$ and s_i^k, is player i's best reply. HARSANYI and SELTEN (1988) also assume that all players $j \notin M$ will use their strategy $s_i^{k'} = s_i^k$. But different from our approach they define the restricted game as the smallest formation $F^M = \times_{i \in M} F_i$ such that F_i contains $s_i^{k'}$ and s_i^k for all active players $i \in M$. Thus every active player i in M can always choose his best reply to any expectation about his opponents according to which every active player stays within the formation F^M and every inactive player $j \notin M$ uses $s_j^{k'} = s_j^k$.

	X_2		Y_2		W_2	
X_1	x	1−x	0	0	0	d
Y_1	0	0	y	1−y	0	d
W_1	c	0	c	0	c	d

Table IV.2.1: A 2–person bargaining game with nonbargaining strategies;

$$1 > x > y > c > 0, \quad 1-x > d > 0, \quad x(1-x) \neq y(1-y),$$
$$\frac{xy}{x+y} < c, \quad \frac{(1-x)(1-y)}{1-x+1-y} < d, \quad \frac{x(1-x)}{y(1-y)} \neq \frac{(x-c)(1-x-d)}{(y-c)(1-y-d)}.$$

To demonstrate the difference between the two definitions, let us consider the game $G = (S_1,S_2;P;H)$ illustrated in Table IV.2.1. There are two players 1 and 2 who can choose between two possible contracts $X = (X_1,X_2)$ and $Y = (Y_1,Y_2)$ of how to divide the total payoff of 1. Player 1 prefers X to Y and player 2 the contract Y to X. Besides proposing contract X or Y by choosing X_i and Y_i, respectively, both players $i = 1, 2$ have a nonbargaining strategy W_i which secures them a positive payoff. Furthermore, let $P_i(s)=1$ for all $s \in S_1 \times S_2$ and $i = 1, 2$. Games of this type have been analysed in great detail by LEOPOLD–WILDBURGER (1982 and 1985) with the help of the Harsanyi–Selten theory.

The game has three equilibrium points, namely $X = (X_1,X_2)$, $Y = (Y_1,Y_2)$, and $W = (W_1,W_2)$, but because of our parameter restrictions W is payoff dominated. It is easy to see that

$$\frac{r_1(X,Y)}{r_1(Y,X)} = \frac{x}{y} \tag{IV.2.1}$$

and

$$\frac{r_2(X,Y)}{r_2(Y,X)} = \frac{1-x}{1-y} \tag{IV.2.2}$$

which implies that X is the ESBORA–solution if

$$x(1-x) > y(1-y) \quad , \tag{IV.2.3}$$

and that Y is the ESBORA–solution in case of the reversed inequality, regardless whether we rely on the preliminary, generalized, new, or the alternative ESBORA–concept.

Let us now consider the restricted game being the smallest formation $F = F_1 \times F_2$ such that $F_i \supseteq \{X_i, Y_i\}$ for $i = 1, 2$. Because of our parameter restrictions we have $F_i = \{X_i, Y_i, W_i\}$ for $i = 1, 2$. That W_i can be a best reply to a mixed strategy q_j of player j ($\neq$ i) with $q_j(W_j) = 0$ is illustrated by Figure IV.2.1 being a familiar diagram in 2–person game theory. Now the definition of player i's individual resistance $r_i(s^{k'},s^k)$ for the resistance comparison of $s^{k'}$ against s^k in the restricted game F^M is

$$\begin{aligned} & r_i(s^{k'},s^k) \\ & = \max\{z \in [0,1] \mid H_i'(s_i^{k'},(zs_j^k+(1-z)s_j^{k'})_{j\neq i}) \geq H_i'(s_i,(zs_j^k+(1-z)s_j^{k'})_{j\neq i}) \text{ for all } s_i \in F_i-\{s_i^{k'}\}\} \ . \end{aligned} \tag{IV.2.4}$$

The difference to definition (I.2.8) is that now player i cannot only switch over to s_i^k but to any other strategy s_i in F_i. For our specific example the new definition implies

$$r_1(X,Y) = \frac{x - c}{x} \quad , \tag{IV.2.5}$$

$$r_2(X,Y) = \frac{1 - x - d}{1 - x} \quad , \tag{IV.2.6}$$

$$r_1(Y,X) = \frac{y - c}{y} \quad , \tag{IV.2.7}$$

$$r_2(Y,X) = \frac{1 - y - d}{1 - y} \quad . \tag{IV.2.8}$$

Thus the new definition implies

$$r(X,Y) = \frac{y(x - c)(1 - y)(1 - x - d)}{x(y - c)(1 - x)(1 - y - d)} \tag{IV.2.9}$$

according to the preliminary, generalized, new, or alternative ESBORA–concept. Equation (IV.2.9) clearly demonstrates that the payoffs implied by the strategies W_i now essentially influence whether X or Y is selected as the solution of the game. X (Y) is the preliminary, generalized, new, and alternative ESBORA–solution if the right–hand side of (IV.2.9) is greater (smaller) than 1.

In general, the computation of the ESBORA–solution will be more complicated if we use the Harsanyi–Selten definition of the restricted game instead of our previous one. First of all it is no longer true that $r_i(s^{k'},s^k) = 1 - r_i(s^k,s^{k'})$ as according to our previous definition. This implies that the normalized individual resistances cannot be determined directly. Furthermore, $r_i(s^{k'},s^k)$ has now to be computed by considering a finite number of inequalities in z instead of only one according to our previous definition (I.2.8). In addition, it is sometimes not easy to determine the restricted game which is closed with respect to the best reply correspondence. Often one has to distinguish many subcases which are defined by the various possibilities for the restricted game (see, for instance, LEOPOLD–WILDBURGER, 1982 and 1985).

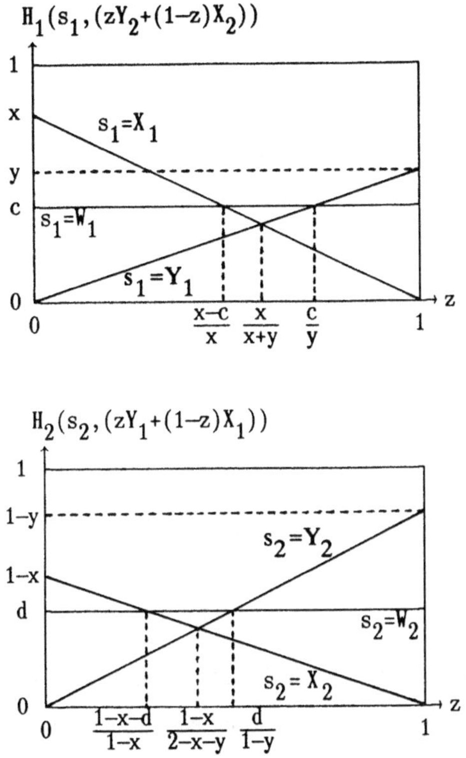

Figure IV.2.1: The best replies of player i to the expectation $(zs_j^k + (1-z)s_j^{k'})_{j\neq i}$ about the opponent j's behavior for the game of Table IV.2.1.

Nevertheless, already our simple example demonstrates that in spite of the greater computational complexity it might be necessary to use the Harsanyi–Selten definition of the restricted game. Consider, for instance, the situation where y–c is very small, 1–x–d relatively large, and y(1–y) > x(1–x). According to our previous definition of the restricted game Y would be the solution. Now contract Y yields a payoff y for player 1 which is only slightly above his maximal sure profit c. Of course, player 1 would have to choose his nonbargaining strategy W_1 to guarantee himself c. Nevertheless, it seems counterintuitive that player 1 should choose the contract which gives him only slightly more than his nonbargaining strategy. Equation (IV.2.9) yields that Y cannot result as the solution if the Harsanyi–Selten definition of the restricted game is used and if (1–x–d)/(y–c) is comparatively large. Thus for many classes of games it might be necessary to use the more complicated Harsanyi–Selten definition of the restricted game instead of our more comfortable, previous definition.

It is probably needless to say that for many of our examples the results do not change if we use the Harsanyi–Selten definition of the restricted game. This is trivially true if all players have just two pure strategies, i.e. $|S_i| = 2$ for $i = 1,\dots,n$. Furthermore, for all unanimity bargaining games the Harsanyi–Selten definition and our previous simpler definition coincide. As a consequence the generalized Nash–property of the ESBORA–theory is not affected if we use the Harsanyi–Selten definition of the restricted games.

3. Mixed strategy equilibria as solution candidates

Our definition of initial candidates fundamentally deviates from the definition of HARSANYI and SELTEN (1988) who do not consider all (uniformly) perfect equilibrium points as solution candidates. The difference results since HARSANYI and SELTEN require an additional stability condition for a perfect equilibrium to become a candidate, namely that it is the solution of a primitive formation (the tracing result of its centroid). Typically this discriminates mixed strategy equilibria, whose support is not contained in a primitive formation, and favors strict pure strategy equilibria. In case of a primitive formation with multiple equilibria it depends, of course, crucially on the selection theory which equilibrium is considered to be the solution of this primitive formation.

We also think of primitive formations as the most basic substructures of games generalizing the idea of strict equilibria (every strict equilibrium generates a primitive formation). Should, however, the requirement of solving a primitive formation be more important than payoff (and/or risk or resistance) dominance? The justification of payoff dominance as a selection criterion is that naturally expectations of all players will focus on equilibria which are not payoff dominated by other equilibria. So why should their expectations concentrate only on those equilibria which are solutions of primitive formations? It was essentially the problem of justifying the priority of the criterion "a solution candidate must be the solution of a primitive formation" which caused us to treat all (uniformly) perfect equilibria as solution candidates whereas perfectness is not sufficient for that propose in view of the Harsanyi–Selten theory.

In the following we want to demonstrate by an example how the different definitions of initial candidates in the Harsanyi–Selten theory and in our theory lead to very different considerations of mixed strategy equilibria and thereby solutions. Thereafter we will discuss how our theory could be based on a definition of initial candidates similar to that one of HARSANYI and SELTEN. The resulting concept will be exemplified by a specific game.

3.1 On mixed strategy solutions

Obviously symmetric games, like 'battle of sexes'–games (see Table I.2.1), must have mixed strategy solutions since the mixed strategy equilibrium point is the only equilibrium point which is symmetry invariant. If a game contains mixed strategy equilibrium points only, it is even more obvious that the solution must be a vector of nonpure strategies. What we want to illustrate here is that the ESBORA–solution can be in mixed strategies in spite of the fact that the unperturbed game has a strict equilibrium point which payoff or resistance dominates all other strict equilibrium points. In our previous examples this phenomenon has been excluded.

Consider the normal form game G illustrated in Table IV.3.1 and completed by $P_i \equiv 1$ for i = 1, 2, and 3. It is easy to see that the mixed strategy vector $q^+ = (q_1^+, q_2^+, q_3^+)$ with

$$q_i^+(X_i) = \sqrt{v}/(1 + \sqrt{v}) \qquad \text{for } i = 1, 2 \qquad \text{(IV.3.1)}$$

and

$$q_3^+(X_3) = 1/(1 + u\sqrt{v}) \qquad \text{(IV.3.2)}$$

is an equilibrium point. The payoff vector $H(q^+) = (H_1(q^+), H_2(q^+), H_3(q^+))$ implied by q^+ is determined by

$$H_i(q^+) = \frac{u\sqrt{v} + uv + 99uv + 100}{u\sqrt{v} + uv + \sqrt{v} + 1} \qquad \text{for } i = 1, 2 \qquad \text{(IV.3.3)}$$

and

$$H_3(q^+) = \frac{v + 2\sqrt{v} + 198\sqrt{v}}{v + 2\sqrt{v} + 1}\ . \qquad \text{(IV.3.4)}$$

100 100 0	Y_3 / X_3	X_2	Y_2	0 100 100
	X_1	u u 1	100 0 100	
	Y_1	0 100 100	100 100 0	
100 0 100				1 1 v

Table IV.3.1: A 3–person normal form game G with $0 < u < 1$, $0 < v < 1$, $198\sqrt{v} \geq 1$, and $u^2 \neq v$.

Since both, u and v, are smaller than 1, equations (IV.3.3) and (IV.3.4), together with the given parameter restrictions, imply that q^+ payoff dominates the two strict equilibrium points X and Y. The same will be true for the ϵ,δ–perturbed games $G^{\epsilon,\delta}$ of game G which shows that q^+ is the ESBORA–solution of G. Observe that neither X payoff dominates Y nor vice versa. Because of

$$\frac{r_i(X,Y)}{r_i(Y,X)} = u \qquad \text{for } i = 1, 2 \qquad \text{(IV.3.5)}$$

and

$$\frac{r_3(X,Y)}{r_3(Y,X)} = 1/\sqrt{v} \qquad \text{(IV.3.6)}$$

it follows, furthermore, from $u^2 \neq v$ that either X resistance dominates Y or vice versa if the preliminary or the generalized weights are used.

This shows that there would be a unique solution in pure strategies if only the two strict equilibrium points were considered as (pre–)candidates. But whereas the Harsanyi–Selten theory only considers X and Y as initial candidates (X and Y are the only solutions of primitive formations), this is not true for the ESBORA–theory.

In principle, a mixed strategy equilibrium point has the same chance to become the solution as a pure strategy equilibrium point. There are mainly two reasons why we have not considered mixed equilibrium points as candidates so far: First of all in many social conflict situations mixed strategy equilibrium points are payoff dominated by pure strategy equilibrium points. On the other hand, in some of our examples we have excluded mixed strategy equilibrium points, which are not payoff dominated by other equilibrium points, in order to avoid complicated case distinctions and lengthy calculations.

Our example demonstrates that any (mixed) strategy equilibrium point has to be expected as the solution if one gives ultimate priority to payoff dominance when comparing two uniformly perfect equilibrium points. Although HARSANYI and SELTEN give higher priority to payoff dominance than to risk dominance, the similar statement for the Harsanyi–Selten theory is not true. This is due to the fact that many mixed strategy equilibrium points are not qualified as solutions of primitive formations (see also GÜTH, 1985).

3.2 Changing the definition of solution candidates

Here we want to indicate how the idea of resistance avoidance can also be used for a theory which only considers solutions of primitive formations as solution candidates. There are essentially two problems of such an approach, namely

(i) to define solutions of primitive formations with multiple equilibria,

(ii) to design a substitution process of solution candidates if, in case of basic symmetries, one cannot discriminate between solution candidates by means of payoff and resistance dominance.

Problem (i) can be easily resolved by adding a penalty term to the payoff function as in (II.5.1) and comparing all equilibria of a primitive formation by means of payoff and resistance dominance as before. It should be mentioned that the new approach would have to rely on payoff functions (II.5.1) including the penalty term only when solving primitive formations with multiple equilibria.

If in case of basic symmetries there are several solution candidates X^i, all being solutions of primitive formations, which neither payoff nor resistance dominate each other but all other candidates, problem (ii) results since one could only arbitrarily select one of them as the solution of the game. Problem (ii) can be resolved by a substitution process of the following form:

(1) The primitive formations F^i, whose solutions are X^i, are neglected in the sense that F^i is not considered as a primitive formation anymore, i.e. F^i is neither in the list of primitive formations nor is a formation, which is nonprimitive only because it contains one of the F^i as a proper subformation, called nonprimitive anymore.

(2) Because of step (1), in a new 'primitive formation' only those equilibria are considered as candidates for solving the formation whose support is not contained in one of the primitive formations F^i eliminated by step (1).

In order to exemplify the new approach relying on a definition of initial candidates similar to that of HARSANYI and SELTEN we want to apply it to the class of games illustrated by Table IV.3.1 where we do not necessarily impose the restriction $u^2 \neq v$.

As the Harsanyi–Selten theory the new approach would consider only X and Y as initial candidates since the mixed strategy–equilibrium described by (IV.3.1) and (IV.3.2) is not qualified as a solution of a primitive formation (its support is not contained in a primitive formation). In case of

$u^2 \neq v$ one therefore would always derive X or Y as the solution of the game.

In case of $u^2 = v$ one cannot discriminate between the two candidates X and Y by payoff or resistance dominance so that X and Y, respectively the formations which they generate, have to be eliminated according to (1). Step (1) yields a unique new 'primitive formation', namely the whole game. Since, due to (2), neither X nor Y are candidates for solving the new 'primitive formation', the solution of this formation and thereby of the game is the only remaining equilibrium point q described by (IV.3.1) and (IV.3.2). Thus different from our usual approach, the mixed strategy–equilibrium is selected as the solution only in the very special situation $u^2 = v$ whereas it was generally selected before.

By this it should have been sufficiently demonstrated how one can use payoff and resistance dominance when solving primitive formations and when comparing the solutions of primitive formations. So there exists a very consistent and convincing way to base our general approach on a definition of initial candidates similar to that of HARSANYI and SELTEN. For many examples such a theory will greatly simplify the task of deriving the solution since certain kind of equilibria (e.g. mixed strategy equilibria whose support is not contained in a primitive formation) can be excluded beforehand. Furthermore, the complicated payoff functions (II.5.1) including the penalty term would only have to be used when solving primitive formations with multiple equilibria (a rare event in all known applications of equilibrium selection theory). Here we have not developed our approach accordingly although more experiences might show that it would have been the better way to focus attention on.

In most of the examples analysed before the new and the previous approach imply the same results. The reason for this is that we could mostly exclude mixed strategy equilibria as being payoff dominated by strict ones. Thus in the final resistance comparisons we only considered equilibrium points qualified as the solutions of primitive formations.

Final Remarks

In the preceding chapters the ESBORA–theory has been formulated and applied to many social conflict situations. It is natural that we have concentrated on games for which the equilibrium solution is typically nonunique. We hope that all examples together demonstrate the applicability of game theory to social decision problems and that they stress the need for accomplishing NASH's program as outlined in the Introduction. Many of our examples have already been analysed with the help of the Harsanyi–Selten theory which made it easy for us to compare the ESBORA–solution to the Harsanyi–Selten solution. Although the ESBORA–theory is closely related to the Harsanyi–Selten theory, the examples demonstrate that the selection behavior of both concepts is quite different. It could be said that the ESBORA–theory owes most of its ideas and tools to the Harsanyi–Selten theory but uses them in a different way. Loosely speaking, the ESBORA–theory could be considered as an equilibrium selection concept determining the solution in a more direct way by the parameters of the game. It is far more easy to see how certain payoff parameters affect resistances and therefore the ESBORA–solution than to find out how the Harsanyi–Selten solution depends on them. Of course, it is even more important to have a theory whose selection behavior is intuitively reasonable. We hope that the few general results in this respect like symmetry invariance, invariance under positive linear transformations, monotonicity of resistance dominance, and the generalized Nash–property, together with the examples, support our belief that the ESBORA–theory provides a reasonable selection concept.

Although we have concentrated on games arising from economic decision problems and social conflict situations the ESBORA–concept is not at all restricted to such problems. Recent applications in the political sciences (e.g. GÜTH, 1988a and b, AVENHAUS, GÜTH, and HUBER, 1988a and b) have shown that, given an appropriate model, also international political decisions could be explained by pure strategic considerations relying on risk or resistance dominance. Till now, our concept has not been adopted to animal conflicts, evolutionary or other biological problems although there seems to be another great area of potential applications (see, e.g., MAYNARD SMITH and PRICE, 1973, SELTEN, 1980, or PARKER and RUBENSTEIN, 1981).

After the first version of the ESBORA–theory in 1982 the concept has been applied in a few publications (GÜTH and SEIFERT, 1984, GÜTH and STEPHAN, 1984, STEPHAN, 1985, GALAHN, 1987, OCKENFELS, 1989) and master theses (GALAHN, 1984, STEPHAN, 1987). Partly we have already mentioned the problems analysed in these studies, e.g. in GÜTH and SEIFERT, 1984, GÜTH and STEPHAN, 1984. Among the studies not mentioned till now STEPHAN (1985 and 1987) analyses the multiplicity of equilibria in fair division games with complete information where infinitely many pricing rules can be distinguished (see GÜTH and VAN DAMME, 1986). The game is rather pathological since minor institutional details as, for instance, the tie breaking rule for equal bids are of special importance for the set of perfect equilibria. The main focus of GALAHN (1987) is to explore the behavioristic aspects of the game theoretic selection approach by analysing experimental results of games with multiple equilibria. OCKENFELS (1989) investigates an oligopoly market with incomplete information about market demand where sellers can decide beforehand whether they want to be informed about market demand or not. A multiplicity of equilibria typically results in situations where the incentive to be informed about market demand decreases with the number of informed sellers whereas information costs do not. In her forthcoming monography KALKOFEN (1989) will examine further theoretical aspects of the ESBORA–concept and apply it to other examples, especially to the whole variety of 2×2–bimatrix games and to some classes of games with (in–)complete information including degenerate cases.

Thus by now we have quite a number of experiences in applying the ESBORA–concept although new examples might reveal new insights which might induce further attempts to modify the concept. If it becomes necessary to improve our concept we will prefer to exploit first of all the possibilities of changing the weights and/or the definition of the restricted game, similarly to our attempts in Parts III and IV, instead of adding completely new aspects to our theory which conceptionally might not be in line with our basic idea of resistance avoidance. In our view, the major advantage of the ESBORA–concept and its main ingredient, the relation of resistance dominance, is the fact that it needs essentially only two instruments, namely a way to measure individual resistances and a method to aggregate them. Although some other possibilities to measure and aggregate individual resistances have been discussed more or less thoroughly, a final judgement about the right method would be premature. In this sense our hope is more to provoke further attempts to select among equilibria than to give final answers.

Notations

Throughout the book standard notations are used as much as possible. The notations specific to games in normal form or in extensive form and to the concept of resistance avoidance are introduced in Part I.

For two sets A and B we define:

$A-B$	$= \{x \in A \mid x \notin B\}$,
$A \subseteq B$	inclusion of A in B,
$A \subset B$	$A \subseteq B$ and $A \neq B$,
∂A	boundary of A,
$\lvert A \rvert$	cardinality of A.

$\mathbb{N}$	$= \{1, 2, 3, \ldots\}$, the set of positive integers.
$\mathbb{R}$	the set of real numbers.
$\mathbb{R}^n$	$= \mathbb{R}\times\ldots\times\mathbb{R}$, n–dimensional Euclidean space.

For $x, y \in \mathbb{R}^n$ let $x \leq y$ be an abbreviation for $x_i \leq y_i$ $(i = 1,\ldots,n)$.

For $x, y \in \mathbb{R}^n$ let $x < y$ be an abbreviation for $x_i < y_i$ $(i = 1,\ldots,n)$.

$\mathbb{R}^n_+$	$= \{x \in \mathbb{R}^n \mid x \geq 0\}$
$\mathbb{R}^n_{>0}$	$= \{x \in \mathbb{R}^n \mid x > 0\}$

The symbols $\rightarrow$, $\uparrow$, and $\downarrow$ mean 'goes to', 'goes to ... from above', and 'goes to ... from below', respectively.

Lower indices usually refer to players, upper indices to a certain numbering. Let $S_i = \{s_i^1,\ldots, s_i^K\}$ be a player i's set of pure strategies. The mixed strategy q_i of player i, determined by $q_i(s_i^k) = z_k$ for $k = 1,\ldots,K$, is sometimes denoted by $z_1 s_i^1 + \ldots + z_K s_i^K$.

References

Aumann, Robert J. (1985): An axiomatization of the non–transferable utility value, Econometrica 53, 599–612.

Avenhaus, Rudolf, Werner Güth and Reiner K. Huber (1988a): Implications of the defense efficiency hypothesis for the choice of military force structures. Part I: Games with and without complete information about the antagonist's intentions, ZiF–Working Paper on Game Theory in the Behavioral Sciences 9, University of Bielefeld.

Avenhaus, Rudolf, Werner Güth and Reiner K. Huber (1988b): Implications of the defense efficiency hypothesis for the choice of military force structures. Part II: A sequential game including the possibility of restructuring forces, ZiF–Working Paper on Game Theory in the Behavioral Sciences 13, University of Bielefeld.

Banks, Jeffrey S. and Joel Sobel (1987): Equilibrium selection in signaling games, Econometrica 55, 647–661.

Bayes, Thomas (1763): An essay towards solving a problem in the doctrine of chances, Philosophical Transactions 53, The Royal Society of London, 376–398.

Bernoulli, Daniel (1730–31): Specimen theoriae novae de mensura sortis, Transactions of the St. Petersburg Imperial Academy of Sciences, 175–192.

Brams, Steven J. (1985): Superpower games – applying game theory to superpower conflicts –, Yale University Press, New Haven – London.

Bronshtein, Ilja N.and K.A. Semendyayew (1985): Handbook of Mathematics, Verlag Harri Deutsch, Frankfurt.

Condorcet, Marie J. Marquis de (1785): Essai sur l'application de l'analyse à la probabilité des decisions rendues à la pluralité des voix, Paris.

Cournot, Augustin (1838): Recherches sur les principes mathématiques de la théorie des richesses, L. Hachette, Paris.

Friedman, James W. (1977): Oligopoly and the theory of games, North–Holland, Amsterdam.

Galahn, Sven (1984): Der Einfluß von Drohungen auf das Verhandlungsergebnis in 3–Parteien Verhandlungssituationen – Eine spieltheoretische und empirische Analyse –, Master Thesis under supervision of Werner Güth, Staatswissenschaftliches Seminar der Universität zu Köln.

Galahn, Sven (1987): Konkurrierende Gleichgewichte in sozialen Entscheidungssituationen – Normative und verhaltenstheoretische Lösungsansätze und empirische Analyse, Verlag Josef Eul, Bergisch Gladbach Köln.

Güth, Werner (1978): Zur Theorie kollektiver Lohnverhandlungen, Nomos – Verlagsgesellschaft, Baden–Baden.

Güth, Werner (1985): A remark on the Harsanyi–Selten theory of equilibrium selection, International Journal of Game Theory 14, 31–39.

Güth, Werner (1988a): Game theory and the nuclear arms race – The strategic position of Western Europe –, European Journal of Political Economy 4, 245–261.

Güth, Werner (1988b): The (stability of the) Western defense alliance – A game theoretic analysis –, ZiF–Working Paper on Game Theory in the Behavioral Sciences 5, University of Bielefeld.

Güth, Werner, Wolfgang Leininger and Gunter Stephan (1988): On supergames and Folk Theorems: A Conceptual dicussion, ZiF–Working Paper on Game Theory in the Behavioral Sciences 19, University of Bielefeld.

Güth, Werner and Hans G. Seifert (1984): Equilibrium selection in bargaining games with unbiased threats, Methods of Operations Research 51, 315–346.

Güth, Werner and Reinhard Selten (1988): Majority voting in the Condorcet paradox as a problem of equilibrium selection, ZiF–Working Paper on Game Theory in the Behavioral Sciences 14, University of Bielefeld.

Güth, Werner and Jürgen Stephan (1984): Equilibrium selection in the one seller and many buyers–game, Journal of Economics (Zeitschrift für Nationalökonomie) 44, 267–281.

Güth, Werner and Eric E.C. van Damme (1986): A comparison of pricing rules for auctions and fair division games, Social Choice and Welfare 3, 177–198.

Harsanyi, John C. (1967/68): Games with incomplete information played by 'Bayesian' players; part I: The basic model, part II: Bayesian equilibrium points, part III: The basic probability distribution of the game, Management Science 14, 159–182, 320–334, 486–502.

Harsanyi, John C. (1975): The tracing procedure: A Bayesian approach to defining a solution for n–person non–cooperative games, International Journal of Game Theory 4, 61–95.

Harsanyi, John C. (1976): A solution concept for n–person noncooperative games, International Journal of Game Theory 5, 211–225.

Harsanyi, John C. (1980): Analysis of a family of two–person bargaining games with incomplete information, International Journal of Game Theory 9, 65–89.

Harsanyi, John C. (1982): Solutions for some bargaining games under the Harsanyi–Selten solution theory, part I: Theoretical preliminaries, part II: Analysis of specific bargaining games, Mathematical Social Sciences 3, 179–191, 259–279.

Harsanyi, John C. and Reinhard Selten (1972): A generalized Nash–solution for 2–person bargaining games with incomplete information, Management Science 18, P80–P106.

Harsanyi, John C. and Reinhard Selten (1977): Simple and iterated limits of algebraic functions, Center for Research in Management Science, Working Paper CP–370, University of California, Berkeley.

Harsanyi, John C. and Reinhard Selten (1988): A general theory of equilibrium selection in games, M.I.T. Press, Cambridge Mass.

de l'Hospital, G.Fr. (1696): Analyse des infiniments petits, Paris.

Kalai, Ehud and Dov Samet (1984): Persistent equilibria in strategic games, International Journal of Game Theory 13, 129–144.

Kalkofen, Brigitte (1989): Gleichgewichtsauswahl in strategischen Spielen, University of Frankfurt/Main, in preparation.

Kohlberg, Elon and Jean–Francois Mertens (1986): On the strategic stability of equilibria, Econometrica 54, 1003–1037.

Krelle, Wilhelm (1976): Preistheorie II. Teil, J.C.B. Mohr (Paul Siebeck), Tübingen.

Kreps, David M. and Robert Wilson (1982): Sequential equilibria, Econometrica 50, 863–894.

Kuhn, Harold W. (1953): Extensive games and the problem of information, in: H. W. Kuhn and A. W. Tucker (eds.) Contributions to the theory of games II, University Press, Princeton, 193–216.

Lensberg, Terje (1987): Stability and collective rationality, Econometrica 55, 935–961.

Lensberg, Terje (1988): Stability and the Nash solution, Journal of Economic Theory 45, 330–341.

Lensberg, Terje and William Thomson (1988): Characterizing the Nash bargaining solution without Pareto-optimality, Social Choice and Welfare 5, 247–259.

Leopold-Wildburger, Ulrike (1982): Gleichgewichtsauswahl in einem Verhandlungsspiel mit Opportunitätskosten, Pfeffersche Buchhandlung, Bielefeld.

Leopold-Wildburger, Ulrike (1985): Equilibrium selection in a bargaining problem with transaction costs, International Journal of Game Theory 14, 151–172.

Mayberry, J.P., John F. Nash and Martin Shubik (1953): A comparison of treatments of a duopoly situation, Econometrica 21, 141–154.

Maynard Smith, John and G.R. Price (1973): The logic of animal conflict, Nature 246, 15–18.

Myerson, Roger B. (1978): Refinements of the Nash equilibrium concept, International Journal of Game Theory 7, 73–80.

Myerson, Roger B. (1984): Two-person bargaining problems with incomplete information, Econometrica 52, 461–487.

Nash, John F. (1950): The bargaining problem, Econometrica 18, 361–382.

Nash, John F. (1951): Non-cooperative games, Annals of Mathematics 45, 286–295.

Nash, John F. (1953): Two-person cooperative games, Econometrica 21, 128–140.

Ockenfels, Peter (1989): Informationsbeschaffung auf homogenen Oligopolmärkten, Physica-Verlag, Heidelberg.

Parker, Geoffry A. and D. I. Rubenstein (1981): Role assessment, reserve strategy and acquisition of asymmetric animal conflicts, Animal Behavior 29, 221–240.

Peters, Hans (1986): Bargaining game theory, Ph.D. Thesis, Maastricht, The Netherlands.

Roth, Alvin E. (1979): Axiomatic models of bargaining, Lecture Notes in Economics and Mathematical Systems 170, Springer-Verlag, Berlin Heidelberg New York.

Rubinstein, Ariel (1982): Perfect equilibrium in a bargaining model, Econometrica 50, 97–109.

Rubinstein, Ariel (1985): A bargaining model with incomplete information about time preferences, Econometrica 53, 1151–1172.

Schmeidler, David (1969): The nucleolus of a characteristic function game, SIAM Journal of Applied Mathematics 17, 1163–1170.

Selten, Reinhard (1965): Spieltheoretische Behandlung eines Oligopolmodells mit Nachfrageträgheit, Teil I: Bestimmung des dynamischen Preisgleichgewichts, Teil II: Eigenschaften des dynamischen Preisgleichgewichts, JITE (Zeitschrift für die gesamte Staatswissenschaft) 121, 301–324, 667–689.

Selten, Reinhard (1973): A simple model of imperfect conpetition, where 4 are few and 6 are many. International Journal of Game Theory 2, 141–201.

Selten, Reinhard (1975): Reexamination of the perfectness concept for equilibrium points in extensive games, International Journal of Game Theory 4, 25–55.

Selten, Reinhard (1975b): Bargaining under incomplete information, a numerical example, in: O. Becker and R. Richter (eds.), Dynamische Wirtschaftsanlyse, 203–232.

Selten, Reinhard (1980a): Oligopoltheorie, in: Handwörterbuch der Wirtschaftswissenschaften 5, Stuttgart et al., 667–678.

Selten, Reinhard (1980b): A note on evolutionarily stable strategies in animal conflicts, Journal of Theoretical Biology 84, 93–101.

Selten, Reinhard (1982): Einführung in die Theorie der Spiele mit unvollständiger Information, Schriften des Vereins für Socialpolitik N.F. 126, 81–148.

Selten, Reinhard and Werner Güth (1977): Risikodominanz in einem Markteintrittsspiel, IMW–Working Paper 63, University of Bielefeld.

Selten, Reinhard and Werner Güth (1978): Macht Einigkeit stark? – Spieltheoretische Analyse einer Verhandlungssituation, Schriften des Vereins für Socialpolitik N.F. 98, 197–217.

Selten, Reinhard and Werner Güth (1982a): Equilibrium point selection in a class of market entry games, in: M. Deistler, E. Fürst and G. Schwödiauer (eds.), Games, Economic Dynamics, and Time Series Analysis – A Symposium in Memoriam of Oskar Morgenstern, Physica–Verlag, Würzburg Wien, 101–116.

Selten, Reinhard and Werner Güth (1982b): Game theoretic analysis of wage bargaining in a simple business cycle model, Journal of Mathematical Economics 11, 177–195.

Selten, Reinhard and Werner Güth (1982c): Original oder Fälschung? – Gleichgewichtsauswahl in einem Verhandlungsspiel mit unvollständiger Information, Schriften des Vereins für Socialpolitik N.F. 126, 153–155.

Selten, Reinhard and Ulrike Leopold (1980): Auswahl eines Gleichgewichtspunktes in einem einfachen Verhandlungsproblem mit Opportunitätskosten, Methods of Operations Research 38, 141–160.

Selten, Reinhard and Ulrike Leopold (1982): Equilibrium point selection in a bargaining situation with opportunity costs, Economie Appliquee, 611–648.

Selten, Reinhard and Ulrike Leopold (1982a): Gleichgewichtsauswahl in einer Gehaltsverhandlungssituation mit unvollständiger Information, Schriften des Vereins für Socialpolitik N.F. 126, 155–161.

Shapley, Lloyd S. (1953): A value for n–person games, in: H.W. Kuhn and A.W. Tucker (eds.), Contributions to the theory of games II, University Press, Princeton, 307–317.

Shubik, Martin (1975): Games for society, business, and war, Elsevier, Amsterdam.

Shubik, Martin (1985): A game–theoretic approach to political economy, Game Theory in the Social Sciences 2, M.I.T. Press, Cambridge London.

Spence, A.M. (1974): Market signalling – Informational transfer in hiring and related screening processes, Harvard University Press, Cambridge, Mass.

Stephan, Jürgen (1985): Pricing in fair allocation games, Methods of Operations Research 54, 457–468.

Stephan, Jürgen (1987): Preisregeln für faire Aufteilungen, Master Thesis under supervision of Werner Güth, Staatswissenschaftliches Seminar der Universität zu Köln.

Sutton, John (1985): Non–cooperative bargaining theory: An introduction, London School of Economics, Discussion Paper in Theoretical Economics, 85–125.

van Damme, Eric E.C. (1983): Refinements of the Nash equilibrium concept, Lecture Notes in Economics and Mathematical Systems 219, Springer–Verlag, Berlin.

van Damme, Eric E.C. (1987): Stability and perfection of Nash equilibria, Springer–Verlag, Berlin.